LIFE AND

LEARNING VII

LIFE AND LEARNING VII

PROCEEDINGS OF THE SEVENTH UNIVERSITY FACULTY FOR LIFE CONFERENCE

JUNE 1997
AT LOYOLA COLLEGE

edited by
Joseph W. Koterski, S.J.

Published by University Faculty for Life
120 New North Building
Georgetown University
Washington, D.C., 20057

Printed in the United States of America
ISBN 1-886387-05-2

LIFE AND LEARNING VII

Table of Contents

PREFACE AND ACKNOWLEDGMENTS   vii
Joseph W. Koterski, S.J.

I. CONTEMPORARY CURRENTS

Where is the Pro-Life Movement Today?   1
Mary Ellen Bork
Why Can't We Love Them Both?   10
John and Barbara Willke
Adoption: Not an Easy Option   25
Adoption: A Personal Perspective   35
Teresa LaMonica

II. PHILOSOPHICAL AND THEOLOGICAL PERSPECTIVES

Coherence and Priority: Evaluating the Consistent Ethic   39
John J. Conley, SJ
The Human Person Exists in Freedom Under the Truth   54
John F. Crosby
Absolute Autonomy and Physician-Assisted Suicide:
Putting a Bad Idea Out of its Misery   65
Francis J. Beckwith
The Incompatibility of Contraception with Respect for Life   80
Kevin E. Miller

III. MEDICAL AND SCIENTIFIC PERSPECTIVES

Mournful Numbers: Quantitative Tools for Combating
the Overpopulation Myth   127
J. T. Maloy
Abortion, Breast Cancer, and Ideology   139
Joel Brind, M.D.
The "Morning-After Pill": Another Step Towards
     Depersonalization?   145
Hanna Klaus, M.D.

IV. RELIGION AND SPIRITUALITY

Catholic Retreat for Post-Abortion Women and Men:
Results and Theological Reflections   150
    William S. Kurz, S.J.
Faith, Suffering, and the Prolife Movement   168
    Sidney Callahan

V. HISTORICAL AND LITERARY PERSPECTIVES

Compulsory Sterilization, Euthanasia, and Propaganda:
the Nazi Experience   187
    Jay LaMonica
Abortion and the Nuremberg Prosecutors: A Deeper Analysis   198
    John Hunt
Principles of American Life: An Archaeology of the Virus
of Negation of Inalienable Rights and its Antidote
in American Literature   210
    Jeff Koloze
The Road to *Roe*: Cultural Change and the Growth of
Acceptance of Abortion prior to 1973   231
    Keith Cassidy

ABOUT OUR CONTRIBUTORS   246

UFL BOARD OF DIRECTORS AND BOARD OF ADVISORS   248

Preface

The present volume contains papers presented at the seventh annual conference of the University Faculty for Life, held on the Loyola College campus in Baltimore, Maryland in June 1997.

Our sincere gratitude is due to Loyola College and especially to the local host for our meeting, Prof. Carol Nevins Abromaitis, Professor of English and Secretary of UFL's Board of Directors. We would also like to thank all the benefactors who have supported our organization and made possible its annual meetings as well as the publication of its newsletter and its annual volume of proceedings. This year we owe a special debt of thanks to the Rord Foundation, to Thomas Ryland, to the Jesuit Community of Loyola College and Fr. Patrick Earl, S.J., its Rector, to the Center for Values and Services at Loyola College and Fr. Timothy Brown, S.J., its Director, and to Martha Cox. Without their generous contributions this meeting would not have been possible.

The first set of essays in this volume bear on some new directions being taken by the Right to Life Movement. Mrs. Mary Ellen Bork reviews the political situation, while Dr. and Mrs. John Willke discuss a promising new pro-life campaign: "Why Can't We Love Them Both?" and Prof. Teresa LaMonica provides both a professional paper about the current state of thinking on adoption and a personal reflection.

On the highly debated topic of physician-assisted suicide, we are pleased to present an article by a frequent contributor to these proceedings, Prof. Frank Beckwith, within a section concerned with philosophical and theological perspectives on the life issues (Conley, Crosby, and Miller). Among the papers written from a medical or scientific perspective (Maloy, Klaus) we also include an important paper by Dr. Joel Brind on the much discussed question of the links between abortion and such current health problems as breast cancer

Two papers in this collection (Kurz, Callahan) deal with issues of faith and spirituality. The paper by Fr. Bill Kurz, S.J., is likely to be of tremendous use to those who work in the healing of post-abortion trauma.

Finally, four splendid papers from the area of history and literature offer deeper understanding of the cultural context for the debates that occur in regard to the great life issues. Two of our essayists (Jay LaMonica and

John Hunt) explore some of the attacks on innocent human life during the Nazi period in Germany, while Jeff Koloze recounts some of the darker periods in our own history. As we commemorate the 25th anniversary of *Roe v. Wade* (1973) in 1998, Prof. Keith Cassidy offers a timely reflection on the road that led to *Roe*.

Joseph W. Koterski, S.J.
Fordham University

Acknowledgments

"Absolute Autonomy and Physician-Assisted Suicide: Putting a Bad Idea Our of Its Misery" by Francis J. Beckwith is a slightly revised version of a piece that appeared in *Suicide: A Christian Response*, eds. Timothy J. Demy and Gary P. Stewart (Grand Rapids: Kregel, 1998) pp. 223-33.

"Abortion, Breast Cancer, and Ideology" by Joel Brind is reprinted with permission from *First Things* (May 1997) pp. 12-15.

WHERE IS THE PRO-LIFE MOVEMENT TODAY?

Mary Ellen Bork

I HAVE OFTEN wondered about Jeremiah's wife and how her attitudes were shaped by reading over his prophecies and living through the many rejections of his message. Living with the author of *Slouching Towards Gomorrah*[1] has taught me to let go of naive optimism and be more realistic—not pessimistic, but realistic—when looking at the state of our culture. When I say, "They don't know what they are saying," Bob will say, "They have an agenda." When I say, "They don't understand," Bob will say, "Yes, they do." I am not a prophet, but looking at the past and present of the pro-life movement I can see that it has a future that may be bigger than anyone has imagined.

The future of the pro-life movement is tied up with other cultural developments at the end of the twentieth century. Many new secular and religious groups have formed for the purpose of revitalizing civil society. Many are against abortion or want it limited. These groups resist the tide of moral relativism and carve out a position of principle and policy, and they work to get their message out, especially to the young. The societal change all these groups want is, as Gertrude Himmelfarb says, not just the revitalization of society but "the far more difficult task of remoralizing it."[2] Resistance alone is insufficient to achieve the larger goal of creating a culture of life.

As the pro-life movement promotes a renewed moral culture, it must resist the utilitarians and the population controllers promoting abortion as a right, a symbol, and a moral value. Political battles are inevitable and necessary to educate the public. Science and technology continue to open new windows on fetal development and the care of neonates. This knowledge adds to our understanding of the miracle of human life. As we look ahead to an enduring defense of life, to what is required in order to face a culture that is "Slouching Towards Gomorrah," the unknown factor is whether we have the courage and fortitude for the task. How do we make a moral argument to people who cannot think morally? How do we speak to a culture that has turned against man himself by allowing a parent to kill the child in the womb?

The judicial imperialism of the Supreme Court has colored the whole history of the pro-life movement. The Court created a constitutional right to abortion and took this issue out of the arena of public debate and action by state legislatures, the normal way in which social issues are usually decided by a democratic people. That is why this issue is so fractious and divisive. The Supreme Court imposed a ruling which was contrary to the moral views of the majority.

Pro-lifers have a difficult time working "the political trenches at the state level or [pushing] for statutory restrictions at the Congressional level."[3] The movement has proceeded on two fronts: a war of conscience and an effort of love to reduce the number of abortions through crisis pregnancy centers and the promotion of adoption. By standing for preserving and respecting innocent life with limited means, it has succeeded in getting a hearing. Its articulate defense of the life issues in the national debate has exposed the euphemisms of the pro-abortionists. The other side has access to large amounts of government and private money and to favorable media coverage. The pro-life movement has not yet succeeded in getting an amendment to the U.S. Constitution that will protect life, nor will that happen any time soon. A cultural divide has opened up that can only be closed by a willingness to recognize the basic facts about conception, the effect of pregnancy on women, and the moral truths surrounding life, death, murder, and responsible love.

In the coming years, the goals of the movement will be the same, but the strategy and tactics will change as politics, politicians, technology, and science change. The movement will have to become larger and work with other groups to persuade greater numbers about its fundamental importance to our future as a democracy. Science and technology are providing us with new knowledge of the life of the fetus and pushing back the time of viability. They are opening the horizon of neonatology and confirming the dangers of abortion and post-abortion syndrome. Information about the complexity of developing life and about ways of healing it when ill shows up the horrors of abortion procedures performed on fetuses of the same age. At the same time there will be still other technologies that destroy life at a much earlier stage of development, such as RU486 and abortifacient vaccines. The question not asked by *Roe* will be challenged by society and denied by pro-abortionists: whether human life begins at conception.

The most recent political success of focusing on an abortion procedure is the debate over partial-birth abortion, another episode in the ongoing battle over whose values are going to guide this country. Most observers agree that "the center of gravity in the abortion debate has shifted, even if only slightly."[4] First, Ron Fitzsimmons, a representative of the national abortion providers' "trade association," admitted that the other side was lying about the numbers of partial-birth abortions. The pro-abortion side lost some of its credibility when he acknowledged that many thousands are performed on healthy women carrying healthy babies. They are performed not just in the third trimester but in mid-pregnancy. Then Senator Daschle's amendment lost, and he voted for Senator Santorum's bill, which passed 64 to 36. The Daschle amendment, viewed as full of loopholes by pro-lifers, does reflect the feeling even in the liberal community that late-term abortions are not acceptable. His amendment barred abortions on viable fetuses and narrowed the exception to cases threatening death or "grievous" physical injury to the woman. He did not include the usual "health" exception. Some pro-lifers like Bill Bennett thought that a compromise could have been reached with Daschle. The White House staff is concerned that the Republicans will use this issue in the '98 elections. Our embattled President will certainly veto the bill.

As it stands now, since the wording of the Senate bill was changed slightly, it will be sent back to the House. The House will vote again and send it to the President. The President has ten working days to veto it. If he does not, it becomes law. If he does veto it, the Senate can vote again and try to get the three additional votes needed to override the President's veto. Some of those who might change are Max Cleland (D-GA), Tom Harkin (D-IA), Bob Graham (D-FL), Bruce Feingold (D-WI), and others.

The two-year debate over the abortion procedure known as partial-birth abortion has seen pro-lifers on the defensive but genuinely successful at educating many people about the true nature of abortion. The use of short TV ads in key states was successful, as were strong statements by religious leaders. Steve Forbes found his voice on this issue and aired ads on 600 radio stations. Doug Johnson of National Right to Life and other groups have kept the spotlight on this gruesome procedure, with the result that some people are learning for the first time just what abortion really is. Jeff Bell, a Republican strategist, says that even many liberal legislators no longer believe that they can defend late-term abortions. It remains to be seen whether President Clinton has noticed.

When the President vetoed the bill last time, he took the occasion to have a press conference in the Oval Office with several women, including three Catholics. He mentioned the religious affiliation only of the Catholics, implying that these women were "reasonable" Catholics, not blind adherents. He tried to win over both sides by claiming that it was an agonizingly difficult decision for him and that it was a rarely used procedure. He claimed that only a few hundred women a year "endure the agonizing decision of delivering a baby with terrible deformities" which would cause the infant to die around the time of birth anyway. Although many doctors have testified that the procedure is never necessary because Caesarian section is always a possibility, the President claimed that these abortions would help women to preserve their ability to have children in the future. "One of these women Mr. Clinton cited as an example of the need for partial-birth abortions has since suffered five miscarriages."[5] The pro-abortionists have also argued that the baby dies peacefully and painlessly from the anesthesia given to the mother before the procedure begins. The American Society of Anesthesiologists has stated unequivocally that their account was "entirely inaccurate."[6]

Why all the lying? Paul Greenberg, a nationally syndicated columnist, said it well. There are a lot of partial truths about partial-birth abortions because "when an ideology runs headlong into fact, it's the fact that must be explained away." The pro-abortionists have known from the beginning that the majority of the American people would not condone abortion. The Court handed them the right, and they have been trying to explain away the facts ever since, their main argument being a woman's so-called "right to choose." A *New York Times* editorial maintained this tradition, saying that both sides have made distortions and evasions. We should not be squabbling over numbers, the editorial insisted, for the principle at stake is privacy: "A ban on the procedure is still an unacceptable political invasion of private medical decisions and an attempt to limit access to abortion."[7] They want to defend a private medical procedure, even if it is infanticide.

Greenberg says that these rationalizations will continue "because every time one is exploded, another has to be invented. And ideology is nothing if not inventive."[8] We do not know what imaginative rationale the White House will come up with, but we know that there will be one. Greenberg wrote: "Partial-birth abortion has long since ceased to be a medical question; it's now an ideological one, and what ideology was ever deterred by mere fact?" I hope that Greenberg is wrong on this issue and that Senator Moynihan's prediction is right that Clinton will change his mind and sign this bill.

On the political front, electing pro-life congressmen and senators is important to winning this cultural battle. During the 1994 elections no pro-lifer lost a seat, which means that no one suffered for holding to a strong pro-life position. Groups are needed like the Susan B. Anthony Fund to raise money to promote pro-life women who are running for Congress. It competes with Emily's List, which raises much more money for the other side. There is much work to be done among Catholics, 64% of whom voted for Clinton in '96.

Looking toward the future, the pro-life movement has learned a great deal in its struggle to present the truth about abortion. Statistics show that there are still many people who are pro-abortion, but they are uncomfortable with that position. They were sometimes turned off by the pro-life focus on the baby and felt that the mothers were being ignored. Dr. John Willke, a former head of National Right to Life, has come up with a third-generation strategy which may be helpful by taking as its theme, "Why Can't We Love Them Both." We need to be concerned for both the mothers and their children. Post-abortion syndrome is pervasive among women who have had abortions and it needs to be addressed. The Willke's have produced a new video and a book that offers guidance to meeting pro-abortion arguments. Reaching that group in the middle will continue to be the main goal of the war of conscience.

Dr. Bernard Nathanson, one of the founders of Planned Parenthood and one of the nation's best known abortionists, changed his mind in 1979 and for the last fifteen years has spoken out on behalf of life. He has reflected on where the movement is now and he sees difficulties for the foreseeable future. This war of conscience is as combustible and as full of incidents of violence as the struggle over slavery. There are many dissimilarities, but the core issue at the center of both struggles is "the definition in moral terms of a human being, and the sweep of natural rights which accompanies that status."[9]

He worries that we may be headed down a bloody road similar to the Civil War. The slavery issue was brought to a focus by the U.S. Supreme Court's 1857 *Dred Scott* decision, which declared blacks, in effect, non-human property. "Free or slave, said Roger B. Taney, the Chief Justice of the Court who wrote the majority opinion, blacks could not be citizens of the United States and therefore could have no legal standing before the Court. Further, he wrote, 'Negroes are so inferior that they had no rights which a white man was bound to respect' and then went on to liken the slave, as pure property, to a mule or a horse."[10] Taney tried to take the issue out of political debate and thereby took away the possibilities of political compromise, which in turn led inevitably to the Civil War.

Like *Dred Scott*, the *Roe v. Wade* decision attempted to remove the issue from public debate and political compromise. Pro-lifers only have the war of conscience as their sphere of action. But in recent years pro-abortionists are trying to constrict peaceful protest and advocacy. It is difficult to get them to attend hearings. Networks refuse to allow pro-lifers to buy time on air for pro-life ads. And there have been campaigns to shut down pro-life protests and pro-life speech. The Freedom of Access to Clinics Act is really an attempt to silence peaceful protest and "sidewalk counseling," not to thwart violence. The media have seized on the incidents of violence committed by the lunatic fringe of the movement and have painted the whole movement as terrorist and fanatical. Dr. Nathanson fears that with the legitimate avenues of protest cut off, extremists and activists with short fuses will resort to more violence. Events of violence by extremists led up to the Civil War, and he is afraid that we may be on the same path.

One of the best things that could happen to defuse this situation would be for the Supreme Court at least to send the question of abortion back to the States and to let the political process work itself out. My husband does not think that this scenario will happen any time soon.

Dr. Nathanson observes a weakness on the other side: underestimating the depth of pro-life commitment to the cause. "Pro-life convictions spring from and have their roots in traditional Judeo-Christian values, in the Bible, in the commanding concept of the immortal soul."[11] He thinks that this is a fatal mistake. The pro-life cause is rooted in people's religious and moral beliefs, and they will continue to resist in a non-violent manner. Whether this can become a creative energy capable of re-orienting the culture remains to be seen.

On our side, we should not underestimate the deepening moral morass of society which must be addressed. The banner of abortion is carried by those who hold to a defiant radical individualism that insists on freedom without regard to truth. Their moral blindness is such that they do not accept the unborn child as a unique and irreplaceable human being. Some do acknowledge the humanity of the child, but not its personhood, and still value its destruction for convenience.

C. S. Lewis was concerned about the trend of moving away from objective moral standards when in 1943 he published the essay "The Poison of Subjectivism." He saw subjectivism as the modern error that leads to the dethronement of reason, and he called it a "disease that will end our species... if it is not crushed."[12] He felt that it leads to a mentality that wants to improve our morality by throwing off the restraints of the past and creating new values. Basic moral premises are given in human experience, and to deny that truth is to risk "the abolition of man." Progressives argue that there is no traditional moral standard because it changes with history, which can be proven false. They also say that to hold to a certain standard is "to stagnate," like water that stands too long. "To infer thence that whatever stands long must be unwholesome is to be the victim of metaphor," says Lewis.[13] Rather, without a permanent moral standard, there can be no progress.

For now the pro-life position is held in contempt by the dominant culture. It is ridiculed as not progressive, as merely neanderthal. We have to make the argument that Lewis made, that the value of the human being is basic to society. It is the "fixed point" against which we can measure our progress. He predicted: "Unless we return to the crude and nursery-like belief in objective values, we perish."[14]

We can now argue from experience that many of the changes we see around us are not progress. Alexandra Colen, a member of the Belgian Parliament, reflecting on recent cases of murder and sexual abuse of Belgian children, wrote in *The Human Life Review*: "It was Christianity that brought a fundamentally different view of humanity.... Our society is gradually becoming a post-Christian society in which there is a return to the pre-Christian vision of man."[15] We object to the rape, murder, and abuse of children, but we do not object to aborting unborn human beings. And we do not object to people being used as objects if they consent to it. Children are seen as property of their parents, as something they have a right to conceive or dispose of as they wish.

Gender feminists have further confused the issue by claiming rights over their bodies to the exclusion of anyone else. The body is their property. Eileen McDonagh has written a book, *Breaking the Abortion Deadlock*,[16] in which she seeks to rewrite the feminine language we use about pregnancy and to replace it with masculine terms of self-defense. The fetus is an invader and the mother's life should be protected from being harmed by this "potential life." She says, "While it is true that preborn human life is dependent on another person's body for its survival, it is hardly true that it is weak and helpless. To the contrary, preborn human life is a powerful intruder upon a woman's body and liberty which requires the use of deadly force to stop."[17]

The pro-life struggle continues world-wide. The population controllers and the feminists after the Beijing Women's Conference have put together a plan of action to ensure that their ideas find their way into the legal structures of all countries. So-called "progress" has become an agenda in which the unborn human person is the enemy, expendable in order to achieve certain totalitarian goals. Totalitarian countries crumbled from within, but their ideas and methods have been taken up by the West, intent on the destruction of its old morality. The significance of the pro-life effort is nothing less than the future of humanity.

NOTES

1. Robert H. Bork, *Slouching Towards Gomorrah: Modern Liberalism and American Decline* (New York: ReganBooks, 1996).

2. Gertrude Himmelfarb, "For the Love of Country," *Commentary* (May 1997) p. 34.

3. Dr. Bernard Nathanson, *The Hand of God* (Washington, D.C.: Regnery, 1996) p. 188.

4. Fred Barnes, *The Weekly Standard* (May 26, 1997) p. 12.

5. Editorial, *The Washington Times* (Feb. 28, 1997) p. 22.

6. *Ibid.*

7. Editorial, *The New York Times* (March 3, 1997) p. A24.

8. Paul Greenberg, "Partial Truth Abortions," *The Washington Times* (Feb. 27, 1997) p. A15.

9. Nathanson, p. 188.

10. Nathanson, p. 188.

11. Nathanson, p. 192.

12. C. S. Lewis, *Christian Reflections*, ed. Walter Hooper (Grand Rapids: William Eerdmans, 1967) p. 73.

13. Lewis, p. 76.

14. Lewis, p. 81.

15. Alexandra Colen, "Some Post-Christian Realities," *The Human Life Review* 23/2 (1997) 59.

16. Eileen L. McDonagh, *Breaking the Abortion Deadlock: from choice to consent* (New York: Oxford Univ. Press, 1996).

17. Tom Pelton, *Harvard Magazine* (March-April 1997) p. 17.

WHY CAN'T WE LOVE THEM BOTH?

John and Barbara Willke

MY MESSAGE TONIGHT is not what I said five or ten years ago.[1] Five or ten years ago my emphasis would have been on the right to life and on saving babies. But now I want to tell those who are involved in women's helping centers that they are doing what I believe is the most important single thing that the pro-life movement is doing in our time. The big problem is that we have not publicized it enough—it's a light hidden under a bushel—and so my message will be very direct. We've got to go out and sing from the housetops about what we're doing—how compassionate we are to women, how we are helping women—not just babies, but also women. Let me develop this point by going back to the beginning.

Barbara and I were already involved before *Roe v. Wade*. We had written *Handbook on Abortion* two years before the Supreme Court decision, and by 1973 it was in ten languages worldwide and had sold over a million copies. But when the Supreme Court decision came down, the pro-life movement began. What were we going to do about this problem? I remember the first meeting we had in my own Cincinnati, less than a month after that court decision. We had a city councilman speak and in the course of his remarks he said, "Well, now you've got to get right down to the precinct and start to work." "Pardon me, sir," a lady asked, "but what's a precinct?" That's where we were back then, 25 years ago.

I think that now we all know what a precinct is. But most folks started literally from ground zero. Everyone was completely shocked and surprised by the decision. There were a few experienced people. We had our share of leaders who came forward at the beginning. We had some excellent lawyers, physician, clergymen—but mostly we were used car salesmen and housewives and butchers and dry-cleaners and teachers and plain, ordinary folks.

I guess Barb and I had a leg up on some. She had been a professor of nursing and headed her department at a college of nursing. I had been

10

doing obstetrics for a long time and had already delivered a few thousand babies. Perhaps we even had it in our blood a little bit, for both of us have siblings who are college professors. We had begun to lecture and teach in the late 1950's, giving pre-Cana marriage-preparation courses. We had written our first book in 1964 about sex education for small children. By the time the abortion issue came along, we were experienced lecturers and had been speaking before large groups in major cities for a decade. In any case, we were among those who sat down and asked what we were going to do about this. Well, it was obvious that we had a *massive* educational job ahead of us. So we looked over the scene and asked what were the arguments that *they* have made that have carried the day, that have influenced the Court to make this decision.

There seemed to be two basic arguments, as we saw them. One was: "It's not a baby yet, just a ball of cells" or "It's not a baby at all" or "It isn't a baby yet" or "It isn't human" or "It isn't alive"—you know that story. We clearly had to answer that one. The second major argument was: "Well, it's only a Catholic issue." That argument has changed over the years to become: "It's only a religious issue" (or, in many areas of the country now, "It's only a Baptist issue," or "an Evangelical issue"). But the only people really standing up out front at the beginning were Catholics. I might add as a postscript (when I speak to Evangelical audiences, I always mention this point) that I think that we have never give due credit to *the* major organization in those early years that stood up and was a major bulwark defending the unborn—the single most important organization was the Knights of Columbus—thank you, guys! For this I usually get a hand from Evangelical audiences, for they know this, and they're quick to show their thanks. I then proceed to explain that, as the 1970's wore on, we had some major Evangelical leaders come forward—Jerry Falwell, Pat Robertson, Francis Shaefer, C. Everett Koop (our former Surgeon General), and others. They stood up to tell their confreres that this was not only a Catholic issue. Rather, it was a very real Christian issue in the broadest sense, and they knew that they needed to come out from within their church walls and go into the marketplace, or the whole nation was going down the tubes. By the time Reagan was elected, they were standing shoulder-to-shoulder with Catholics and have continued to grow in numbers and influence ever since.

But let's go back to the two questions. How do you answer those two questions, the two that convinced the Court? The first one we answered scientifically, biologically, medically. Like others who had been on the speaking circuit, Barb and I had never used pictures or slides, but at that point we quickly assembled a series of accurate, scientific pictures of the developmental phases of a fetal baby, and we started using them in our lectures: "Here is a developing baby at six weeks.... Here is one at eight weeks..." and so on up the time-line. "Here's a premature baby at 20 weeks." The set of slides we put together caught on like wild-fire. If you travel the world, you'll hear about Willke slides. Overseas it's almost a generic term. What these slides did was to tell the audience, through scientifically accurate photographs, that this is in fact a living human being from the first cell stage and that biologically there is really no question about this.

We elaborated the point: "This is when we have recorded the first brain waves, at six weeks.... Here is when we detect the first heartbeat, at three weeks...." And so we taught, by pointing out that here is this and here is that. As the years went on and many of you became involved in this project, this first question became *the* central core question that the pro-life movement spoke of and answered. We were certainly helped immensely by ultrasound, by fetoscopy, and by all the other brilliant diagnostic medical advances that have been developed in the last decade or two. If somebody in a debate before a college audience were now to say, "Well, we don't know when human life begins," we would get a titter through the audience. What rock did the person who said that crawl out from under? Is that Rip Van Winkle? In Washington we would say that "it wouldn't pass the smile test." It's such a stupid comment that people smile at it. For today to say that you don't know when human life begins is either to demonstrate that you're ignorant or that you're lying, because everybody knows when human life begins.

A couple of weeks ago Barbara was at Miami University in Oxford, Ohio, where she also spoke at a high school. Both groups gave her the same reaction. When she asked, "How many of you have seen a picture of an unborn baby on ultrasound?", one-third of the kids apparently had seen a still picture from a sister or an aunt or someone who had been in for an ultrasound test while they were pregnant. Barbara then asked,

"How many of you have heard the heartbeat of an unborn baby?" Over half of those in the audience had heard the heartbeat. And so, with the help of technology over the years, and with the help of all of you, we have succeeded in answering the first question. All the pro-aborts can now say is, "Well, yes, it is a living human, but a woman has a right to do it anyway." In any case, the first question has been answered.

Let's talk about the second point: "It's only a Catholic issue" or "only a religious issue." Well, this question was devastating. If we make it a religious question, and only a religious question, there will be one person who will say, "Hey, I'm a Catholic, and I believe what my church teaches—this is human life, and it's wrong to abort." But there will also be someone who says, "Well, I'm something else, and I think it's okay to do abortions, and that's my religious belief." The second would say to the first: "We're not going to impose our morality on you. You act according to your belief, but don't impose your morality on us. Both of us can then believe and act according to our own beliefs." This is the whole dimension of "choice"—neither should impose his morality upon the other. If we make it only a religious question, we lose.

And so, for at least the first decade, whenever we'd have a debate or a panel discussion, they would always want a priest up there and in uniform (collar and everything) because if they could get a Catholic priest up there, they were halfway home before anybody opened their mouths. Of course, we would at least try to get a minister up there. But, of course, that wasn't the answer either because it was still seen as a religious issue.

What was our answer to that? Our answer tended to follow the answer we gave to the first question: "Is it human life?" *Yes*. "From conception?" *Yes*. "Therefore, it's human from the beginning?" *Yes*. Since these are humans, this is a human rights issue. (That's the term used in Europe. Here we call it a *civil* rights issue.)

Now, 30 years ago—not too long after Martin Luther King and the passage of the Civil Rights Act of the 1960's—friends of Dr. King would come to him when he was agitating on behalf of equal rights for minorities and say "Look, Dr. King, we're with you. We understand the problem of segregation of black people, and we think that there should be equality and equal opportunity. We're with you, but, look, you can't impose this by law. You have to change minds and hearts. This is a change that must come, but it will only come slowly, through education, witness, and so on." King had an answer for that. He said, "I know a law cannot make you love me, but a law can prevent you from lynching me." For many of you, this may be the first time you've heard his comment, but that was not true 30 years ago. Many remembered it in the years just after that, and so we often quoted Dr. King. It had not been that long since the Congress had passed the Civil Rights Act. Since they did make *laws* to protect civil rights, we said, "Since this is a civil rights issue, we can and should make a law to protect the civil rights of the unborn." In short, we're still working on the answer to the second question, but we've come a long way.

Let's sum up. What was the effect of our method of teaching back then? In retrospect, it was spectacularly successful. If you were a raw audience who came to one of our lectures back then and if we were given an hour with you, we'd spend 30 minutes proving that this is a kid, and then we'd spend the other 30 minutes partly on civil rights and partly talking to you about abortion and its social consequences. If we were effective and if you were reasonably receptive, the overwhelming majority of the audience would walk out the door saying, "Yep, they laid it on the table. That is a baby. Yes, abortion kills a baby, and that's wrong. Therefore, *we must stop abortions*." It sounds like a very simple intellectual equation: convince the audience that this is a baby, convince them that this is killing, and that it is not just a religious issue, and they will walk out concluding that we had to stop abortion.

Using that method of education, we slowly began (and always this "we" is being used corporately here) to convert a nation. We were slowly becoming successful. And then something changed. I had been President of National Right to Life for ten years. I was probably in a better position to observe this change than most other people, and I'm a slow learner, but it did slowly sink in. This was the end of Reagan's time and the beginning of Bush's term.

There was a meeting in New York in the late 1980's, called by Bill Moran, who was then head of New York Planned Parenthood. He called together all of his fellow-travelers. We have been told that the whole abortion industry was there: the National Abortion Rights Action League (NARAL), the National Organization of Women, the YWCA, the

Women's Political Caucus, the various professional abortion groups, the American Civil Liberties Union, and all the rest. They were all there. Moran told them that they were in big trouble, that in his eight years in office Reagan had appointed two-fifths of all federal judges, and that now it was Bush's turn. Bush was popular, and he might get a second term. If so, that would be eight more years, and another two-fifths of the federal judiciary could be replaced by anti-abortion types. "Never forget," he said, "the federal judiciary has given us everything we have today, and they have guaranteed for us the right to abortion. But if the federal judiciary, which has been our friend, is replaced by those who are anti-abortion, the judges could take from us what they have given us." They knew that they "had" the support of over 90% of the media, almost 100% of the major foundations, most of academia, and much of the government. All of these were sympathetic to the cause, but he noted that this issue had never had majority support among the grassroots people of America. If they lost the judges and did not have support in the grassroots, the pro-abortion cause would lose. What to do? They didn't know the answer, but they did know that they had to find out if there was a way to influence the grassroots. And so they went for it. They got the best Madison Avenue types, they used focus groups, polling, market-testing, and other sophisticated techniques.

We know that NARAL alone anted up $500,000. Apparently the others also gave large sums. The research took two years. To put it briefly, the answer consisted of three suggestions. Suggestion #1: never talk about what's inside of the woman. Well, they never did so if they could help it. They knew that if they argued whether or not this was a baby, the pro-life side would win.

Suggestion #2: quit talking about abortion. Quit talking about abortion? Yes! You see, *they* (that is, *us!*) have framed the question before the American public. The question is: "Is abortion right or wrong?" They were told that when the argument is about whether abortion is right or wrong, the pro-life people win. So the advice was to quite arguing about whether abortion is right or wrong. Just don't talk about abortion at all.

Suggestion #3: change the question. Instead of arguing whether abortion is right or wrong, the advice was to change the question and move the debate to a question about women's rights: "Does a woman have the right to have an abortion?" Label it a matter of *choice*. Call yourselves *pro-choice*. Emphasize that the government should stay out of this very private matter. Keep repeating that the woman's right to choose is a greater right than the fetus's right to live. "Change the question."

Here's how this hit me. I was debating Faye Wattleton on a national talk show. The moderator asked her a question. She smiled and said, "Oh, that's a good question, but before I answer it, let's be very clear. The real question here—the central, the only important question—is this: does a woman have the right to choose? And should we or should we not keep the government out of this very private matter? Okay, now your question." And then she answered the question. In fifteen minutes we heard that same comment two more times. This happened again when I faced Kate Michelman, and then Pat Ireland, and then others. I'm a slow learner, but something began to penetrate my thick head. They've changed their line. They were all doing it. I didn't realize how devastating it would be, but devastating it was.

As an example, let's look at Tom Harkin, Senator from Iowa. Some of you may remember that Roger Jepsen, the incumbent, had been involved in a scandal. Harkin was a congressman when re ran for that seat. Harkin had a pro-abortion voting record, but in the election he held himself out as being pro-life. I can still see the full-page ad: Tom with his wife and handsome children, and in the background a Catholic church. He was going to do everything he could to stop abortion. He ran on a pro-life platform. He won. That was in 1984. He continued to vote pro-abortion. When he was up for re-election in 1990, he ran on a pro-abortion platform, accepted money from the pro-abortion groups, and spoke at their meetings and conventions. This time he ran as "pro-choice" and was re-elected. If he had done that in 1984, he would have had no chance of winning. He did it in 1990 and he won, and he won again in 1996. My point is that something happened during those years.

Back when Reagan was finishing his second term, we had a twenty-to thirty-vote pro-life margin in the U.S. House of Representatives. By the time Bush finished his term, we had a twenty-vote deficit. Something happened to our politicians during those years. What happened was that the pro-aborts had changed the question. I tried to keep track of this. My guess was that they must have spent as much as $50 million. Think of 12 full-age ads, the best that Madison Avenue can give you, in *The New York Times*, at $80,000 a pop. Multiply the cost of these ads by running them in almost every paper in the United States, for that's what happened.

As an example of such an ad, here was a picture of a well-dressed lady—she could have been a debutante—with the proper jewelry and everything, looking out through some bars. She's in jail because of those anti-choice laws. There was another one of Jesse Helms in bed in the middle between a handsome husband and wife—Washington invading your privacy—this sort of stuff. Clever, good, effective. And you know what? At least for people in politics, they did change the question. They also changed it for many people in the United States.

What had happened was that many of the politicians getting this barrage of propaganda came to the conclusion that we had pulled the tail of the pro-abortion tiger once too often and that the tide of pro-choice was going to sweep everything before it. Being convinced of this, the mugwumps jumped. A mugwump is a species of political bird who sits on the fence with his mug on one side and his wump on the other. Wherever the wind blows is where the mugwump jumps.

I was finishing ten years as President of National Right to Life. Barbara and I finally had an empty nest, and I was tired of commuting every week. But I started to see clearly what was happening about the time I was leaving. For a variety of reasons I knew that National Right to Life wasn't in a position to do what was needed. So, after I left office, I went from one organization to another—by this time I knew everybody in the movement, of course. Let's take just one example. Tom Glessner was head of the Christian Action Council (now called CareNet). Then it was still a viable lobbying group. Tom and I had been good friends. I spent some time with him and went over all of this, as I saw it. I said, "Tom, you're a good one. You're Evangelical, you're developing crisis pregnancy centers out there—can't you take this on?" "Oh, Jack," he said, "we have too tight a budget. We just let somebody go. I can't begin to do it here," he said, "you do it." Then I went to Concerned Women for America, to those dear friends of ours, the LaHayes, and talked to Beverly. I said, "You're the perfect one to do so. You're a woman's group." "Oh," she said, "Jack, look, we're doing this and that, and our budget's such and such. You do it."

I went from Catholic leaders to the head of the Southern Baptists and to others, but I kept getting the same answer. I finally got the message. Somebody upstairs was telling me that if I didn't do it, it wouldn't get done. So I started Life Issues Institute. And, almost miraculously, within the very first few months, I had two checks (one requested and one absolutely unexpected) that totaled $175,000. What I then did was what they had done. I began with polling, then moved on to focus groups and discussion groups, and then to designs, market-testing, and so on. Let me reduce this to two questions. The answers were startling.

We asked, "Do you have an opinion on abortion?" If they said, "Yes, I'm pro-life," we said, "Thank you for your cooperation, but we can't use you." If they said that they were pro-choice, "Thank you for your cooperation, but we can't use you." These were each about 25% of the total. The balance, some 50%, answered, "Well, I really haven't made up my mind yet." We used to call these undecided people "the mushy middle." Now we call them "the conflicted middle."

The "conflicted middle" did not really like abortion. They really did not think that it ought to happen and they would not want their daughters to have one. But if she said that she had a right to do it, this group reluctantly said, "Yes, she has that right." The one thing that came through as an absolute was that both sides thought that adoption was the greatest thing since sliced bread. But, of course, Planned Parenthood has been dumping on adoption all these many years, and it is not a very popular option today for young ladies.

But, in any case, the point was that the general public was not listening to us anymore. We were at an impasse. Our challenge was: "How do we get them to listen? We don't lose debates on points, but how do we get them to listen?" And so we went back to work—more research and more time. Let me condense this part of the story.

We have had a little triumvirate in Cincinnati for many years now. We do most of the thinking at Life Issues Institute. Market-testing was through Cincinnati Right to Life. My dear Barbara has been their volunteer Executive Director for 27 years. It is the largest city Right to Life group in the world. It has published 80,000 newsletters a month for the last 25 years and it puts out a lot of other educational material. First we did the design, then Barbara printed and did the market-testing. For instance, in the Cincinnati area she tested 25 different billboards on the theme we were working on until we came to the right one.

Much of the problem boiled down to what *they* thought about *us*. You see, they thought we were violent, that we shot abortionists, that we burned down clinics. And, furthermore, we weren't compassionate to women. They really didn't think that we were too well educated. We were mostly kookie religious zealots, and we weren't compassionate to women. Everything we touched was colored by that same "we weren't compassionate to women." Everything. It finally got through our thick heads that this was why the barrier had gone up. They weren't listening to us because they didn't think we were compassionate to women. It's like what Bush told me after I spent thirty minutes trying to convince him to drop his rape exception. He said, "Well, Doc, you're probably right. I can't answer your arguments. You've got it all there, but I'm going to keep my position." Why? "I guess the best I can say is some kind of gut compassion for women." He stayed with that position.

But that was echoed again and again. We were not compassionate to women. My heavens! Look what's out there! We have almost 4,000 pregnancy help centers in the United States. We've only got 3,000 Right to Life chapters and groups. So we have more offices dedicated to helping the women than we have offices dedicated to stop the killing. And who staffs them? Well, go to the typical crisis pregnancy center of Birthright. They are 98% female. Yes, they may have a male treasurer, and every now and then they'll let a man do something else. But this is a woman's world. Let's take a Right to Life group. We've got 25 members on the board of Cincinnati Right to Life, and three-fourths are women. I still represent Ohio on the board of National Right to Life—it is three-fourths women. Anywhere in the country you go, it's the same. If you take that sex-ratio and put these huge pieces together, we see that 80% of the activists in the pro-life movement in the United States are female. And a majority of the hours expended in the United States by the pro-life female is spent helping women! A minority of our time is spent trying to stop the killing.

And we're not compassionate to women? That's the centerpiece of our movement. That's what I meant when I started by telling you that you who staff the pregnancy centers are the cutting edge of the pro-life effort in our time. But this has been absolutely a very well-kept secret. Nobody knows it. And so we decided that our job was to brag about it, to get up and tell people about this. We then came up with a slogan and used it as the title of our new book this past year. It is *Why Can't We Love Them Both*. We also made a slide-set and a video with the same title. Cincinnati Right to Life has made this slogan available commercially on bumper strips, pin-on buttons, paper stickers, parade posters, and full-size billboards. This theme was tested through Cincinnati Right to Life. Now we finally have an effective answer. And so for the best answer today, when they say, "But a woman has a right to choose..." we suggest that you say, "But why can't we love them both?"

If I leave you with one thing tonight, let me say this. When we talk about the baby and killing, we win. When we talk about a woman's choice, we lose. They have even changed their title. They're pro-choice—we're anti-choice. Don't help them change the question, please. Every time you call them "pro-choice," you help them change the question and you help them kill babies. And I'm sure that's the last thing you want to do. So if you walk out of here with any resolution at all, please *never again call them pro-choice*. Call them pro-abortion, but don't ever call them pro-choice again.

Let me give you one example of how this is effective. Barbara and I have a rather unique situation at the University of Cincinnati. As a large public university, it has some 35,000 day students. A professor there called us up about 15 years ago. He was part of a prominent Jewish family that helped Planned Parenthood. He was agnostic and pro-abortion. He said, "Doctor, I have a rather unique class at the University—900 students and everyone gets a B. Nobody flunks if they just behave themselves. Class attendance is compulsory." He has it in a big auditorium, as you might guess. The students are not necessarily from church choirs. It's a snap course—they get a good grade. They just have to be there and behave themselves because he's a tough disciplinarian. If he's walking down the aisle and somebody makes a noise behind him, he'll spin around, point to that student, and say "You, what's your number? 385? Out!" And they're out. So they behave themselves.

His aim is to teach them public speaking and how to sell ideas in the public arena. He said, "I hear that you and your wife are very effective in presenting your case. I'd like you to speak. I'll give you a full hour. You can use anything you want to—slides, movies, whatever. Do your damn'dest. Planned Parenthood will be here next week." And so he gave us free time in front of 900 students. We have repeated this class for the last 15 years. Just as a sideline, Barbara asked a generous donor to pay for a handbook on abortion for each student. That's been done every year since, and I'm sure it has saved many babies.

This lecture has given us a platform that kept repeating each year. Through it we were able to try out certain ideas on the students. We were always fairly effective. After all, we have been lecturing for 40 years, and one does gain a certain ability to do this sort of thing. We were always able to hold their attention. They always took the books. Then about four years ago, Barbara and I looked at each other over the supper table the night after this class and agreed, "That was a difficult class." We blamed it on the kids.

We thought that this was just a different class. There had been some rumbling. The questions were sharper, and some of them were angry questions. We answered the rape question and got an "Oooo." After that lecture Barbara and I looked at each other and said, "Boy, that was a bummer of a class!" We blamed them. But the same thing began to happen elsewhere too. The next year was a little bit worse. Finally, after more of this, we got the picture—it was us.

Here's the structure we had been using. We began with slides of the number of abortions and live births. Then for thirty minutes, using slides, we proved that this was a living human from the first cell stage. After this we discussed and showed discrimination on the basis of race (the holocaust), skin color (slavery), disability (fetal malformation), and compared discrimination in these cases to discrimination in regard to "place of residence and age" (abortion). Then successively we met and answered the social questions regarding rape, back alley abortions, unwanted pregnancy, choice, population, imposition of morality, and so on. We then showed and explained the types of abortion. Barbara finished by offering them a wallet-sized card listing pregnancy help centers, offered our book, and so on, and then moved on to questions.

But this presentation was not working the way it used to work. We were right in the middle of our research at that point, and so we put the results of our research to use. The following year we made a change. Here's what we did. Barbara started with five minutes of telling them how compassionate we are to women. "We understand the agony of her decision. We stand *with* her, not against her. We want to help her. We really don't think that there is such a thing as a convenience abortion. This is a painful thing for any woman at any time. We think it's time to discuss compassionate alternatives like adoption. Why can't we love them both?

Then we told them how many abortions there were. *Then* we proved it was a baby. *Then* we went through the social questions. We spent more time on choice. We cut back on discussing abortion, showing the abortion pictures only briefly. At the end Barbara took five minutes explaining post-abortion syndrome and how it affects a woman. When she was done, I spent the last five minutes telling them how they could help such a woman. I detailed the steps of treatment and the fact that most doctors don't have time or don't know enough to help her properly. I was specific in saying that you, her roommate, her sister, or her friend are the one who can do the most. I outlined the steps for getting rid of the denial and bringing it to the surface, and then going through a grieving process. Even if she is not churched, we found out that she needs to accept Divine forgiveness. The next step, for those who can, is forgiving others, and finally the most difficult step—to forgive herself. I explained how those listening could help her go through these stages and how, at every stage, it takes time, it takes *your* shoulder, it takes *your* sharing some tears with her, *your* prayers with her.

Then we passed out the little wallet card with crisis pregnancy addresses and asked for questions. There were only two and it was over. The prof came up to us excited. He said, "Willke's, did you see what happened? Not a single girl asked a question. They took the books and filed out like out of a funeral home." Since then we have repeated this numerous times, and we keep getting the same result.

The difference in what we are doing now is that we start by telling them that *we* are the compassionate ones. There are almost 4,000 pregnancy help centers. There are only 3,000 Right to Life chapters. The pregnancy centers are staffed over 95% by women. Some 80% of the total personnel in this movement are women, and well over half of the total effort expended in this movement is expended in helping women. People are absolutely blown away by this. They come up afterwards and say, "Wow, I never knew you liked women. That's amazing! Why haven't we been told this?"

All right, how do *you* apply this? You're a preacher? Start with compassion to women, forgiveness by God, to the women there. You're at a home-and-garden show and you start to talk with some of the other women. It used to be that we'd advise you to start with "Yes, but do you know that's killing babies? Do you know there's a heartbeat at...?" Stop! Don't start that way now. Now you want to start by saying, "You know, one of the things that's not really known is how compassionate the...." Now when they come back and say, "Yes, but a woman should have the right to choose," you say, "But why can't we love them both?" They have had a one-liner, but now you've got one.

Let us leave you with something *very* important. If you remember *nothing* else you've heard here, remember this: when we argue whether it's a baby, we win. When we argue on choice, we tend to lose. So please, *never again call them pro-choice*. Every time you do, you help them to change the question, and you help kill babies. Obviously, that's the last thing you want to do. So *never again call them pro-choice*.

Finally, let me answer the "choice" question specifically. A woman says that she has the right to choose. What is her choice? Well, she *is* pregnant. Left alone, in a number of months she's going to have a baby. So what is her choice? Her only choice is how the baby is coming out—alive or dead, crying or in pieces. And so the right to choose is a right to choose to kill your own offspring. This is one way of answering the question.

Let's try another answer. Here's a group of young men. They've just formed a new organization. The title of it is The Right to Rape Club. We hear about this and we ask, "How can you justify this?" They say, "Well, really, the paramount question here, the central and only question, is who has the right to choose. We fellows think we have the right to choose to rape women, and we think we ought to keep the government out of this very private matter. Furthermore, we think we ought to appropriate some tax money to build hygenic centers where we can rape them safe and legal." Now let the audience pause just a moment and think, how are they going to respond to that? They'll be a bit incredulous at first and then reply "But rape is *wrong!*" Note the sequence of this thinking here. They guys said *the* central question was the right to choose to rape, and you said "but rape is wrong."

Let's substitute bank robbing. If they think that they have a right to choose to rob banks, you respond "But robbing banks is wrong." Try driving a hundred miles an hour down Main Street, and then try having an abortion. In any morally laden human action, the first question is not "Who's allowed to do it?" but "Is the action permissible?" Only then do you get to the second question, which is "Who is allowed to choose to do it?" Sometimes, when you structure the argument this way, the lights really go on for some people. They say, "Golly, I never thought of it that way." So this is another way to answer the "choice" question.

Let me finish with a comment from Richard John Neuhaus, a great civil rights activist from years ago who has remained very prominent over the years. Here's what he said as he finished a talk not so long ago:

So long as we have the gift of life, we must protect the gift of life. So long as it is threatened, so long must it be defended. This is the time to brace ourselves for the long term. We are laying the groundwork, the foundations for the pro-life movement of the 21st Century. Pray that the foundations are firm, for we have not yet seen the full fury of the storm that is upon us.

But we have not the right and not the reason to despair, if we understand that our entire struggle is premised—not upon a victory to *be* achieved, but a victory that has *been* achieved. If we understand that, far from despair, we have the right and reason to rejoice that we are called at such a time as this—a time of testing, a time of truth. The encroaching culture of death shall *not* prevail, for we know that the Light shineth in the darkness, and the darkness shall not overcome it. The darkness will never overcome that Light.

NOTES

1. This paper was given by Dr. John and Mrs. Barbara Willke together, speaking from a single microphone. But the continuing back-and-forth dialogue of the presentation made it extremely difficult to transcribe. Accordingly, the diction has been changed by the Willke's to read as a first-person address even though the actual presentation was thoroughly a "team-effort."

ADOPTION: NOT AN EASY OPTION

Teresa LaMonica

ADOPTION IS A VIABLE OPTION in our society today but one that holds lasting consequences for all those involved in the adoption triad: birth parents, adoptive parents, and the adoptee. One should not underestimate its effect on any of these parties. Like organ transplants, there are definite benefits for the recipient but a high cost to the donor. The act of adoption always exacts a cost from someone. Even in the best scenarios, where there is much preparation and support, there is a process of grieving that must be worked through for all those involved. This article will attempt to dispel some of the commonly held myths about adoption and look at the process through the perspective of each member of the adoption triad.

ADOPTION

Adoption is not a 'one-time deal.' The implications are life-long and often very painful. It is a process that affects the adopted child, adopted parents and birth parents throughout their entire lives.[1] Extended family members are affected as well; siblings lose or gain siblings and grandparents lose or gain grandchildren. One's viewpoint clearly defines how happy or sad an occasion it is. While adoption is often a necessity, the extreme act of giving up a baby or sometimes an older child does not lessen the pain involved.

Adoption requires the birth mother (and sometimes the birth father, if he is involved) to relinquish all legal rights to be parents. I was thirty-five years old and in the search process for my first-born child when I realized the difference between 'relinquishment' and 'adoption.' Adoption is the process where the adoptive parents (or single parent, as in many cases today) legally take over all rights of parenting the child *after* the child has been relinquished by the birth parents. The child is the one adopted, and usually has little or no say about any of this—a reason that many adoptees voice later as the need for control over meeting or not meeting their biological parents.[2]

Shlomith Cohen describes adoption as "... a situation where the process of developing a relationship with parents (adoptive ones) is intertwined with loss and restitution."[3] The adoptee must struggle with issues of rejection and abandonment, no matter how loving and caring the adoptive parents are. Adoptive parents must strike a balance between treating the adopted child as overly "vulnerable" while still being realistic about inevitable loss and rejection that may be felt at different stages in the child's life.

That adoption is a perfect or easy solution is a myth. Silverstein and Demick write that "adoption is a process that requires complex emotional compromise."[4] Professionals who deal with the adoption process should be sensitive to the complex issues of all members in the triad. Adoptive parents, for the most part, must accept a lost opportunity to conceive and a decision to raise another couple's child. Birth parents must give up their own child and the opportunity to raise that child. The adoptee often fares the worst since he has no choice in the matter. He has lost the opportunity to be raised by his own parents and must be raised by others unrelated to him. Silverstein and Demick discuss "...three emotional arenas in which all triad members are repeatedly engaged: loss and grief; bonding and attachment; and denial and shame." That all those working with the adoption recognize each of these is essential.

Adoption has been a harsh reality since the beginning of time. Even the Old Testament has the story in which Moses was left in the bulrushes by his mother in a desperate act to save his life. His life ended up quite differently because of this, and history can thank his adoption experience for the chain of events that followed. Even in more modern times many women may find themselves in desperation due to finances or social pressures where taking care of a child is just not possible, and sometimes even dangerous.

Myths about adoption abound. Although the social stigma of unwed motherhood has lessened considerably, it is a misconception that it no longer exists. Another misconception is the idea that a woman who gives up her baby for adoption can simply "put it behind her." Well-intentioned professionals foster this myth by giving advice to the birth mother to "get on with your life" or (worse yet) not even to acknowledge that they are mothers at all. To adoptive parents, well-meaning friends and relatives say things like "he looks so much like you, he could be your own" just as they are struggling with trying to feel like he *is*. Adoptees, even when "grown up" are still called "adoptive children," as if their adoptive status cannot be outgrown.[5]

One of the biggest myths of all, and perhaps the most harmful, is that adoption will be a perfect solution. There is no perfect family, and sometimes adoptive matches can be far less than perfect, particularly if reasons for the adoption are not in the best interest of the child or if expectations are unrealistic. Like any family, adoptive families have their share of divorces and family dysfunction. While there is often a chance for a better life for the adopted child, there are still no guarantees. Adoptive families carry their own set of problems and are not immune from the same sort of stressors which the birth mother has. The birth mother who gives up her child so that he will have two parents may find that in reality he has only one. No longer can it be assumed that the adoptive couple will be male and female, as many homosexual and single parents are opting to adopt. Similarly, a child who is placed for adoption because a single mother cannot bear to have him all day in day care while she works is often surprised to learn that he fares the same in his new adoptive home with parents of much greater means.

Slogans such as "adoption not abortion" do nothing to dispel another myth, namely, that there is nothing in between. There are certainly more options than that. "Have the baby or abort" would be a better, more accurate saying, for not every baby that is unplanned and not aborted would be better off being adopted.

DIFFERENCES IN THE 90'S

One of the biggest and most controversial changes in the field of adoption, and still a matter of controversy, has been the "open adoption." In 1986 Curtis defined open adoption as "the personal contact or sharing of information between the adoptive parents and birth mother during the adoption with the possibility of communication after the adoption is finalized."[6] There is as much variation in the amount of openness and communication in open adoption as in the types of adoption themselves. Not everyone agrees that open adoption is for the best, for there can be problems in a more open communication system between adoptive parents and birth parents. Openness may vary from just having a "say" in picking out the adoptive parents to meeting them and continuing a life-long communication, usually limited, with the adoptee and adoptive parents.

Closed adoptions do still exist but are often thought to be the most painful of all for the birth mother, in that little or no say is given to the birth mother (or birth father, for that matter) in the selection of the adoptive parents who will raise the baby. In a closed adoption, there is usually no contact again with the baby or the adoptive parents once the adoption papers are signed. Birth mothers typically voice their lamentations over "not knowing whether or not their child is dead or alive, let alone how he is growing up."[7] In a closed system, the baby is usually adopted with the birth parents having little or no say in the whole process. This point was brought home to me a few months after I had been reunited with my child. The adoptive father had called one evening to offer my husband and me tickets to a performance that evening. When I declined because I had no babysitter for my other three children, he very kindly offered to come over and babysit. I immediately made up an excuse because "I didn't know him that well." I hung up the phone and painfully realized the irony of having let this man, as a perfect stranger to me, adopt my child and raise him the rest of his life. Over the years, we have become good friends and I am sorry that I never had the opportunity to have gotten to know him and his wife before they took my child to be their own—I may have had less pain and anguish over the years.

There are many different types of adoption today. Edward Schor comments that "today an adoptable child is one who is acceptable to the parents, who can give and receive love, and who can benefit from family life."[8] This would certainly represent the ideal scenario and a variation from the past.

In the 1800's and early 1900's male children were adopted to help out in farms and female children to be companions for the woman in the home.[9] Then size and strength were important. Today most infertile couples want to adopt an infant and the younger the better. The infant supply has diminished in this country as the lives of more babies are terminated by abortion. As abortion has become more acceptable in this country, many women have become unwilling to bring a baby to term, especially if they may not keep it. Adoption has become less acceptable as an option for unwanted pregnancies, and more women are now risking social stigma and financial burdens so as to raise their own babies, despite the odds. Adoption of older children and infants who have physical or mental handicaps have become more common, as the availability of healthy infants has decreased.

In the 1990's the creation of families by any and all reproductive means has added new meaning and complications to the adoption process. Babies born from gamete donation, *in vitro* fertilization, and donor insemination are some of the ways in which new technology has changed adoption.[10] Legal battles over who holds adoption rights of frozen embryos have posed new ethical dilemmas. The use of surrogate mothers and artificial insemination by sperm donor have created other battles over adoption rights. Adoption *in utero* has become a new concept, as more and more embryo banks are set up posing new ethical dilemmas in adoptions today.

International or foreign adoptions have become popular as the waiting-list for healthy infants grows longer and longer.[11] These adoptions pose many problems of their own, for these children often enter the country with many special needs.[12] Perhaps one day there will be a trend where infertile couples begin to 'adopt' the pregnant teenager or help support the pregnant woman in financial trouble, in essence 'adopting' a grandchild as a novel approach to adoption. In my mind, this would be the ideal.

AGENCY VS. PRIVATE ADOPTION

The process of adoption continues to involve either private means or an agency. Both must follow adoption laws within their states. Private adoption usually cuts down some of the waiting period as well as the screening process for adoptive parents. This can be beneficial, but it can also cause problems, particularly if the screening process is sketchy and if little preparation is done in the way of counseling for either party.

Adoption through an agency, serving as an intermediary between parties, usually provides more counseling to both the adoptive parents and the birth parents. This is not always the case, however, and there can be problems with both systems. A reputable adoption should provide a better system of checks and balances for all involved, as well as counseling for both the birth mother and the adoptive parents. Most agencies encourage relinquishment papers to be signed only after delivery, whereas many of the private adoptions encourage legal agreements before birth, often causing many problems later on when a woman changes her mind. I have been saddened by what I call the "vulture" mentality when well-meaning adoptive parents wait outside (and sometimes even inside) the delivery room for their new baby, before the birth mother has even had a chance to say goodbye! While infant bonding is important, it is often overemphasized within this context, sometimes with dire results. Again, professionals who work with adoptive parties should keep in mind the needs of each in order to provide a healthier outcome for everyone. All in all, one of the most hopeful trends in adoption is the gradual shift from adoption in order to provide a baby for a childless couple to "what's in the best interest of the child."[13]

THE ADOPTION TRIAD: BIRTH PARENTS

Regardless of the type of adoption procedure, each of the members of the adoption triad is affected. "Birth parents have lost a child, and with it, a sense of personal moral worth and integrity."[14] Lauderdale and Boyle describe definite phases of grief which birth mothers go through. While many have de-emphasized the pregnancy experience and some the birth experience, almost all could remember vividly every detail of their babies.[15] A few who did not see their babies after birth suffered lasting grief over this. Those women who felt pressured by the agency or others to relinquish their babies experienced longer periods of grief and lasting bitterness over the experience.[16] The women who had more of an open adoption process, with some say in the birth and placing of their infants, also experienced intense grief but for shorter periods of time and with more of a sense of peace later on.

The relinquishment—the actual signing away of parental rights—was considered as the "culmination" period by Lauderdale and Boyle. Most described this experience as "numbing" while some depict it as an "out-of- body experience," followed by intense grief.[17] For myself, I remember seeing my hand sign my name on the form to "give up my baby" as if I was outside myself. Even small decisions ever since have often been fraught with anxiety for me. Birth mothers "do not put relinquishment lightly behind them—they suffer a lingering sense of loss and have continued needs for support and counsel."[18] Cushman states that this grieving and mourning are necessary in the relinquishment process, and if denied there will be serious consequences later on.[19] Unfortunately, support for birth mothers is not always available after the baby is given up. The adage "get on with your life now" is somehow not enough.

THE ADOPTION TRIAD: ADOPTIVE PARENTS
Adoptive parents have their own struggles. Happy to have a baby or child "of their own," they are constantly reminded of the child's lineage from another family, with roots different than their own. The adopted baby or child does not enter the adoptive family with a "clean slate," but brings physical and personality ties to another family.[20] The adoptive parents come with a history of their own: "they have lost their sense of reproductive competence and the child of their fantasies," a child that is seen as a linear extension of themselves.[21] Acknowledging these differences, rather than denying them, is healthier in the long run.

Psychological problems and marital conflict is common with fertility problems in spouses, but the study by Abbey and colleagues shows that, particularly for the woman, an improved well-being is found after the adoption.[22] This is not as apparent with the husband, perhaps because of the new stress of having a child and the demands made on the marriage. Similar stressors have been found after a new baby is brought home for both adoptive parents and birth parents. A study by Gjerdingen and Frobey also show some similarities between adoptive mothers and other new mothers in terms of fatigue (though not as much) and reluctance to go back to work.[23] Those who work with adoptive parents need to help these parents set realistic expectations for having a new baby at home just as they do for other new parents.

THE ADOPTION TRIAD: ADOPTEE
Adoptees must deal with the loss of their original family and the knowledge that for some reason, known or unknown, they did not want them. "The child has lost a set of parents, a sense of roots...."[24] Their connection to their genetic and cultural family is lost. Much of the

rationale behind older adoptees' search for their biological families is to re-establish these ties and to gain a sense of identity.

According to Cohen, the adoptee "must integrate two factors into his life: a bond with the original parents, along with its loss and rejection, and the adoption of new ("alien") parents.[25] Although raised by one set of parents, the adoptee continues to feel the influence of both sets throughout his life. One set is known while the other stares back at him from the mirror each day. With usually only a meager set of facts given to him about his original parents, the adopted child will attempt to fill in the rest through his imagination. "Themes of abandonment and rejection abound, no matter how muted by fantasy.... They are inevitable."[26] Hajal and Rosenberg describe different development stages in the adopted child's life where the adoption issue seems to peak. Adoptive parents who are aware of these stages can help their child go through these more easily. Acceptance of the need for information, especially as the child approaches adolescence, is very important, particularly in terms of "identity formation."[27] Identity is the "essence or core of the person," as defined by Lord and Cox.[28] The adoptive parents who recognize the adolescents' need to find their roots as a basis of increasing their own identity will only enhance their relationship, not split it. Hajal and Rosenberg quote Lipton in their article by reminding us that "the bonds that tie are of the heart."

Different stages in each of their lives will hold new adjustments, ones that can be met successfully, once understood. It is important not to oversimplify the adoption process or to glorify it. It remains both a complex issue and one that is often a double-edged sword—carrying with it potential for both happiness and pain. Understanding the different perspectives of each member of the adoption triad and the unique problems of each will help us all to be more sensitive to adoption.

NOTES

1. E. Schor, "Adoption and Foster Care" in Green and Haggerty, *Ambulatory Pediatrics* (Philadelphia: N.B. Saunders, 1990).

2. Adoptive Birth Parent Support Group (ABSN), Washington Chapter (1997).

3. S. Cohen, "Trauma and the Development Process: Excerpts from an Analysis of an Adopted Child" in *Psychoanalytical Study of Children* 51 (1996) 287-302.

4. Dr. R. Silverstein and J. Demick, "Toward an Organizational Relational Model of Open Adoption" in *Family Process* 133/2 (1994) 111-24.

5. See E. Schor, cited in n.1 above.

6. J.L. Lauderdale and J.S. Boyle, "Infant Relinquishment Through Adoption" in *Image: Journal of Nursing Scholarship* 26/3 (1994) 213-17.

7. *Ibid.*

8. E. Schor, cited in n.1 above.

9. P.T. Castiglia, "Adoptive Families" in *Journal of Pediatric Health Care* 8/4 (1994) 181-83.

10. I. Craft, E. Fincham, and T. Al-Schwaf, "Adoption *in utero*" (editorial) in *British Medical Journal* 304/6830 (1992) 839.

11. See P.T. Castiglia, cited in n.9 above.

12. See I. Craft *et al.*, cited in n.10 above.

13. Committee on Early Childhood, Adoption, and Dependent Care, "Initial Medical Evaluation of an Adopted Child" in *Pediatrics* 88/3 (1991) 642-44.

14. See E. Schor, cited in n.1 above.

15. See J.L. Lauderdale, cited in n.6 above.

16. M. Resnick, R. Blum, J. Bose, M. Smith, and R. Toogood, "Characteristics of Unmarried Adolescent Mothers: Determinants of Child-Rearing versus Adoption" in *American Journal of Orthopsychiatry* 60/4 (1990) 577-84.

17. J.L. Lauderdale, cited in n.6 above.

18. E. Schor, cited in n.1 above.

19. L. Cushman, D. Kalmuss, and P. Namerow, "Placing an Infant for Adoption: the Experiences of Young Birth Mothers" in *Social Work* 38/3 (1993) 264-72.

20. E. Schor, cited in n.1 above.

21. *Ibid.*

22. A. Abbey, F. Andrew, and J. Halman, "Infertility and Parenthood: Does Becoming a Parent Increase Well Being?" in *Journal of Consulting and Clinical Psychology* 62/2 (1994) 398-403.

23. D. Gjerdingen and D. Froberg, "The Fourth Stage of Labor: the Health of Birth Mothers and Adoptive Mothers at Six Weeks *Post Partum*" in *Family Medicine* 23/1 (1991) 29-35.

24. E. Schor, cited in n.1 above.

25. Cohen, cited in n.3 above.

26. E.B. Rosenberg and T.M. Homer, "Birth Parent Romances and Identity Formation in Adopted Children" in *American Journal of Orthopsychiatry* 61/1 (1991) 70-71.

27. F. Hajal and E.B. Rosenberg, "The Family Life Cycle in Adoptive Families" in *American Journal of Orthopsychiatry* 61/1 (1991) 78-85.

28. R. Lord and C. Cox, "Adoption and Identity: A Case Study" in *Psychoanalytic Study of Children* 46 (1991) 355-67.

Adoption: A Personal Perspective

Teresa LaMonica

I CALLED HIM ELDON PATRICK. He was born on March 1, 1972. He was the most beautiful baby I had ever seen. He had blonde hair and blue eyes, and he was my first child. As my dad handed him to me to hold for the first time, I suddenly knew that all the difficult months before and even the recent labor were all worth it. I knew at that moment that I would never feel greater love than I felt for this child in my arms. I also knew that in just six weeks I was expected to say goodbye to him forever.

Eldon and I stayed in the hospital for three days, getting to know each other, and I savored every moment with my new son. Then I returned to St. Ann's Infant and Maternity Home, where I lived with Eldon for the next four weeks—a procedure encouraged by St. Ann's. I resumed high school (in the little tutorial classroom at the end of the hall), and between classes I visited and fed my baby. The nurses in the nursery took care of him the rest of the time. At night I would come in and rock him and talk to him and sing to him for hours. These were precious moments which I have cherished a lifetime.

When he was six weeks old, I signed my name to a form which stated that I relinquished all my rights to be his mother. We had discussed all of my options many times and yet we always arrived at the same conclusion: there was no way that I, a 17 year-old single mother, could raise a baby by myself. But right at that moment that was exactly what I wanted to do—more than anything. I was told that I was being unselfish by giving him a better life in a better home. Yet my heart told me different: only I could love him best! Feeling defeated and numb, I signed the papers which said that he was no longer mine.

I went to the nursery and I walked over to my baby, lifted, held him, and rocked him. I sang to him one last time, a favorite song which my father had always sung to me, and I told him how much I loved him. I prayed that he would somehow sense this love and hold it in his heart always. I whispered "I love you" as I kissed him goodbye. Never had a goodbye been so sad, so heart-wrenching, and so painful as that. I walked down

35

the hall as if in a dream, as if part of me was being left behind—forever.

Mom was somber and I felt dead inside as we started the long trip home. My sadness increased with each mile we drove. It was years before I would realize how much pain my parents had also had over this goodbye, the loss of their first grandchild.

My mother broke the long silence between us by saying, "Teri, I know you will see him again." Whether she was saying that to comfort me or to help both of us, I'll never really know. Either way, her words gave me a glimmer of hope and I resolved to get on with my life, as long as I knew that one day I'd see my child again. I'd be ready.

I knew I would never forget my son—nor did I want to. There was so much of life that I wanted to share with him. "Please, God," I prayed, "I want so much to see my son again. Help me to get through the years until I do. I ask that you guide him and bless him in his new life. May he always know that I love him and let him know You in his life."

I did "go on with my life": college, dating, nursing, and then graduate school. I started and directed a pregnancy center, Birthright in North Carolina, and later I became a pediatric nurse practitioner. Eventually, I married and had another son, Gabriel, and then two beautiful daughters, Anna and Laura. Once again, I felt the joy of being a mother. I was happy and complete—*almost*.

On March 1, 1990 Eldon turned 18! My usual custom on his birthday all these years had been to attend early mass, to spend some time by myself, and later to write him a letter. I sent some of these to the adoption agency in hopes that one day he might be able to read them. But this birthday was different—I could hardly contain my excitement because I knew I could finally let myself believe I would be seeing him again! Little did I know that Eldon's adoptive father was at that time trying to find me!

The next day I started my search, with the help of my husband, Jay, and my search advisor from the Adoptee-Birthparent Support Group. My parents helped by offering their babysitting services. Originally, I thought Eldon would just "look me up" when he was 18—I had always believed this—but it was Jay who suggested that I should be the one to look him up since I had been the one to "give him away."

My first step was to go to the adoption agency—the last word I had of Eldon was when he was 18 months. The social worker had kept me informed of his progress at intervals in the beginning, but I was politely discouraged about calling very much after that. They had received my letters over the years, and they were still in his file. They were able to tell me about the last time they had talked to the adoptive parents—it was when he was 3 years old and "he was doing well then." There wasn't much else that they could tell me, for that was the last they had heard from them and it was still a closed adoption. They also did not mention that his adoptive father was also trying to locate me.

The search process was more emotionally difficult than I had anticipated. It brought back painful hurts, but now that they were uncovered, they slowly started to heal. I began a journal to him, explaining the search and filling him in on my life since we left off. I stayed awake many nights, remembering my son and I cried a lot. I had a great sense of anticipation, of excitement, and of pain. Less than four months after my search had begun, I located him! His name was now *Robert* and he lived less than eight miles away!

REUNION

Our reunion came two months later—it was a bit slow for me but a much needed time interval for him. Robert's dad arranged a brunch on Sunday and invited Jay and me to their house. As Robert and I saw each other for the first time in 18 years, we stared and then laughed as we realized how similar our looks and gestures were. We talked, sitting out on the grass in his front yard for hours, while Jay and his dad talked indoors. Robert talked about his family—his mom and dad and brother Kenneth. His parents had separated many years before and he had stayed with his dad, while his brother lived with his mom. He told me about his friends, his girlfriend, his truck, how glad he was to be out of high school, and his dog, Blackie. He said he always "knew" I would find him. He seemed to be such a handsome, happy, normal kid that I couldn't help but be proud of him.

All too soon it was time to go. It would have been wonderful to have him jump into the back of our Toyota and come home with us forever, but I knew he had another family now. He had tears in his eyes as we hugged and I said, "I love you." He said, "I love you too, Mom." I knew that he meant it and that somehow all through the years he had sensed my love for him after all. I knew then that the bond we had made years ago when he was a baby had never completely been broken. I knew that we would always stay part of each other's lives.

Saying goodbye, I hugged his dad, and Robert shook hands with Jay. As we drove away, I watched his father casually slip an arm around him. As we waved goodbye, tears were in his eyes, but there was happiness on his face. I am forever thankful that God had answered my prayers. He guided and blessed my son and allowed me to find him—my miracle had happened!

POST-SCRIPT

The author is a pediatric nurse practitioner and has served on the nursing faculty at Georgetown University as well as the UFL board. Robert has become much a part of his "extended family." Since meeting his birth father and his family, he has also become much a part of their lives. The adoptive family has been more than welcoming in this, and we all share a closeness based on a common interest and love for one fine son! We have all been truly blessed!

COHERENCE AND PRIORITY:
EVALUATING THE CONSISTENT ETHIC

John J. Conley, S.J.

IN THE 1980'S THE "CONSISTENT ETHIC OF LIFE" emerged as a theoretical and practical movement within the Catholic community. Crystallized in a series of addresses by Joseph Cardinal Bernardin,[1] the consistent ethic offered a moral and political linkage among a variety of human life-issues: abortion, euthanasia, war, and capital punishment. This ethical position immediately provoked intellectual controversy. Supporters such as J. Bryan Hehir,[2] Sidney Callahan,[3] and Ronda Chervin[4] touted the value of a comprehensive defense of human life across a spectrum of issues. Critics such as James Gustafson,[5] Richard McCormick,[6] and John Finnis[7] analyzed the defects of such a global ethic. In the practical arena, the consistent-ethic perspective animated such activist groups as Just Life and the Seamless Garment Network.[8] In many pro-life circles, however, the ethic received a critical reception,[9] inasmuch as it risked displacing the primacy of the abortion issue in a welter of secondary concerns.

Less than a generation after its emergence, the consistent ethic is already showing the signs of its age. One of the key contexts for its elaboration, the imminent danger of nuclear attack in the Cold War, is now of historical interest. One of the pressing contemporary threats to human life, euthanasia in the form of physician-assisted suicide, was scarcely an issue at its birth. Nonetheless, due to its ambitious scope and wide influence, the consistent ethic merits careful analysis.

CORPUS

The purpose of this paper is to provide a critique of the consistent ethic as a tool to defend the right to life. The major object of this critique is Bernardin's collection of writings devoted to this topic. Bernardin's version of the consistent ethic is important both because of its influence and because of its theoretical sophistication. Bernardin provides the clearest outline of the consistent ethic in five addresses: Fordham

(1983);[10] St. Louis (1984),[11] Seattle (1986),[12] Portland (1986),[13] Chicago (1987).[14]   Important applications of the consistent ethic emerge in addresses on abortion (Kansas City, 1985),[15] pornography (Cincinnati, 1984),[16] poverty (Catholic University, 1985),[17] the death penalty (Chicago, 1985),[18] health care (Chicago, 1985;[19] New York, 1986).[20]

Throughout this canon, Bernardin sketches the tenets of this ethic on several distinctive levels. First, at the level of vision, the ethic provides an account of the dignity of human life and the attitude of respect which cherishes it. Second, at the level of moral principle, the ethic identifies certain negative and positive rules of action enjoined by this respect. Third, at the level of application, the ethic examines the linkage among various life-issues. Finally, at the political level, the ethic studies the translation of its vision and norms into specific public policies.

ANTHROPOLOGICAL VISION
At the level of vision, Bernardin insists upon the sacred and social nature of human life. "Catholic social teaching is based on two truths about the human person: human life is both sacred and social. Because we esteem human life as sacred, we have a duty to protect and foster it at all stages of development, from conception to natural death, and in all circumstances. Because we acknowledge that human life is also social, society must protect and foster it."[21] The consistent ethic offers a comprehensive account of the sacredness of human life: it is imperative in each person from conception until death. It cannot be limited to the adult, the born, the conscious, or the healthy.

The consistent ethic also insists upon the social framework of this sacred life. Its defense and promotion at each stage of development is properly a concern of the entire community. It cannot be relegated to the voluntary concern of private individuals.

Especially in his later addresses, Bernardin stresses that this vision of the sacredness and sociability of life is a vision proper to human life alone. It is the personal nature of this life which merits such careful defense. "The theological assertion that the person is the *imago Dei*, the philosophical affirmation of the dignity of the person, and the political principle that society and state exist to serve the person—all these themes stand behind the consistent ethic."[22] Against the criticism of James

Gustafson[23] that the life of the individual person must be weighed against other social goods, Bernardin insists that "in moments of conflict between the individual and the social, the individual must predominate for it is here that the fullest presence of the Divine is to be encountered."[24] In other words, the consistent ethic's vision of the sacredness and sociability of life is not a sacral vitalism. Its vision places the individual person, the irreplaceable image of God, at the center of its metaphysics, ethics, and political program.

ETHICAL NORM

At the level of moral principle, Bernardin underlines a key negative norm for human action: One may never directly kill an innocent human being. "The basic moral principle that the direct killing of the innocent is always wrong is so fundamental in Catholic theology that the need to defend it in the multiple cases of abortion, warfare, and the case of the handicapped and the terminally ill is self-evident."[25] He underlines that "The inviolability of innocent human life is a fundamental norm."[26] In these passages, the central moral principle tied to respect for life is the categoric refusal to kill directly an innocent. It is adherence to this norm which simultaneously protects the child in the womb, the civilian in wartime, and the patient with Alzheimer's.

Bernardin's defense of the absoluteness of this norm is adamant. He explicitly refutes the position of Richard McCormick,[27] a moral theologian who had argued that this rule can admit of rare exceptions. "I think that the reduction of the prohibition against the intentional killing of the innocent to a status less than an absolute rule is not correct.... Because of my experience with this specific moral dilemma of deterrence and because I find the prohibition against the intentional killing of the innocent a crucial element across the spectrum of the consistent ethic, I find myself not persuaded by Fr. McCormick's recommendation."[28] For this version of the consistent ethic, the norm against direct homicide of the innocent is absolute.

In other passages, Bernardin provides norms for action far broader than that presented in the traditional rule against direct killing of the innocent. In several addresses, Bernardin summarizes the Catholic norm as a more general repugnance toward all deliberate homicide. He presents "the traditional Catholic teaching that there should always be a *presumption* against taking human life, but in a limited world marked by the effects of sin there are some narrowly defined *exceptions* where life can be taken."[29] Further, he argues that these permissible exceptions have been progressively narrowed by the magisterium. Two examples are the narrowing of "just war" causes to one (defense of the innocent) and the prudential judgment of recent popes and bishops that capital punishment, although theoretically legitimate, should be abandoned in favor of less violent means of punishment.[30] In his 1986 New York address, he further restricts the scope of these exceptions: "Life itself is of such importance that it is never to be attacked directly."[31] Without yielding to pacifism, such broad norms do suggest a heightened animus against all voluntary homicide and an erosion of the strict distinction between innocent and aggressive life which informed the traditional norm.

Not only does Bernardin underline the negative norms regarding homicidal action. He also sketches the positive duties which the conscientious person must exercise in the defense of human life. In numerous speeches, Bernardin ties concern for the right-to-life to concern for quality-of-life issues which promote and enhance human life. The 1986 New York address is typical. "I would like to examine...the relationship between 'right to life' and 'quality of life' issues. If one contends, as we do, that the right of every unborn child should be protected by civil law and supported by civil consensus, then our moral, political, and economic responsibilities do not stop at the moment of birth! We must defend that *right to life* of the weakest among us: we must also be supportive of the *quality of life* of the powerless among us: the old and the young, the hungry and the homeless, working mothers and single parents, the sick, the disabled, and the dying. The viability and the credibility of the 'consistent ethic' principle depends primarily upon the consistency of its application."[32] In this perspective, the positive duties to nurture the lives of the vulnerable emerge as correlative with the negative duties of avoiding unjustified homicide.

ANALOGY OF LIFE
At the third level of analysis, Bernardin specifies the linkage among a variety of human life-issues from the consistent-ethic perspective. In his

later addresses, he cautions that such linkage requires careful analogical reasoning, that is, a prudent recognition of the discontinuities, as well as the similarities, between these various questions of life-endangerment and life-diminishment.[33]   Nonetheless, the ethic tends to highlight the similarities, thus breaking the left/right opposition which tends to isolate particular life-issues according to narrow ideological interests.

The linchpin of this linkage is the key moral norm against the direct killing of the innocent. This norm guides human action across a wide spectrum of life-issues. "The more explicit connection is based on the principle which prohibits the directly intended taking of innocent human life. The principle is at the heart of Catholic teaching on abortion; it is because the fetus is judged to be both human and not an aggressor that Catholic teaching concludes that direct attack on fetal life is always wrong.... The same principle yields the most stringent, binding, and radical conclusion of the pastoral letter [on war and peace]: that directly intended attacks on civilian centers are always wrong....The use of this principle exemplifies the meaning of a consistent ethic of life. The principle which structures both cases, war and abortion, needs to be upheld in both places."[34] This norm illuminates the moral similarities among direct abortion, active euthanasia and counter-civilian warfare, without ignoring the ethical issues (such as the ordinary/extraordinary means distinction in euthanasia) which are proper to only one area of human life dilemmas.

In other passages, however, the linkage is far broader. Respect for life involves respect for the life of the aggressor, hence opposition to the death penalty. "We have also opposed the death penalty because we do not think its use cultivates an attitude of respect for life in society."[35] The defense of the right to life entails support for the quality of life of the vulnerable. "Those who defend the right to life of the weakest among us must be equally visible in support of the quality of life of the powerless among us: the old and the young, the hungry and the homeless, the undocumented immigrant and the unemployed worker."[36] Opposition to direct homicide of the innocent should foster repugnance toward the homicide of the aggressor and positive support for the development of the lives of the most fragile members of society.

Bernardin further extends this linkage to include what he terms "life-diminishing" as well as "life-threatening" activities. As examples of such life-diminishing issues, he lists "prostitution, pornography, sexism, and racism."[37] Opposition to these evils is tied to opposition to direct killing of the innocent because such social evils radically diminish the value of the life of the persons affected by them. "The comprehensive moral vision, which the consistent ethic of life promotes, demands that we work together to eliminate the evils of obscenity, pornography, and indecency even as we address the other evils which threaten and diminish life in today's society."[38]

Bernardin does recognize that not all issues bear equal prominence in this analogy of life. "A consistent ethic of life does not equate the problem of taking life (*e.g.,* through abortion and in war) with the problem of promoting human dignity (through humane programs of nutrition, health care, and housing.)"[39] Nonetheless, the general tenor of Bernardin's analysis is to present the consistent ethic of life as a broad vision of strict opposition to direct homicide of the innocent, general repugnance to all deliberate homicide, and positive action to promote human life through social protection and combat against a wide variety of social ills. Individual and corporate witness on behalf of life which lacks such linkage would appear to lack consistency and credibility.

POLITICAL TRANSLATION

At the last level of analysis, Bernardin studies the translation of the ethic's moral principles into public policy. Two attitudes mark this analysis. On the one hand, Bernardin insists that the integral respect of human life must manifest itself through a broad civic network of laws and institutions. He underscores the role of the Church as advocate and critic in the state's construction of a life-respecting polity. On the other hand, the Cardinal recognizes that the moral and political orders are not coterminous. The finite resources of the state and the principle of subsidiarity place limits upon the power of the state to defend and promote life. Moreover, the pluralistic and individualistic cast of American society makes the translation of moral principle into civil law even more problematic.

In numerous passages, Bernardin indicates the breadth of the civic programs which flow from the respect of human life. The Seattle address presses a typical case. "If one contends, as we do, that the right of every fetus to be born should be protected by civil law and supported by social consensus, then our moral, political, and economic responsibilities do not stop at the moment of birth. Those who defend the right to life of the weakest among us must be equally visible in support of the quality of life of the powerless among us: the old and the young, the hungry and the homeless, the undocumented immigrant and the unemployed worker. Such a quality of life posture translates into specific political and economic positions on tax policy, employment generation, welfare policy, nutrition and feeding programs, and health care."[40] The consistent respect of life expresses itself as advocacy both for laws which ban unjustified homicide (such as abortion) and for social-welfare programs which sustain the lives of the marginal.

In many addresses, Bernardin extends the defense of human life to concerns outside of the immediate area of homicide, such as pornography[41] or the employment policies of hospitals.[42] He justifies the breadth of the interventions of the American bishops in both domestic and foreign policy as a faithful political translation of a consistent respect for life. "On issues as diverse as abortion, Central America, nuclear war, and poverty, failure of the bishops to speak would be a dereliction of civic responsibility and religious duty."[43] Effective promotion of life demands such comprehensive political witness.

Political, as well as moral, commitment to defend life requires consistency in its principles and applications. The issue of political consistency is especially acute in one's posture toward the extent of state authority in life-related questions. One cannot support a maximalist polity in one area, then suddenly tout a minimalist polity in another. "Consistency means we cannot have it both ways: We cannot urge a compassionate society and vigorous public policy to protect the rights of the unborn and then argue that compassionate and significant public programs on behalf of the needy undermine the moral fiber of society or are beyond the proper scope of governmental responsibility."[44] In this political consistency, the ethic defended by Bernardin rejects both the liberal refusal to oppose certain types of homicide (abortion, euthanasia) under the rubric of privacy and the conservative refusal to oppose certain types of life-sustaining institutions (social welfare programs) by an appeal to economic freedom. The consistent-ethic perspective clearly endorses substantial state intervention both to repress all homicide of the innocent and to foster the security of the marginal.

Despite the effort to deduce political from moral commitments, Bernardin recognizes that the moral and political orders are not identical. Following the position taken by the American episcopate in their pastoral letter on war and peace,[45] he concedes that the public-policy conclusions which the bishops support as applications of moral principles do not enjoy the same authority as the principles themselves. Differences in analysis of empirical facts, in prudential judgment regarding feasibility, and in political philosophy can lead Church members, let alone the general public, to divergent positions on public-policy solutions. A realistic appreciation of the gap between the clarity of the moral order and the ambiguity of the political realm must govern debate on the translation of the consistent ethic's moral imperatives into a civic code.

Several factors limit the capacity of the state to defend and promote life. One is the radical difference in scope between the moral and the civic orders. "Although the premises of civil law are rooted in moral principles, the scope of law is more limited and its purpose is not the moralization of society. Moral principles govern personal and social human conduct and cover as well interior acts and motivation. Civil statutes govern public order; they address primarily external acts and values that are formally social."[46] In order to support the passage of a law, it is not sufficient to show that the action which is the object of the law is destructive or supportive of human life. One must show that the action is central to the social order itself and that the legislation will not produce even worse consequences. In American society, it is further necessary to demonstrate why the proposed legal remedy to the life-endangering evil should override the usual presumption on behalf of individual freedom.

In evoking the limits of the state in developing a pro-life civic code, Bernardin also appeals to a traditional tenet of Catholic social doctrine: the principle of subsidiarity. According to this principle, the state should not attempt to do what is proper for certain intermediate bodies (family, guild, church) to do. In the field of life-related actions, this principle indicates that certain of these actions, especially those of a more social-welfare nature, should be left primarily to the care of these intermediate bodies rather than to the direction and possible abuse by the bureaucratic state. "We cannot be consistent with Catholic tradition unless we accept the principle of subsidiarity. I fully support a pluralist social system in which the state is not the center of everything."[47] Private groups play a key role in promoting human life, one which should not be supplanted by the state. Nonetheless, Bernardin immediately cautions about the misuse of this principle. "I do not want the principle of subsidiarity used in a way which subverts Catholic teaching on the collective responsibility of society for its poor. I am not endorsing a concept of decentralization or federalism which absolves the government from fulfilling its responsibilities."[48] Despite his affirmation of the principle of subsidiarity as a brake upon state power, Bernardin clearly refuses to accept it as a tool to abolish or reduce the substantial social-welfare duties proper to the state.

CONTRIBUTIONS

More than a decade after its emergence, the strengths and weaknesses of the consistent ethic appear in bolder relief. If Bernardin's version of the ethic provides a clear framework for pro-life activism, its ambiguities have not receded with age.

In the Bernardin account, the consistent ethic provides several theoretical resources for the moral and political defense of human life. First, the ethic details a vision of the pre-eminent value of life. Not only does it evoke the sacredness of life. It details the distinctive value of human life as a unique person made in God's image. The spiritual powers of intellect and will, proper to the person alone, ground the defense of human life against aggression as a supreme moral obligation. Moreover, Bernardin repeatedly emphasizes the social, as well as the sacred, character of human life. The exercise of these personal powers—their careful gestation as well as their immunity from assault—requires careful legal protection and generous social tutelage. At the level of vision, the consistent ethic explicitates the global attitude of reverence toward the good of personal life which must inform the debate over moral rules and civic code.

Second, the ethic affirms a cardinal moral rule which cuts across the spectrum of human life-issues: One may never directly kill an innocent human being. It is this norm which grounds complete opposition to direct abortion, active euthanasia, and the direct killing of civilians in warfare. Adherence to this rule in all questions regarding homicide is the touchstone of moral consistency. Such an emphasis upon precise norms saves Bernardin's ethic from remaining at the vague level of general sentiments. His defense of the absolute and exceptionless nature of such norms, against the "lesser of evils" position of proportionalists, provides a steely clarity to the consistent ethic's account of human action.

Third, the consistent ethic carefully welds right and duty together in the human life arena. Respect for life entails both defense of the right of the innocent to live, from conception until natural death (hence, right as immunity from aggression), and the duty to foster this life through personal and corporate acts of nurturance (hence, commitment to social welfare). Consistent moral action, as well as equitable political translation of this action, turns upon the balanced synthesis of these rights and duties.

Fourth, the ethic provides a sophisticated measure of political consistency. This consistency does not involve uniformity in adherence to the civic application of certain principles concerning human life. It requires coherence in one's fundamental posture toward the state. One cannot insist upon a maximal state in the repression of murder (for example, through state bans on abortion and euthanasia) and a minimal state in the area of social welfare. Conversely, one cannot endorse a massive welfare state to promote life while denying the state competence to outlaw abortion and euthanasia in the name of privacy. Both the typically liberal and conservative accounts of the state fall radically short of the fundamental coherence, a coherence at the level of polity, demanded by the consistent ethic in its account of political authority and mission.

LIMITATIONS
Despite its contributions, this ethic manifests several major weaknesses. A certain theoretical haziness blunts its political effectiveness.

First, Bernardin compromises the clarity of the rule against direct killing of the innocent by arguing, in certain passages, against all deliberate acts of homicide. He rightly claims that the terrible power of modern warfare has narrowed the acceptable grounds for recourse to war. He also rightly notes that, while the state in principle has the right to execute criminals, a compelling prudential case can be made for the renunciation of this right. But such a heightened attention to the life of the aggressor should not abolish or diminish the decisive moral difference between the rights of the innocent and those of the aggressor, especially in situations of immediate life-endangerment. Unfortunately, certain vague formulae in the Cardinal's addresses, such as opposition to all direct homicide, suggest such a leveling. Not surprisingly, such broad strictures undercut the firmness of the traditional moral norm and foster a political program so vast that it risks impotence.

Second, the intertwining of the negative and positive duties concerning the good of life may suggest a certain equivalence regarding the two. As John Paul II argues in *Evangelium Vitae*,[49] however, the similarity between these two sets of duties is not exact. The negative duty to avoid murder, that is, the direct killing of the innocent, is absolute. It binds all without exception. The positive duties to foster life, however, have a looser scope and force. One may rightly choose among these obligations, such as the duty to feed the poor or to educate the ignorant. The precise nature of these obligations is often elusive, varying according to the resources of individuals and societies. While Bernardin does argue that all of these duties do not possess the same moral absoluteness, his constant interlacing of the negative duties against homicide with the positive duties toward social welfare tends to suggest a moral equivalence among them. The absoluteness of the duty to avoid murder (and the unique moral gravity of murder) tends to be effaced in a congeries of duties to perform the corporal works of mercy.

This tendency to level all life-related duties becomes especially problematic in the political arena. It is relatively easy to outline the state's duties to defend the right-to-life of the innocent. This entails a legal code which recognizes the right-to-life of each citizen from conception until natural death and a judicial framework for the prosecution of assaults against this fundamental right. While individuals may dispute the merits of 'imperfect' legislation in this field, the *telos* of the state in this regard is clear. But when the state ponders social welfare policies in this area, the proper outcome is inevitably hazier. People equally committed to the good of life may legitimately disagree on the desirability and details of particular laws concerning education or health. The principle of subsidiarity and the role of the intermediate bodies raise serious questions regarding the prerogatives and limits of the state in such life-enhancing areas. While Bernardin, especially in his later addresses, does recognize such ambiguities, he tends to minimize them in the name of the state's duties toward the common good. This political minimization of legitimate pluralism concerning the state's role in fostering social welfare reflects the problematic fusion of positive and negative duties toward human life on the level of moral obligation.

Third, the version of the consistent ethic supported by Bernardin appears to lack political prudence. The art of government is not the simple capacity of the legislator to turn moral desiderata into civil law. It is the power to prioritize. It is the ability to distinguish between grave and minor evils, more urgent and less urgent concerns in a given society. It is the prophetic discernment about which questions of justice demand immediate consideration and which, for the moment, may remain legitimately in the background. Since the late 1960's, especially since the *Roe v. Wade* decision (1973), the American bishops have placed such a priority upon the question of abortion. They have emphasized that the sudden disenfranchisement of an entire class of citizens and the legacy of 1.5 million abortions a year constitute a cataclysmic assault upon human rights. In many recent documents the bishops have labeled abortion "the pre-eminent civil rights issue of our age." In Bernardin's version of the consistent ethic, however, abortion appears to lose its priority. Against the criticism of pro-life activists, Bernardin insists that a global concern for the value of life only heightens the case against abortion. In practice, however, the linkage of abortion to a myriad of other issues gravely weakens the primacy of the struggle against abortion. In the subordination of abortion to a long list of social welfare concerns, the scandal of the state's complicity in murder is effectively occulted. Such a political leveling of the abortion issue inevitably tends to justify the position of "pro-choice" Catholics that their witness to life is found in other substantial patches of the seamless garment.

Finally, the very criterion for the development of this ethic—consistency—is a remarkably thin and formal one. It is a necessary but insufficient condition for developing an adequate ethic of life. Divergent moralities of life, perfectly consistent within themselves, can arrive at contradictory principles. The pure pacifist position, supported by thinkers such as the Mennonite John Yoder,[50] provides a coherent condemnation of all deliberate homicide by an appeal to the sacrificial love of one's enemy. In perfect internal coherence, it rules out all voluntary recourse to abortion, euthanasia, war, or lethal police action. The neo-libertarian position, defended by the philosopher Ronald Dworkin,[51] exhibits a similar, if diametrically opposed, consistency. According to this perspective, the right-to-life is proper only to the self-conscious human being. Adult autonomy and self-determination are the key goods for state protection. In this schema, abortion and euthanasia are easily tolerated, while recourse to war may be justified.

In order to elaborate an adequate ethic of life, consistency alone does not suffice. To justify Bernardin's version of the consistent ethic, it is necessary to address the more substantive issues of why human life enjoys such pre-eminent value, of why the direct killing of the innocent is an absolute norm, and of why the state must firmly oppose every instance of such a gravely unjust act. Emphasizing too strongly the value of consistency in human life ethics may lead the Church to comfort a moral pluralism and a libertarian polity which it must contest.

NOTES

1. Cf. Joseph Cardinal Bernardin, *Consistent Ethic of Life* (Kansas City: Sheed & Ward, 1988). This volume assembles the major speeches of Bernardin on the consistent ethic and the scholarly responses to his position presented at a colloquium at Loyola University of Chicago on November 7, 1987. Hereafter cited as CEL.

2. Cf. J. Bryan Hehir in CEL 218-36.

3. Cf. Sidney Callahan in CEL 237-44.

4. Cf. Ronda Chervin, *The Consistent Life Ethic: Understanding the Issues* (Ligouri: Ligouri Press, 1990).

5. Cf. James Gustafson in CEL 210-17.

6. Cf. Richard McCormick in CEL 96-122.

7. John Finnis in CEL 182-95.

8. For a journal devoted to news and analysis of such consistent-ethic activism, cf. *Harmony* (P.O. Box 210056; San Francisco, CA 94121-0056).

9. Cf. the publications of the American Life League during the 1983-88 period for a selection of essays criticizing the consistent-ethic approach as subversive of work against abortion and erosive of the distinction between innocent and aggressive life.

10. Cf. CEL 1-11.

11. Cf. CEL 12-19.

12. Cf. CEL 77-85.

13. Cf. CEL 86-95.

14. Cf. CEL 245-56.

15. Cf. CEL 20-26.

16. Cf. CEL 27-35.

17. Cf. CEL 36-48.

18. Cf. CEL 59-65.

19. Cf. CEL 49-58.

20. Cf. CEL 66-76.

21. CEL 88.

22. CEL 79.

23. Cf. James Gustafson in CEL 196-209.

24. CEL 250.

25. CEL 23.

26. CEL 23.

27. Cf. Richard McCormick in CEL 96-122.

28. CEL 81.

29. CEL 5.

30. Cf. CEL 5-6.

31. CEL 70.

32. CEL 70.

33. Cf. CEL 80-83.

34. CEL 8.

35. CEL 7.

36. CEL 7.

37. CEL 30.

38. CEL 34.

39. CEL 15.

40. CEL 82.

41. Cf. CEL 27-35.

42. Cf. CEL 66-75.

43. CEL 43.

44. CEL 82.

45. Cf. CEL 43.

46. CEL 92.

47. CEL 42.

48. CEL 42.

49. John Paul II, *Evangelium Vitae* #57.

50. Cf. John Howard Yoder, *The Politics of Jesus* (Grand Rapids: Eerdmans, 1972).

51. Ronald Dworkin, *Life's Dominion: An Argument about Abortion, Euthanasia, and Individual Freedom* (New York: Knopf, 1993).

THE HUMAN PERSON EXISTS
IN FREEDOM UNDER THE TRUTH

John F. Crosby

WE ALL KNOW HOW OFTEN it happens that the freedom of human persons is asserted in such a way as to undermine pro-life positions. Whether it is the objective moral wrong of abortion and euthanasia that we affirm, or whether it is the legal proscription of them that we propose, we can expect to hear in response that our affirmations and proposals interfere with the freedom of the human person. To some ears the very idea of the objectivity of the moral law sounds coercive; these are the people who think that the freedom of persons requires that all truth and value be relative to persons, that each person have his own truth and his own system of value.

Years ago I was greatly struck by an essay of the enormously influential legal positivist, Hans Kelsen, who gave what seemed and still seems to me a paradigmatic expression of this philosophy of personal freedom. In his "Absolutism and Relativism in Philosophy and Politics,"[1] Kelsen takes absolutism in politics to mean simply the rule of a totalitarian tyrant over his subjects. Absolutism in philosophy means simply that truth and being are understood as independent of the human mind that discovers them, it means that the human mind is measured by truth and being and is not the measure of them. Then Kelsen connects the two absolutisms like this: if we understand the human mind as measured by truth and being, then we subject man to truth and being *in the same slavish way in which people are subjected to the totalitarian state that dominates and manipulates them.* The undeniable servitude that he sees in the totalitarian state is for him an image of a kindred servitude that he sees in our relation to a mind-independent order of truth and being. Hence Kelsen also affirmed a correspondence between the freedom of persons in a democratic regime and the relativity of truth and being to man. Human persons are free in relation to truth and being—free with a freedom analogous to that of the citizens in a democratic state—only if each of them is himself the source of truth and being. Now such a position obviously puts an end to our pro-life position. My pro-life position is only true for me, but I would impose it wrongly on you, violating your freedom as person, if I assume that it is true simply speaking and hence also true for you, and if I therefore expect you as a rational being to share a pro-life stance.

Our task in the pro-life movement is to show that the freedom of persons is in reality not harmed but protected and perfected by depending on what John Paul II likes to call "the truth about good." In fulfilling this task we must resist the temptation to fudge on personal freedom and to be suspicious of the growing understanding of it in our time. One has only to look at Vatican II's "Declaration on Religious Liberty" to see this growth at work in the Catholic Church. We have to make our own this development with respect to freedom. And so we must not say that truth is more important than freedom, but rather that truth and freedom should not be played off against each other, since they in fact perfect each other.

Of course, you and I will want to ask: how can people possibly think that they are oppressed by the fact that they cannot make up their own truth about existence and the moral order of the world? Whence this fear not just of an error in moral principle but of moral truth itself? C.S. Lewis undoubtedly speaks for us when in *The Abolition of Man* he shows in the most convincing way that it is not living by the objective moral law, which he calls the *Tao*, that oppresses our freedom; what oppresses us is rather repudiating the *Tao*. He shows that if we will not live within the cosmos of objective value, we are inevitably abandoned to our arbitrary likings and aversions, which in turn has the effect of handing us over to those natural causes (such as the weather, heredity, digestion) that make things agreeable or disagreeable to us. But to live by being pushed back and forth by natural causes is to live a life utterly unworthy of a person who is called to freedom.[2] Only the *Tao* gives us an alternative to the indignity of being ruled by nature; it is therefore the principle of our freedom. And so we to whom this seems self-evident are left puzzled at the claim that objective moral truth is the enemy of our freedom.

Our puzzlement is all the greater when we think more concretely about moral truth. Take the basic moral principle that persons are never to be used as instrumental means but are always to be taken as their own ends.

We human beings did not posit this principle, we have no power to revoke it; our highest wisdom is to discover the dignity of the person on which it rests. We are subject to moral judgment when we act against it, which means that this principle measures us and not the other way around. It has all the objectivity and universality that Kelsen dreads—but is he right in saying that we are enslaved to it when we order our lives according to it? Of course, if someone coerces us to live according to it, then it may be that we stand in a servile relation towards the coercing person. But take all the conscientious people who need no coercion to try to live according to it: they suffer no heteronomy at all as a result of living according to a principle whose authority they experience as lying beyond all human willing. The fear of heteronomy is particularly absurd when the principle is applied to oneself: I ought never make a mere means of myself. Although I am not the measure of even this moral norm—I am bound to respect myself even if I want to throw myself away, and I am in the wrong even if I do make myself the slave of some master—it is nevertheless not a norm that can be reasonably said to weigh oppressively upon me as some foreign force.

Why, then, do people feel cramped in their freedom by a moral law presenting itself as objectively and universally valid? It is tempting to answer merely in moral terms, saying that they want to be free to do whatever they feel like doing and that the moral law obviously interferes with their unbridled gratification. There are, of course, those who will brook no hindrance to the fulfillment of their "unbitted lusts." But there are others, such as Kelsen, who have plausible reasons for setting freedom against truth, and these deserve to be taken intellectually seriously. Let us try to engage them in discussion, and let us do so by identifying the circumstances under which the objectively valid moral law really can be confining for persons.

1) It goes without saying that persons suffer if certain precepts are erroneously put forth as belonging to the moral law. Thus if one reads into the moral law a puritanical aversion to sex and the body, then one harms oneself by subjecting oneself to the moral law thus understood. Indeed, people will be particularly harmed by the fact that the erroneous conception of the body is invested with the authority of the moral law. It is one thing for someone to say that he despises the body, it is another

thing for someone to present his despising of the body as being in accordance with the truth about the human body and hence as binding on all human beings. With this moral claim his erroneous conception gains entrance into the consciences of people, thus harming them at their deepest level. It is all-important that we "get it right" when we proclaim the moral law. This much is fairly obvious.

2) Can it ever happen that the moral law becomes oppressive to persons even when they commit no error about its content? I submit that it can and that we have in fact arrived at an all-important point in the discussion of freedom and truth.

Let us think of the child early on in its moral development. At first the child does not fully understand all that it is taught; it takes over the way of life proposed by its parents, but not because it understands what they understand, but rather because it at first exists as a kind of moral extension of them. The child's "conscience" is a kind of internalized parental voice; it is not yet the voice of the child himself. If this state of conscience, normal as it is in the young child, were to continue into later life, we would all agree in seeing in it a serious moral immaturity. If even as an adult the former child continues to be inhabited by his parents and their traditions, which continue to speak through him in place of his own moral voice; if he fails to become a free citizen in the moral universe; if he fails to develop for his part the same relation to morality that they have; if he fails to gain that independence from them that befits his distinct personhood, then we do indeed have to say that the morality he learned at home has become oppressive to him. In his best moments he will feel weighed down by a morality that he has not been able fully to make his own. If he has studied philosophy he might even speak of the "heteronomy," the foreignness of all the moral precepts he carries around with him. It is a heteronomy that becomes still more painful if others put pressure on him to conform to this morality or if they try to coerce him to live in accordance with it. But even without being subject to pressure and coercion he has plenty of heteronomy to suffer.

Let it again be noted that the precepts are not oppressive for him because they are false—let them all be as true as ever the moral precepts of human beings can be—they oppress him because he has never learned how to speak in his own name in professing them. The truth, which is supposed to make us free, has not made him free.

It can hardly be denied that people today are more sensitive than they were formerly to this heteronomy; they do not want to live their whole moral lives as the moral extension of some tribe or tradition; they sense more keenly than ever the moral indignity of a tribal solidarity that interferes with them being their own persons. They have an instinctive aversion to all unjustified coercion. And I think we have to admit that this growing need for a certain moral independence represents an entirely positive development. If it is positive for people to awaken from their immersion in social groups, where they feel themselves to be mere parts of a social whole, and to discover themselves as distinct, incommunicable, unrepeatable persons, then it is positive for them to want to have a conscience which is their own moral voice and not someone else's. This striving for greater moral authenticity is nothing but a positive moral sign of our times. The Vatican Council's "Declaration on Religious Liberty" is a capital expression of this sign.

We come now to the supremely important question: how does a person, oppressed by the heteronomy we have described, break through to the desired moral independence, or as we could as well say, to the desired moral autonomy? Some say that he posits his own morality, setting up a moral universe that is true for him but perhaps not true for anyone else. They evidently think that if the moral law is objectively and universally valid, it must remain outside of us in a heteronomous way; that morality can become our own only if it is of our own making. We need to understand this plausible logic that drives some people's thinking away from the freedom of persons to a subjectivism of truth and value.

But is this logic irresistible? Does an objectively valid moral law have to remain heteronomously outside of us? Can it not be brought inside of us without being eliminated as objectively and universally valid? Can we not come to own it in some way other than enacting it for ourselves? We can indeed! We can take it into ourselves, living and thriving as irreducibly distinct persons, *in virtue of understanding the objectively valid moral law*. There is an understanding of moral norms and ideals whereby we do not posit, enact, or otherwise set up the norms and ideals, but rather find them as already given, but find them in such a way that we approve of them and take them into ourselves, making them the innermost principles of our acting. If these norms did not already exist, we would make them exist by setting them up; since they already exist, we ratify them, willing them not because someone else inhabiting us wills them, but entirely in our own names. This means that we can satisfy the thirst for freedom, autonomy, and authenticity without subjectivizing moral truth. Let moral truth be understood, let the goods and values calling for certain actions be experienced, and moral truth will be internalized in us, or (as we could just as well say) we will come to stand within it. We will possess it in a manner appropriate to our being distinct persons; we will show forth our personhood in our way of holding it. Go back for a moment to the case of moral immaturity discussed above; if only the person who continues to live in unquestioning solidarity with his tribal traditions can come to understand the moral point of the traditional way of life, he can come to will it in his own name and to will it as much in his own name as anyone else could will it for him. It is not necessary that he break with what he has grown up with; he may, of course, have to do that, but it may also be that he can take over much of it, making it his own in a properly personal way.

An example. A person grows up learning the norms of chastity. At first he remains strongly tethered to his parents, his conscience in matters of chastity being to a great extent their internalized voice. He comes into adolescence and is capable of understanding more and more the moral rhyme and reason of chastity. Suppose that he is not encouraged to grow in this understanding and that his parents proclaim the prohibitions connected with chastity in an arbitrary way—in response to his questions they have nothing better to offer than "because I said so." Then chastity begins to present itself to this adolescent as "one long no" (Wojtyla) and begins to be experienced as oppressive. This does not just mean that chastity is difficult to live; "oppressive" here has the very different sense of remaining painfully outside of the adolescent because of an apparent meaninglessness; it is the oppression of heteronomy. What effects the transition from heteronomy to autonomy? Does the adolescent have to devise his own truth about sexuality? No, it suffices that he understand the truth that already exists and that is founded in the nature of man and woman as persons. In understanding it he makes it his own and lets it become the innermost principle of his acting. He takes it into himself, yet without interfering in any way with its objective validity. Others can take it into themselves, and yet there remains one truth about chastity that is between, or rather above, all men and women. It is, then, not truth in the abstract but truth as understood, as internalized, that sets us free.

3) But there is another consideration that lies behind the fear that truth is the enemy of freedom. As Charles Taylor has shown, a new understanding of each human person as an unrepeatable individual has emerged in the last two centuries:

Herder put forward the idea that each of us has an original way of being human. That each person has his or her own "measure" is his way of putting it. This idea has entered very deep into modern consciousness. It is also new. Before the late eighteenth century no one thought that the differences between human beings had this kind of moral significance. There is a certain way of being that is *my* way. I am called upon to live my life in this way, and not in imitation of anyone else's.[3]

Thus one now stresses that each human person is a human being in his or her own unrepeatable way. Human persons are not just instances or specimens of the human kind, but there is something in each person that cannot exist again in any other human being, something that is incommunicably, unrepeatably each person's own. We can hardly understand the dignity of each human person without understanding this unrepeatable selfhood of each one.

Max Scheler has developed this idea by saying that each human person has his or her own unique moral calling or set of moral tasks. This means that a person does not just have to fulfil universal norms that bind him as they bind everyone else, but also has to fulfil certain personal norms that bind only him and no one else. Maritain says that no one knew about these personal norms like the saints did:

The saints always amaze us. Their virtues are freer than those of a merely virtuous man. Now and again, in circumstances outwardly alike, they act quite differently from the way in which a merely virtuous man acts. They are indulgent where he would be severe, severe where he would be indulgent.... What does that signify? They have their own kind of mean, their own kinds of standards. But these are valid only for each one of them.... This is why we utter something deeper than we realize when we say of such acts that they are admirable but not imitable. They are not generalizable, universalizable. They are good; indeed, they are the best of all moral acts. But they are good only for him who does them. We are here very far from the Kantian universal with its morality defined by the possibility of making the maxim of an act into a law for all men.[4]

As I say, the basis for these highly personal moral tasks is the unrepeatable personal identity of each person: as each person is unrepeatably himself, so he has moral tasks entrusted only to himself.

Now we can understand why the talk of the moral law as universally binding can seem threatening to those who are keenly aware of the unique moral calling that grows out of their unique personhood. We can understand why they can perceive a certain antagonism between the universality of the moral law and the unrepeatable individuality of each person. Above, it was the objectivity of the moral law that seemed threatening, that seemed to keep the moral law heteronomously outside of the person; here, it is the universality of the moral law that threatens, and it threatens by seeming to have a depersonalizing effect on those who conform to it. But here as above, it seems that moral truth is in some way at odds with man as person and that it has to be subjectivized or relativized so as to be brought into harmony with our personhood.

I would respond by saying, first of all, that a personal moral task that only I have is in its moral validity in no way subjective in the sense of subjectivism, or relative in the sense of relativism, just as the fact of my unique personal identity does not constitute evidence in support of subjectivism or relativism. For example, Socrates had a philosophical mission in Athens that no one else had. Let us assume that Socrates could have never discovered this mission by applying moral universals to himself, but discovered it only by taking account of who he unrepeatably was. This mission was nevertheless an objective moral reality; it was not indeed an instance of a moral universal, but it was just as objective as if it were such an instance. Socrates found this mission *given* to him, and precisely not devised or chosen by him, or revocable by him. He was aware of falling under judgment if he should betray his mission. Thus he was aware of still standing *under* moral truth in being bound to do what only he was bound to do. Objective moral truth does not always only exist as universal; it also exists in the more concrete-personal form that

Scheler and Maritain pointed out. Thus it does not have to be subjectivized in order to be adapted to unrepeatable persons.

And I have another response to make to this latest attempt to construe
some antagonism between personhood and truth. As Scheler pointed out,
*the unique moral task of a person presupposes all the universal moral
norms and never contradicts these.* Thus, for example, Socrates
presupposes that knowledge of truth is in principle (or in other words
universally) good; his unique task of raising questions of fundamental
truth with his fellow Athenians does not make sense apart from this
universal. Nor does Socrates ever feel entitled to violate some universal
in the pursuit of his personal mission. Karl Rahner has explained as
follows the relation of the personal tasks to moral universals.[5] He says
that when we have applied to our concrete situation all the relevant
universals, it commonly happens that several courses of action remain
open to us; the universals do not always specify only one morally
acceptable action but can often be fulfilled by several actions. It is,
Rahner says, only within these several actions that I ask which one befits
me as the unique person that I am. Thus my moral life is first of all
governed by those norms that bind me as they bind all other human
persons; only then is it also governed by norms more uniquely my own.

It follows, then, that we can recognize uniquely personal moral tasks and
at the same time still affirm universal norms, such as the norm that
innocent persons must never be directly killed. Indeed, such norms are
presupposed by the more personal moral calls which some people receive
and are never contradicted by these. We can even recognize more clearly
than earlier generations recognized that I cannot lead a full moral life
exclusively on the basis of universal moral norms, that personal moral
tasks play a larger role in the moral life than had been appreciated. I can
even think that I live and thrive more truly as person on the basis of this
enhanced understanding of the moral life. And with all of this I do not
cease to recognize universal moral norms, nor do I ever depart from the
objectivity of the moral law. For all the personalism of my ethics, I have
nothing at all to do with ethical subjectivism and relativism.

Let us conclude. We have found three ways in which the moral law,
understood as objectively and universally valid, can be harmful for
persons and their freedom. If one makes a serious mistake about some

content of the moral law, one is liable to suffer from living under a distorted moral law. Secondly, if one fails to develop a moral mind of one's own, one will experience the moral law as painfully outside of oneself. And finally, if one thinks that the moral law consists exclusively in universal norms, one will feel overlooked as an unrepeatable person. But none of these problems requires the subjectivization or relativization of the moral law. We have instead to determine rightly the contents of the moral law; we have to *understand* the moral law, thus letting it become the innermost principle of each person's moral life; and finally we have to recognize that the moral law, besides binding me as it binds everyone else, also calls me in a personal way.

When in the course of our pro-life work we hear people play moral freedom off against moral truth, we should listen closely to hear if they are perhaps thinking of one of these ways in which moral truth really can interfere with moral freedom. If they are, then there is a core of truth in their protest against the moral law; we have to know how to retrieve this core of truth even as we defend the moral law to them. Charles Taylor practices this strategy admirably in his *The Ethics of Authenticity.* He wants to find certain noble moral aspirations at work in the culture of authenticity despite all the subjectivism, relativism, and narcissism that disfigure it. He thinks that such often-criticized aspects of this culture are not the whole story and that in the midst of them important moral insights are struggling to be born. We need to know how to point out to our contemporaries the path leading from these insights to the fullness of the truth about freedom and law.

NOTES

1. In Hans Kelsen, *What is Justice?* (Berkeley: Univ. of California Press, 1957).

2. See especially C.S. Lewis, *The Abolition of Man* (New York: MacMillan, 1976), pp. 72-80.

3. Charles Taylor, *The Ethics of Authenticity* (Cambridge Univ. Press, 1991), pp. 28-29.

ABSOLUTE AUTONOMY AND PHYSICIAN-ASSISTED SUICIDE: PUTTING A BAD IDEA OUT OF ITS MISERY*

Francis J. Beckwith

PERHAPS THE MOST SIGNIFICANT and influential contribution that contemporary bioethicists have made to the medical community is their affirmation that a fundamental principle of medical ethics is the principle of respect for autonomy (or patient autonomy).[1] The implementation of this principle, though not entirely unproblematic,[2] has been instrumental in empowering patients and moving medicine away from physician paternalism.

Dr. Jack Kevorkian and his attorney, Geoffrey Fieger, have made much of the principle of autonomy in their defense of physician-assisted suicide. In a talk given at a National Press Club luncheon on July 29, 1996, Fieger states:

I have been at the center of this along with Jack Kevorkian for the last six years, and I am telling you, I have never heard a rational argument why a mentally competent, sick or dying person does not have an absolute right, under certain controlled circumstances, to end their suffering without government. I don't see how rationally you can make an argument in this country, where over 20 years ago, it was declared a fundamental right for a woman to control her own uterus and make decisions about an unborn child.

At the same luncheon, in a reply to a question posed by the moderator, Ms. Sonja Hillgren, Dr. Kevorkian was much more candid than his attorney:

MS. HILLGREN: Many questioners have asked about your religious beliefs. I think you've articulated them, describing yourself as an agnostic. Can you tell us your underlying philosophical belief?

65

DR. KEVORKIAN: Yeah, it's quite simple: Absolute personal autonomy. I'm an absolute autonomist. Do and say whatever you want to do and say at any time you want to do or say it, as long as you do not harm or threaten anybody else's person or property.

This exchange was followed by audience applause. Although he claims to perform physician-assisted suicide on suffering people with terminal illnesses,[3] his application of the principle of autonomy, which he calls absolute autonomy, allows him to practice his specialty on a much larger constituency, including the depressed, the downtrodden, and the emotionally vulnerable; that is, pretty much any "rational" person who wants to exercise his or her right to absolute autonomy. This is not to say that Dr. Kevorkian in fact has helped or will help terminate such people. It just means that Dr. Kevorkian's lone moral principle, if it is truly the only legitimate moral principle, justifies such behavior.

Although there are some bioethicists who believe that physician-assisted suicide in some cases may be morally permissible, they employ other ethical principles in their moral decision-making and conclude in many cases that physician-assisted suicide is morally impermissible.[4] These other ethical principles include the principles of beneficence, nonmaleficence, and justice. However, the view that Kevorkian and his attorney defend seems not to take this nuanced approach. It is crass and absolutist.

The principle of respect for autonomy, though a legitimate moral principle of medical ethics, if affirmed unrestrained by any other consideration, logically entails absolute personal autonomy, resulting in absurd counter-intuitive consequences. Absolute autonomy trumps every other moral principle, every view of the human person which does not enshrine autonomy, as well as any concern, interest, or values of the community. In short, Kevorkianism is a dangerous and narrow dogma crushing in its path, in the name of tolerance and openness, every thoughtful notion or value which its proponents find disagreeable.

Although I believe that a good moral and legal case against physician-assisted suicide can and has been made,[5] my concern in this essay is the misuse of the principle of respect for autonomy by Dr. Kevorkian as well as the courts.

ABSOLUTE AUTONOMY AS A CONSTITUTIONAL RIGHT

Contemporary jurisprudence is headed in a troubling direction. Although many see Kevorkianism as an ethical aberration, there is reason to believe that absolute autonomy is becoming the primary dogma by which courts, especially the U.S. Supreme Court, adjudicate issues of great moral and social importance.

In the 1992 case which held *Roe v. Wade* (1973) as precedent, *Planned Parenthood v. Casey*, the Court departed from its 1973 appeal to the right to privacy and instead grounded abortion rights in an appeal to near absolute autonomy which it believes it has found in the Fourteenth Amendment of the U.S. Constitution:

Our law afford constitutional protection to personal decisions relating to marriage, procreation, family relationships, child rearing, and education.... These matters, involving the most intimate and personal choices a person may make in a lifetime, choices central to personal dignity and autonomy, are central to the liberty protected by the Fourteenth Amendment. At the heart of liberty is the right to define one's own concept of existence, of meaning, of the universe, and of the mystery of human life. Beliefs about these matters could not define the attributes of personhood were they formed under compulsion by the State.[6]

Although political philosopher Hadley Arkes says that "this is the kind of sentiment that would ordinarily find its place within the better class of fortune cookies,"[7] this passage from *Casey* was taken to heart by Judge Stephen Reinhardt of the Ninth Circuit Court of Appeals, in the March 6, 1996 ruling of *Compassion in Dying v. Washington*, in which the judge not only affirmed a constitutional "right to die," but also called the state's motivation for banning physician-assisted suicide "cruel": "Not only is the state's interest in preventing such individuals from hastening their deaths of comparatively little weight, but its insistence on frustrating their wishes seems cruel indeed."[8]

Two years prior to this ruling, Judge Barbara Rothstein of the U.S. District Court in Seattle struck down the state's ban, employing the logic of *Casey*:

Like the abortion decision, the decision of a terminally ill person to end his or her life "involves the most intimate and personal choices a person can make in a lifetime," and constitutes a "choice central to personal dignity and autonomy."[9]

In supporting this decision, philosopher Ronald Dworkin makes a similar appeal, though emphasizing the state neutrality articulated in *Casey*:

> Our Constitution takes no sides in these ancient disputes about life's meaning. But it does protect people's right to die as well as live, so far as possible, in the light of their own intensely personal convictions about "the mystery of human life." It insists that these values are too central to personality, too much at the core of liberty, to allow a majority to decide what everyone must believe.[10]

What makes these decisions particularly troubling is that they concerned a case in which a pro-euthanasia organization, Compassion in Dying, had sued the state of Washington over a statewide 1991 referendum in which the voters "had reaffirmed the provision of the criminal code that outlawed persons in its jurisdiction from 'knowingly causing or aiding other persons in ending their lives.'"[11]

Consider also a New York case, *Quill v. Vacco*, decided in the Second Circuit Court of Appeals. In that case, the court ruled that "the state of New York violates the equal protection clause of the Fourteenth Amendment with its prohibition of assisting suicide. By permitting patients to refuse treatment at the end of life, but not allowing physician-assisted suicide, the state unfairly treats similarly situated persons." The court did not take seriously the traditional distinction between passive (letting die) and active (killing) euthanasia. Like the Ninth Circuit and the District Court in Seattle, the Second Circuit appealed to *Casey*. Writing for the majority, Judge Miner, asked the question, "What concern prompts the state to interfere with a mentally competent patient's 'right to define [his] own concept of existence, of meaning, of the universe, and of the mystery of human life,' when the patient seeks to have drugs to end life during the final stages of a terminal illness?" The answer, according to Judge Miner, is "None."[12]

Philosopher Russell Hittinger, a critic of the case, explains the judge's reasoning: "[G]iven two patients, each of whom can define the meaning of the universe, the state of New York violates equal protection when it allows one to 'define' himself by having treatment withdrawn [i.e., passive euthanasia] while it forbids the other to 'define' himself by requesting that a physician assist his suicide [i.e., active euthanasia]."[13]

The courts are apparently saying that the community, moral considerations, and/or certain views of what it means to be a human person, however well-grounded philosophically and/or historically, are to be discarded and replaced with "absolute autonomy." The courts also seem to be saying that the people, whether through the legislature or through referendum, have no legal means by which to fashion the moral and social parameters of their communities or to redress what they perceive as harmful to the public good as well as to their character-shaping institutions (e.g., the family, medicine, school curricula, the arts, higher education), since there is no objective good, only the unencumbered individual armed with his absolute autonomy.

Because these cases were decided in federal appeals courts on matters of constitutional law, they are legally significant, for they are, in the words of Hittinger, "authoritative renderings of the fundamental law."[14] However, the U.S. Supreme Court seems for the time being to have rejected the "absolute autonomy" interpretation of *Casey* when on June 26, 1997 it overturned the lower federal courts' rulings both in *Quill* and *Compassion in Dying*. Nevertheless, it is an interpretation which finds acceptance among some of the more influential social and legal philosophers.

WHAT'S WRONG WITH ABSOLUTE AUTONOMY?
There are many reasons why absolute autonomy is flawed, both legally and morally, some of which I have already alluded to. Consider just the following four.

1) *Absolute autonomy is based on a dogma for which its proponents typically provide no reason.* Remember Dr. Kevorkian's comments at the National Press Club luncheon: "I'm an absolute autonomist. Do and say whatever you want to do and say at any time you want to do or say it, as long as you do not harm or threaten anybody else's person or property." Although many people believe this, why is it any better than alternative

dogmas, such as this one? "Do and say whatever you want to do and say at any time you want to do or say it, as long as you do so consistent with what is morally correct and with living in a community of other persons, including one's family, neighborhood, and church, synagogue or mosque."

Of course, Kevorkian and Fieger may find this alternative too constraining. But why should that matter? After all, maybe this dogma truly describes what really is while Kevorkianism does not. And if that is the case, then Kevorkianism puts people in bondage to an autonomy that is wholly unnatural, since human freedom may not be freedom at all if the will is antiseptically amputated from moral and social obligations and institutions which inform, empower, and nurture personal virtue. Consequently, what Kevorkian and Fieger find as liberating may in fact lead to cold and unnatural solitude, denying to the good doctor's patients the perspective that human life in community is much more than isolated individuals making choices for their unencumbered selves.

Recall Mr. Fieger's bold confession: "I have never heard a rational argument why a mentally competent, sick, or dying person does not have an absolute right, under certain controlled circumstances, to end their suffering without government." Well, we have yet to hear and are still awaiting Mr. Fieger's and his client's rational argument for absolute, unrestrained, unencumbered personal autonomy. Evidently, Mr. Fieger believes that mere assertion rather than rational argument is sufficient to justify his position, though it is not adequate for his opponents. Although Fieger and the courts would like you to think otherwise, Kevorkianism is not the default position. It too must be supported by rational argument.

2) *Kevorkianism is counter-intuitive.* In order to appreciate this flaw, consider the following fictional scenario. Imagine that you are a physician working the emergency room at a large urban hospital. Three paramedics wheel in an unconscious 33 year-old man who has taken an overdose of barbiturates. Other than his drug overdose, he is in excellent physical condition. You tell your colleagues that he can be saved if his stomach is pumped immediately. As you are preparing the patient for the procedure, a nurse shows you a note that she had found in the young

man's pocket. The note reads:

> If you find me before I die, please do not pump my stomach. I know exactly what I'm doing. My girlfriend, Rebecca, has broken up with me and life no longer has any meaning. I read somewhere that life's meaning and purpose is subjective, so you have no right to judge whether the reason for killing myself is serious or silly. Also, I recently read in a book by a Michigan pathologist, and during law school the legal briefs of his attorney, that each of us has a right to absolute personal autonomy. During my years in law school I also studied numerous U.S. Supreme Court and Federal Court decisions. One of them, *Planned Parenthood v. Casey*, said that "at the heart of liberty is the right to define one's own concept of existence, of meaning, of the universe, and of the mystery of human life." So, according to my concept of existence, life only has meaning if Rebecca loves me. Rebecca doesn't love me. So, life has no meaning *to me*. Now that may seem like a dumb reason for me to kill myself. But, I have absolute autonomy to do whatever I want with my body. I choose to kill my body. If you pump my stomach, you violate my autonomy. If I survive, I will sue you for violating my Fourteenth Amendment right to absolute autonomy and to define my own concept of existence, of meaning, of the universe, and of the mystery of human life.

Do you pump the young man's stomach? If you say yes, then you believe that it is perfectly appropriate for people, such as physicians, to make judgments about what sort of reasons are good or bad when another person is trying to justify killing himself. Although you may believe that in some circumstances physician-assisted suicide is justified, you don't believe that the principle of respect for autonomy is absolute and that nothing else should be considered.

On the other hand, if you say no, then you must take the counter-intuitive position that nothing counts except personal autonomy. You have to assert that medicine as a profession has no purpose other than to facilitate the wants of patients, no matter how fanciful or foolish they may appear to most people. You must also assert that the individual has no obligations to others, such as family, friends, and community, which should be enforced by law and/or custom, since such an enforcement would violate the individual's absolute autonomy. Also, you must hold that family, friends, and community should not be encouraged by law and/or custom to consider how the individual's actions, such as committing suicide for foolish reasons, affect the moral ecology of important social institutions, such as medicine and family, and the future generations which will inhabit these institutions, as well as how such actions may affect the spiritual and/or moral well-being of the individual who commits them.

The person who says no to pumping the young man's stomach is forced to admit that there is no such thing as public and private virtue which transcend the desires of the individual. There is no good to which society should strive, human life is not inherently sacred, and no view of human nature is correct if it does not allow for absolute autonomy; there are simply unencumbered autonomous selves exercising choices in light of their "own concept of existence, of meaning, of the universe, and of the mystery of human life." This view is so counter-intuitive it is incredible that otherwise intelligent people should even consider it a viable alternative in social ethics.

3) *When courts appeal to absolute autonomy as a "neutral position" they violate their primary reason for this appeal.* Recall the Supreme Court's assertion from *Casey*:

At the heart of liberty is the right to define one's concept of existence, of meaning, of the universe, and of the mystery of human life. Beliefs about these matters could not define the attributes of personhood were they formed under compulsion by the State.

The Court is asserting the primacy of personal autonomy over the metaphysical question of personhood in order to affirm that the state should remain neutral when it comes to ultimate philosophical questions. The problem, of course, is that this appeal to autonomy is far from neutral, for it assumes a view of reality, a view of the person in particular, which is secular,[15] anti-communitarian,[16] and metaphysically libertarian. That is to say, the Court is answering some ultimate philosophical questions in a way that is consistent with the Court's own metaphysical predilections, which are far from neutral. If the Court's members were not so philosophically untutored (with the exception of Justices Scalia and Thomas), it would not be unreasonable to say they were intentionally trying to hoodwink their constituency.

Consider an ironic example. By affirming that human beings are the sort of beings that can be autonomous, the court apparently is presupposing a libertarian view of human freedom, which can be defined in the following way:

[G]iven choices A and B, I can literally choose to do either one, no circumstances exist that are sufficient to determine my choice, my choice is up to me, and if I do one of them, I could have attempted to have done otherwise. I act as an agent who is the ultimate originator of at least some of my own actions.[17]

But this view of human freedom, which is apparently a necessary condition for the Court's view of personal autonomy, seems to be best established philosophically by a particular view of the human person, substance dualism,[18] a view which, many philosophers have argued, is inconsistent with mind-body physicalism[19] and property dualism,[20] two views of the human person which deny the independent existence of the soul (or mind).

Yet if this is the case, then the court must presuppose a particular view of the human person which *by definition* excludes other views from the purview of constitutional consideration. Ironically, according to some scholars, substance dualism entails the prolife (anti-abortion) view that the fetus is a human person.

Therefore, one could argue that the court cannot get its "personal autonomy" justification of abortion rights (or for that matter, physician-assisted suicide, if it chooses to justify it on the same basis as abortion rights) without at the same time implicitly passing negative judgment on certain views of the human person that are associated with secularism and atheism (i.e., mind-body physicalism and property dualism) while implicitly establishing a view of the human person that is not only associated with theistic perspectives (i.e., substance dualism) but also seems to lend support to the claim that fetuses are human persons and that abortion is therefore homicide.[21] Other ethicists have argued that substance dualism also counts against physician-assisted suicide as well as active euthanasia in general.[22]

The Court, therefore, in holding up personal autonomy as the basis for deciding not to overturn *Roe*, which it may employ to support physician-assisted suicide as a constitutional right, made a philosophical assumption about the nature of the human person which is *inconsistent with* mind-body physicalism and property-dualism, both of which deny libertarian free will,[23] even though the Court claimed that beliefs about such things could not be "formed under compulsion by the State."

It seems, then, that when the courts affirm absolute autonomy in the name of neutrality they are not being neutral at all; rather, they violate their primary reason for this appeal.

4) *Since Kevorkianism is based on the dubious presumption that suicide ends suffering, Dr. Kevorkian's patients may not be truly acting autonomously.* Mr. Fieger states in his National Press Club speech: "Make no bones about it; we're involved in a fight here. This is not the right to commit suicide. This is not the right to obtain the right to suicide, physician assisted suicide. It is the right not to suffer."

Don't forget that Dr. Kevorkian is an agnostic when it comes to questions of ultimate concern. Thus, he does not deny the existence of God or the afterlife, he merely claims that he doesn't know if there is a God or an afterlife. But according to the major Western religious traditions, including the orthodox versions of Christianity, Islam, and Judaism, there is a place of eternal torment for those who are not redeemed. And according to Dr. Kevorkian, since he is an agnostic, there *may be* such a place. In the Gospel of Matthew (chapter 25), Jesus says it is reserved for the Devil and his angels as well as those Christ never knew, which may include a large percentage of Dr. Kevorkian's patients. If that is the case, then by assisting in their suicides, the good doctor may be leading them into greater suffering, violating, according to Mr. Fieger, their "right not to suffer." And since Dr. Kevorkian is doing so while admitting he is totally ignorant of the spiritual requirements for entering, let alone knowing the existence or non-existence of, the afterlife, one wonders if one can truly say that his patients are acting autonomously, i.e., making free choices with informed consent.

CONCLUSION

Even though it has support in both the federal courts and the popular culture, Dr. Jack Kevorkian's appeal to absolute autonomy to justify physician-assisted suicide, whether in the social or legal arena, is fatally flawed for at least four reasons: (1) absolute autonomy is based on a dogma for which its proponents typically provide no reason; (2) absolute autonomy is counter-intuitive; (3) when courts appeal to absolute autonomy as a "neutral position" they violate their primary reason for this appeal; and (4) since the appeal to absolute autonomy is motivated by the dubious presumption that suicide ends suffering, Dr. Kevorkian's patients may not be truly acting autonomously.

NOTES

* This essay is a slightly revised version of a piece that appeared in *Suicide: A Christian Response*, eds. Timothy J. Demy and Gary P. Stewart (Grand Rapids: Kregel, 1998) pp. 223-33.

1. For a defense and explanation of the principle of respect for autonomy, see Tom L. Beauchamp and James Childress, *Principles of Biomedical Ethics*, 3rd ed. (New York: Oxford, 1989) pp. 67-119.

2. See, for example, Edwin R. Dubose, Ron Hammel, Laurence J. O'Connell, eds., *A Matter of Principles? Ferment in U.S. Bioethics* (Valley Forge: Trinity Press International, 1994).

3. The question of what constitutes suffering as well as the question of pain management and how each relates to the moral and legal justification of physician-assisted suicide are outside the scope of this paper, though they are vitally important questions. For an informative discussion on these questions as they relate to the legal and political debate, see Robert Spitzer, "The Case Against Active Euthanasia" in *Life and Learning IV: Proceedings of the Fourth University Faculty for Life Conference*, ed. Joseph W. Koterski, S.J. (Washington, D.C.: University Faculty for Life, 1995) pp. 80-97.

4. For example, Beauchamp and Childress (*Principles of Biomedical Ethics*, p. 112) write: "Although respecting autonomy is more important than biomedical ethics had appreciated until the last two decades, it is not the only principle and

should not be overvalued when it conflicts with other values....In many clinical circumstances the weight of respect for autonomy is minimal, while the weight of nonmaleficence or beneficence is maximal. Similarly in public policy, the demands of justice can outweigh the demands of respect for autonomy."

5. See, for example, Spitzer, "The Case Against Active Euthanasia"; John J. Conley, "Libertarian Euthanasia" in *Life and Learning IV*, pp. 73-79; Victor Rosenblum and Clark Forsythe, "The Right to Assisted Suicide: Protection of Autonomy or an Open Door to Social Killing?" in *Do the Right Thing: A Philosophical Dialogue on the Moral and Social Issues of Our Time*, ed. Francis J. Beckwith (Belmont: Wadsworth, 1996) pp. 208-21; J.P. Moreland, "James Rachels and the Active Euthanasia Debate" in *Do the Right Thing*, pp. 239-46; and Patricia Wesley, "Dying Safely: An Analysis of 'A Case of Individualized Decision Making' by Timothy E. Quill, M.D." in *Do the Right Thing*, pp. 251-61.

6. Justices Sandra Day O'Connor, Anthony Kennedy, and David Souter in "Planned Parenthood v. Casey (1992)" in *The Abortion Controversy: A Reader*, eds. Louis P. Pojman and Francis J. Beckwith (Boston: Jones & Bartlett, 1994) p. 54.

7. Hadley Arkes, "A Pride of Bootless Friends: Some Melancholy Reflections on the Current State of the Pro-Life Movement" in *Life and Learning IV*, p. 19.

8. As quoted in Russell Hittinger, "A Crisis of Legitimacy" in *First Things: A Monthly Journal of Religion and Public Life* 67 (November 1996) p. 26.

9. As quoted in Timothy Egan, "Federal Judge Says Ban on Suicide Aid is Unconstitutional" in *The New York Times* (5 May 1994) p. A24.

10. Ronald Dworkin, "When Is It Right to Die?" in *The New York Times* (17 May 1994) p. A19.

11. Hittinger, "A Crisis of Legitimacy," p. 26.

12. *Ibid.*

13. *Ibid.*

14. *Ibid.* In his article, Hittinger cites other cases as well as showing how the courts have arrived at their present state. See also Robert H. Bork, "Our Judicial Oligarchy" in *First Things: A Monthly Journal of Religion and Public Life* 67 (November 1996) 21-24; and Hadley Arkes, "A Culture Corrupted" in *First Things: A Monthly Journal of Religion and Public Life* 67 (November 1996) 30-33.

15. The Supreme Court's bias in favor of secularism is made clear in recent comments made by Justice Anthony Kennedy, who said that it is a religious belief to hold that "there is an ethic and morality which transcend human invention" (as quoted in Hittinger, "A Crisis of Legitimacy," p. 27). It is not very difficult to imagine the Court, using Justice Kennedy's reasoning, to dismiss out of hand any ethical position which does not assume naturalism as a worldview on the basis that it violates the Establishment Clause of the First Amendment. The Court could then ignore, rather than take the time to refute, the arguments put forth by the proponents of a non-naturalistic ethical position. So, in theory, the Court, on the basis of metaphysical bias alone without the benefit of reasoned argument, can dismiss an ethical view, which may be more philosophically and constitutionally justified in comparison to its rivals, merely because it does not presuppose the truth of naturalism. This is intellectual fascism.

16. In his critique of John Rawls's political philosophy, Michael Sandel makes a similar point by arguing that Rawls's view of the person (which Sandel refers to as "the unencumbered self"), far from being the neutral view that Rawls claims, is anti-communitarian. See Michael Sandel, *Liberalism and the Limits of Justice* (New York: Cambridge Univ. Press, 1982). See also Sandel's popular treatment of how this view of the self has negatively affected American political discourse, *Democracy's Discontent* (Cambridge: Harvard Univ. Press, 1996), as well as Mary Ann Glendon, *Rights Talk: The Impoverishment of Political Discourse* (New York: The Free Press, 1991).

17. J.P. Moreland, "A Defense of the Substance Dualist View of the Soul" in *Christian Perspectives on Being Human: A Multidisciplinary Approach to Integration*, ed. J.P. Moreland and David M. Ciocchi (Grand Rapids: Baker, 1993) p. 71.

18. On this matter, John Mitchell and Scott B. Rae write that "a necessary condition for libertarian free will is the existence of an agent (e.g., agent-causation or noncausal agent theory); and a substance ontology of the agent is arguably a necessary condition for agency theory." (John A. Mitchell and Scott B. Rae, "The Moral Status of Fetuses and Embryos" in *The Silent Subject: Reflections on the Unborn in American Culture*, ed. Brad Stetson [Westport: Praeger, 1996] p. 22). Because a defense of substance dualism is outside the scope of this paper, see Moreland, "A Defense of the Substance Dualist View of the Soul," and J.P. Moreland, "A Contemporary Defense of Dualism" in *Philosophy: The Quest for Truth*, 3rd ed., ed. Louis P. Pojman (Belmont: Wadsworth, 1996).

Moreland defines substance dualism in the following way: "Substance dualism holds that the brain is a physical substance that has physical properties and the soul is a mental substance that has mental properties. When I am in pain, the brain has certain physical (e.g., electrical, chemical) properties, and the soul has certain mental properties (the conscious awareness of pain). The soul is the possessor of these experiences. It stands behind, over, and above them and remains the same throughout my life. The soul and the brain can interact with each other, but they are different entities with different properties." (Moreland, "A Defense of the Substance Dualist View of the Soul," p. 61)

19. Mind-body physicalism is the view that the human person is merely a physical brain with no mental properties as well as no underlying non-physical substance or human nature. "The only things that exist are physical substances, properties, and events. When it comes to humans, the physical substance is the body or brain and central nervous system. The physical substance called the brain has physical properties, such as weight, volume, size, electrical activity, chemical composition, and so forth." (Moreland, "A Defense of the Substance Dualist View of the Soul," pp. 58-59)

20. Proponents of property-dualism assert that "there are some physical substances that have only physical properties. A billiard ball is hard and round. In addition, there are no mental substances. But there is one material substance that has both physical *and* mental properties—the brain.... The brain is the possessor of all mental properties. I am not a mental self that *has* my thoughts and experiences. Rather, I am a brain and a series or bundle of successive experiences themselves." (Moreland, "A Defense of the Substance Dualist View of the Soul," p. 60)

21. For a defense of substance dualism as it pertains to the human personhood of the fetus, *see* Mitchell and Rae, "The Moral Status of Fetuses and Embryos," and J.P. Moreland and John Mitchell, "Is the Human Person a Substance or a Property-Thing?" in *Ethics & Medicine* 11:3 (1995) 50-55.

22. For a defense of substance dualism as it pertains to the question of physician-assisted suicide, see J.P. Moreland, "Humanness, Personhood, and the Right to Die," *Faith and Philosophy* 12.1 (January 1995) 95-112; and Scott B. Rae, "Views of Human Nature at the Edges of Life: Personhood and Medical Ethics" in *Christian Perspectives on Being Human*, pp. 235-56.

23. On this matter, Moreland points out that "if physicalism is true, then determinism is true as well. If I am just a physical system, there is nothing in me that has the capacity to freely choose to do something. Material systems, at least large scale ones, change over time in deterministic fashion according to the initial conditions of the system and the laws of chemistry and physics." (Moreland, "A Defense of the Substance Dualist View of the Soul," p. 71) Concerning property dualism, Moreland states that since this view maintains that mental properties are

the result of physical causes (whether one takes an epiphenomenal or a state-state causation view), mental states (or mental agents) do not cause anything but are themselves caused by physical events. Consequently, human beings are not truly free moral agents. (*Ibid.*, pp. 71-73)

THE INCOMPATIBILITY OF CONTRACEPTION WITH RESPECT FOR LIFE

Kevin E. Miller

ONE MIGHT SUPPOSE that increasing the availability and use of contraception[1] would decrease the abortion rate. In view of such a supposition, it is very often suggested that those wishing fewer abortions, whether for moral or medical reasons, should promote access to contraception, even as a matter of public policy. At the very least, it is suggested, opposition to contraception should not be linked with opposition to abortion; opponents of abortion should, as such, prefer contraception as a lesser evil.[2] And many of the groups that comprise the pro-life movement have adopted a strategic neutrality toward contraception in order, at best, to encompass people who are not opposed to contraception and, at least, to avoid alienating them.[3] Even though this neutrality probably does not often reflect agreement with the above premise about contraception and abortion—indeed, even though this neutrality probably often coincides with opposition to contraception on its own terms—it does reflect an implicit assumption that opposition to abortion does not, either theoretically or practically, itself entail opposition to contraception.

Now in fact, increased acceptance and use of artificial methods of contraception seems to correlate to some degree with increased acceptance of and recourse to abortion.[4] But since in any case causality cannot be demonstrated from correlation alone, it seems to me that to explore the possibility and nature of a link between abortion and contraception and to determine what abortion opponents should, as such, do about contraception, it is, finally, necessary to develop a moral evaluation of contraception and to inquire whether the precise manner in which contraception is contrary to human goodness, if it turns out to be so contrary, is related to the evil of abortion. I shall in this essay undertake such an inquiry and argue that the use of contraception promotes dispositions that are contrary to those necessary for respect for life and therefore required for what Pope John Paul II has called a "culture of life."[5] Consequently, the pope has been right to say that pro-life strategy must, in fact, include teaching the unacceptability of contraception (EV #13, 97; cf. 88).

My argument will be presented in four parts. The first will assess a proposal that contraception is itself contralife. I shall show that this argument is inadequate. A more adequate argument will require an analysis of the manner in which marital intercourse serves human goodness, since contraception affects the act of intercourse, and not merely accidentally. I shall allow John Paul's writings, especially some of his pre-papal philosophical work, to guide this analysis, not as an appeal to authority, but because one finds in them a detailed and especially insightful account of the issue, and because he has shown a concern about contraception that is a manifestation of this insight. Thus the second part of this essay will present some features of John Paul's philosophical anthropology and the starting point of his corresponding personalistic ethics.[6] The third will use this ethics to evaluate marital love, intercourse, and contraception. In these parts I shall explain that marital intercourse modified by contraception is immoral for the reason that it objectively embodies a disposition toward one's spouse that treats this person as an object of use rather than love, and therefore not as a person.

In light of this evaluation of contraception, the fourth part will return to the question of whether the dispositions embodied and therefore promoted by contraception are compatible with respect for life. Here I shall argue, again following the pope, that it is precisely use of persons, as opposed to love for them, that is most fully manifest in disrespect for life. It follows that, while the disposition toward one's spouse objectively embodied by contraception is specifically different from the disrespect for life embodied by abortion, the two dispositions are nevertheless related—both are species of a general disposition toward use rather than love of persons. Acceptance and reinforcement of this disposition, as by contraception, leads ultimately to the deaths of those who are most vulnerable, especially the unborn. I shall suggest some implications for pro-life efforts.

I. THE PROBLEM OF THE RELATIONSHIP
        BETWEEN CONTRACEPTION AND LIFE ISSUES

One argument for the evil of contraception that implies a very close linkage between it and abortion is the now-well-known argument of a school of moral theorists whose founding member is Germain Grisez.[7] According to this argument, the primary evil of contraception is that it is itself contralife. If this is true, then acceptance of contraception entails acceptance of a contralife principle, and it is easy to see how this could pave the way for acceptance of, *inter alia,* abortion. In fact, this argument is inadequate, but explanation of its inadequacies will not only clear the way for the pope's more adequate but more complicated argument, but also help to introduce the key features of that argument.

Grisez and his co-authors have argued that contraceptive behavior is, by definition, chosen to impede the coming to be of a new life that might result from some other behavior.[8] Thus it involves a contralife will, a "practical hatred" similar to that in homicide.[9] But human life is a human good, and the coming to be of human life is included in this good.[10] And a will or choice contrary to this good can never be rationally justified. There can be no standard by which rationally to compare the reason not to contracept (the good of human coming to be) with a reason to contracept.[11] "Therefore, [contraception] is contrary to *reason itself,* and so it is immoral."[12]

This approach is problematic on more than one level. To begin with, the moral theory it employs can be questioned. While the recent explication of the argument of Grisez and his colleagues that I have summarized does not explicitly invoke Grisez's concept of "basic goods" that serve as *per se nota* principles of practical reason,[13] "human life" seems to function in their argument as such a good.[14] According to Grisez's theory, one may never will directly against such a good.[15]

This theory in fact seems necessary to ground the comparison of contraception with homicide. For it is clear that the actions chosen in homicide and in contraception differ, at least in that the former ends an existing life while the latter prevents a non-existing life from coming to exist. Homicide therefore does a kind of injustice that is not done in contraception. To minimize the moral relevance of this difference requires recourse to a moral theory that reduces the injustice of homicide to an expression of a will contrary to the good of life. Thus, Grisez and co-authors respond to the objection that homicide and contraception differ in their relation to human life by arguing that "homicide is wrong not only because it involves an injustice, but also because it carries out a nonrationally grounded, contralife will—a will that the one killed not be.... Thus, even if contraception does no injustice to anyone, it is wrong because it necessarily involves a nonrationally grounded, contralife will—the same sort of will which also is essential to the wrongness of... homicide in general."[16]

A problem with this theory is that it envisages goods, like "life," only abstractly, apart from their relation to existing human or other beings.[17] This raises the question of the relationship between such goods and morally good action. Contrary to Grisez's claim, it is simply not clear that it is contrary to moral reason to act against such a good.[18] One cannot begin moral theorizing with such goods. One must begin with the human person (and other beings) as good and conceive morally good action as action in harmony with its good.[19] Thus, deliberate homicide is evil (when it is evil) not because it is "contralife" but because it is "contralife" in an unjust way —because it is inordinate (unjust) to intend directly to take the life of an (existing) innocent person.[20] In light of this objection, one should say that Grisez and his colleagues' analysis of contraception begs the question of why contraception is a *morally inappropriate* "contralife" action.[21] To the extent that it does so it also leaves obscure the possible connection between abortion and contraception.

Questions can also be raised concerning Grisez and his colleagues' treatment of contraception itself. Closely related to the above objection is the more specific issue of whether, if contraception is contralife, this is the primary evil of contraception. Grisez and his co-authors discuss the effects of contraception on the sexual act and on spouses as partners in that act, but they also maintain that contraception "is not a sexual sin."[22] In fact, they say, "Contraception is related to marital acts only instrumentally."[23] The latter statement is correct (and they rightly conclude that contracepted intercourse cannot be justified by the principle of double effect, which requires precisely one action with multiple effects, not multiple actions). But it does not follow that the primary evil of contraception could not be its effects on intercourse as an act of the spouses themselves, rather than its relationship to the life that could result from fertile intercourse. This is rather an assumption than a conclusion.

Grisez and co-authors say that in contraception, by definition, "one's relevant immediate intention... is that... prospective new life not begin."[24] This is not sufficiently precise, and further precision clarifies that the authors are wrong to assume that contraception is not primarily a sexual sin. It can more precisely be said that the most immediate relevant intention in contraception is *to modify* (extrinsically or intrinsically) *acting persons'* (spouses') *potentialities* vis-à-vis *intercourse so that* "prospective new life [will] not begin."[25] With this clarification it becomes obvious that one should examine as matter for moral evaluation what contraception, in seeking to impede the genesis of life, does to intercourse as an act of the spouses.[26]

As a final consideration, Grisez and his co-authors contend that the use of natural family planning (NFP) to postpone childbearing[27] is not objectively contralife as contraception is. Indeed, establishing this difference is a primary purpose of their efforts.[28] Their argument is that what is chosen in NFP is to abstain from something not itself morally obligatory, namely, fertile intercourse. This, they say, is done "with the intent that the bad consequences of the baby's coming to be will be avoided, and with the *acceptance as side effects* of both the baby's not-coming-to-be and the bad consequences of his or her not-coming-to-be."[29]

The characterization of "the baby's not-coming-to-be" as a "side effect" of avoidance of "the bad consequences of the baby's coming to be" is not credible, since the former is the means to the latter and is chosen for the sake of the latter. And NFP involves even more immediately the choice of certain methods which provide a couple with the information needed to time intercourse to avoid fertility. It is not clear that choosing not to have recourse to naturally fertile acts *qua* fertile, in order to avoid further consequences of fertility, is any less "contralife" than choosing to render a naturally fertile act infertile, to the same end. So if in fact contraception were evil because "contralife," NFP would also be evil. NFP does, however, differ from contraception with respect to its relation to the natural (in *at least* the sense of "biological") potentialities of the acting persons. NFP does not modify these potentialities *vis-à-vis* intercourse as does contraception. Here again is matter for moral evaluation.[30]

Now it is clear that contraception (as also NFP) can be *subjectively* contralife. Pope John Paul speaks in *Evangelium Vitae* (#13) of what is perhaps most likely to underlie this, saying that "contraception and abortion are often closely connected, as fruits of the same tree.... [I]n very many... instances such practices are rooted in a hedonistic mentality unwilling to accept responsibility in matters of sexuality, and they imply a self-centered concept of freedom, which regards procreation as an obstacle to personal fulfillment. The life which could result from a sexual encounter thus becomes an enemy to be avoided at all costs, and abortion becomes the only possible decisive response to failed contraception." It might be added that the very actualization of contralife selfishness by the practice of contraception could probably exercise it, so to speak, making it a stronger disposition, and so make people more accepting of its more radical actualization in abortion. But the pope also teaches that "from the [objective] moral point of view contraception and abortion are *specifically different* evils: the former contradicts the full truth of the sexual act as the proper expression of conjugal love, while the latter destroys the life of a human being; the former is opposed to the virtue of chastity in marriage, the latter is opposed to the virtue of justice and directly violates the divine commandment 'You shall not kill.'"

Yet John Paul does not view the connection between abortion and contraception as only subjective. He suggests that precisely contraception's opposition to "the virtue of chastity in marriage" grounds its objective incompatibility with respect for life. For he says in his explanation of what is necessary to bring about a transformation of culture into a culture of life, "The trivialization of sexuality is among the principal factors which have led to contempt for new life. Only a true love is able to protect life. There can be no avoiding the duty to offer... an authentic *education in sexuality and in love,* an education which involves *training in chastity* as a virtue which fosters personal maturity and makes one capable of respecting the 'spousal' meaning of the body" (EV #97). As I shall show, contraception *qua* unchaste, *qua* opposed to "true love," to a right respect for the (embodied) person, is already the beginning of the hedonism or self-centeredness of which John Paul has spoken.[31]

Fully to explicate his insights into the connection between abortion and contraception requires elaboration of the meaning of spousal love and contraception's effects on it.[32] John Paul's understanding of these matters is developed at length in his pre-papal works, especially *Love and Responsibility.*[33] This pre-papal thought has informed philosophically his papal treatment of the issues. I shall, in the next sections of this essay, present the key steps in the argument, which include (1) a philosophy of the human person and the ethical requirements corresponding to the person, the primary one being the "personalistic norm," and (2) an examination of marital intercourse in relation to the human person and the personalistic norm, with development of more specific norms concerning contraception (and NFP) insofar as these bear upon the personalistic meaning of intercourse. I shall then consider the significance of these (personalistic) norms for the abortion issue.

Contrary to the suggestion of Grisez and his co-authors, who admirably present some personalistic concerns about contraception,[34] that these concerns do not ground an adequate moral evaluation of contraception because people could (and do) "redefine marriage" to avoid "faith's teaching about what marriage is" (which requires that personalistic values be honored),[35] I shall clarify that it is precisely the requirements of adequate personalistic ethics that constitute an argument against a vision of marriage and sexuality that could encompass contraception. I shall also try to clarify the important role of nature in John Paul's argument, the normative status of nature being a major philosophical issue today (including in Grisez's work, since he self-consciously avoids both deriving goods from an account of human nature, and speaking of the natural structure of actions).[36]

II. PERSON, NATURE, THE PERSONALISTIC NORM, AND LOVE

What is signified by calling the human being a person? "Person" is not simply a synonym for "human being," although all human beings are persons. For the opposite is not true: not all persons are human beings. The Father, Son, and Holy Spirit are persons, but divine beings and therefore divine persons (though the Son has, since the Incarnation, a human nature as well as a divine one). Indeed the theological and philosophical importance of the word "person" has owed especially to its role in Trinitarian theology. Some non-human creatures, the spiritual creatures we call "angels" from their office as messengers, are also persons.

What divine persons, created spiritual persons, and human persons have in common is that each has an intellect and a will (cf. LR 21–22). So profound are the implications of this that personhood is rightly called a mode of being. Rationality, which results from having an intellect and a will, is not something superadded in us to otherwise integral animal natures. Rather, as what is distinctive about our natures,[37] it makes us fundamentally, and so as wholes, different from (non-human) animals. It is the core of our being—our being, therefore, human "persons." Our embodiment with all that it entails is certainly not accidental to ourselves; yet our intellect and will give us an "interior life" or "spiritual life" (LR 22–23), so that even in our embodied life we are akin not only to other embodied creatures, the (non-human) animals, but to spiritual beings.

The interior or spiritual life of intellect and will does not, however, close persons up within themselves. On the contrary, precisely this life confers upon persons an intimate contact and involvement with the world outside themselves that non-persons could never attain, since persons can know other beings (beyond being moved in other ways, including through sensation), and persons can also choose to act to bring about desired states of affairs among beings (LR 23–24). Furthermore, knowledge can guide choices. Knowledge of truth or being brings with it also knowledge of goodness or value.[38] We must choose to act in ways that either are or are not in conformity with that truth or goodness, and therefore in ways that are or are not ordinate to ourselves as beings fundamentally capable of knowing truth and striving for goodness—ways that objectively are or are not fulfilling of ourselves as persons.[39] Failures in this regard threaten our own integrity profoundly.[40] "Consequently, every being—or, more precisely, the essence, or nature, of every being—can serve as the basis of an ethical norm and of the positing of norms."[41]

The nature of these norms becomes particularly important when the object of a human act is another human being, a person.[42] The personhood of the human being, constituted by the life of intellect and will, grounds a moral norm unlike those grounded by other beings. The inseparable connection between the interior life of the person and the person's relationships with other beings means that "personality is *alteri incommunicabilis,*" not communicable to others (LR 24). For to the extent that you "act" solely insofar as you are responding to (my) force, to that extent do you not act *as a person*.[43] And to that extent also are the relationships constituted between you and other beings (including me) by such actions not properly personal relationships. Your personhood—your ability to establish certain kinds of relationships—is not something that anyone else can exercise for you. *When the object of an action is another person, this character of personhood must be respected.* This fundamental ethical requirement[44] is expressed by what John Paul has called the "personalistic norm."

The good of the person entails the good of human nature as a whole, not only of its distinctly personal dimension (LR 229–30). All of "human nature actually exists always in a concrete *suppositum* that is a person,"[45] which as a person has value.[46] Personal interiority and incommunicability is respected only when we respect the entire being that this spiritual life binds together and informs. We may contrast the respect owed to those dimensions of our nature that we share with animals, with the respect owed to these dimensions of a (non-human) animal's nature. We do owe respect to animals, and indeed to all beings, and therefore are not at liberty to treat them arbitrarily (cf. EV #42). We may not, for example, take an animal's life for no good reason. We may, however, do so for a good reason. We may say that nothing about the nature of an animal precludes our regarding it as a source of food or other important human goods, or even as something to be destroyed if it is dangerous or even, sometimes, merely annoying. This is not true of a human person.

But respect for dimensions of nature below the distinctly personal, while necessary, is not sufficient. Nature itself calls for the elevation and integration of respect for all of human nature into respect for the person as such, or conformity with the personalistic norm.[47] Furthermore, full explanation of the evil inherent in any action bearing upon another person that is "contrary to nature" must include reference to the manner in which such an action is contrary to the personalistic norm.[48]

The personalistic norm can be formulated substantively in at least two equivalent ways. The first, and negative, form makes more explicit reference to the norm's basis in the nature of the person. Treating persons as persons means not acting upon them apart from their knowing and willing participation in the end of the action, so that their "part" in the action is also a properly personal one. This is reflected in the norm: "[W]henever a person is the object of your activity, remember that you may not treat that person as only the means to an end, but must allow for the fact that he or she, too, has, or at least should have, distinct personal ends" (LR 28). That is, persons must not be used, since to "use" is to treat as merely the means to an end (LR 25, 41). This norm is respected even by God, who created us as personal beings and who, consistently, "does not [even] redeem man against his will" (LR 27).[49]

If use of a person violates the personalistic norm, the norm's second, "positive form," which clarifies how it is fulfilled, "confirms this: the person is a good towards which the only proper and adequate attitude is love" (LR 41). To see how love is the opposite of use requires a proper understanding of the word "love." "[L]ove is always a mutual relationship between persons... based on particular attitudes to the good, adopted by each of them individually and by both jointly" (LR 73, emphasis deleted). It is necessary to attend to the phrase, "attitudes to the good." "The good" encompasses not only or even primarily some extrinsic object of (coincidentally shared) pursuit, but also, more importantly, one's partner in that pursuit (and, necessarily, *qua* person, not *qua* means). Accordingly, "[m]an's capacity for love depends on his willingness consciously to seek a good together with others, *and to subordinate himself to that good for the sake of others, or to others for the sake of that good*" (LR 29, emphasis added). That is, the pursuit of good that constitutes a loving relationship is not a selfish pursuit in which another person is still used as a means, if perhaps willingly and so more decorously—it is a pursuit for the sake of one's partner as much as of oneself; and, even insofar as a good is pursued for one's own sake, it is sought in a manner that gives primacy to the good of the partner. In true love "[i]t is not enough to long for a person as a good for oneself, one must also, and above all, long for that person's good" (LR 83). Love involves "the drive to endow beloved persons with the good" (LR 138).

Now in the subordination to the other that is essential to love, one endows the other not only with extrinsic goods, but with one's own good *qua* person. Thus the personal self-donation that "is impossible and illegitimate in the natural order and in a physical sense, can come about in the order of love and in a moral sense" (LR 96–97). This self-donation is the way—the only way—to self-fulfillment. I cannot substitute for someone else's personhood, nor vice-versa: this expresses "natural" incommunicability. Were I to use another, in this use the other would be less than a person, and I would be neither giving nor receiving person-hood. But when I subordinate my personhood to another's in pursuit of some common good, the other as a partner in this pursuit remains a personal good, and one even more fulfilled by the good bestowed and pursued (cf. LR 82–83). Then my own personhood can in turn live more fully in that of the other.[50] This is "the law of *ekstasis*": "the lover 'goes outside' the self to find a fuller existence in another" (LR 126). It reflects the Gospel that one who loses one's life will save it (LR 97). And love "does not merely mean that [persons] both seek a common good, it also unites [them] internally" (LR 28). In sum, "only the spirituality and the 'inwardness' of persons"—conferring as they do a mode of being that is at once incommunicable and relational, each characteristic necessary for the perfection of the other[51]—"create the conditions for mutual interpenetration" (LR 131).[52]

It is crucial to add at this juncture that love is expressed or withheld by the action one chooses (moral object), not only by the further intention for the sake of which one chooses an action. This further intention is morally important. But an action itself constitutes a relationship between the self and the other, a relationship that is already either one of love (or incipient love since a good further intention is also necessary) or of use. For an action intends to affect the other, independent of the further intention for the sake of which the effect is chosen, and some intended effects of human acts are only uses, not bestowals of personal good.[53]

Furthermore, a personal action contributes to the formation of a settled disposition (*hexis, habitus*) on the part of the acting person.[54] Such dispositions themselves can be dispositions of love or use. Right (virtuous) relationships with others require right dispositions; the truest love comes from a true heart.[55] But right dispositions are also "practical": while not essential for right action, they make it easier. This practical importance increases as temptations to act wrongly in a given sphere of life increase. And the various kinds of actions that come under the headings of "love" and "use" are related to each other in such a way that to become disposed to one kind of act of love or of use might in fact dispose one to love or use in general.

Finally, love can and must become a sociocultural reality, not only an individual one. Societies, from the small (families) to the large (nations), are not simply sums of their (individual human) parts; precisely as societies do they correspond to irreducible human needs, and so have their own proper "subjectivities."[56] Yet they are nonetheless human entities, dimensions of human activity and life, and so must respect the personalistic norm. Indeed they attain their meaning and integrity only by respecting this and related norms.[57] Societies not "disposed" to love, as we might say, by being informed by these norms degenerate into "structures of sin," themselves using persons (EV #12) and encouraging individuals also to use rather than love.[58]

III. SEXUAL LOVE AND CONTRACEPTIVE USE

The anthropological and ethical considerations I have outlined can be applied to marital sexuality and to the problem of contraception. As I shall proceed in this section to explain, the pursuit of pleasure cannot found a loving relationship between persons. If pleasure is the ultimate goal of sexual activity, that activity can only be use. Yet marital sexuality can found that realization of love in which the self is most fully given to the other. This is so because of the good of procreation. Procreation is of more than merely biological significance for the human person; it is of existential significance. And the good of procreation is self-transcendent and common (since a child, a new person, transcends either parent's individuality) as well as intimately personal. With this good as its natural purpose, sexuality can and must be approached in accordance with the personalistic norm as well as the other requirements of nature. And contraception, but not NFP, destroys the relationship of this good to the acting person so as to leave pleasure as the sole or highest goal of intercourse. Accordingly, contracepted intercourse, and contraception insofar as it envisages such intercourse, is an act of use, incompatible with love.

That pleasure or enjoyment does not found love, so that one may not treat sexuality and marital intercourse in particular as means to pleasure as the primary end, can be seen by considering first that pleasure is in no way trans-subjective (LR 37, 156–57). When "John" experiences pleasure, his pleasure is just and never more than, precisely, "his." It cannot be "Jean's" as well. Intercourse in which each partner seeks primarily his or her own pleasure must therefore be egoistic and an act of use, not loving and unifying.

And egoism is not transformed into altruism if the partners each simply agree either to allow the other to pursue pleasure, or even actively to seek to bestow pleasure on the other, with pleasure still the primary end. It might be thought that each partner could then be said to be pursuing the pleasure of both. But there is no such thing as "the pleasure of both." Each partner will be striving for merely a coincidence of two pleasures, each pleasure remaining wholly subjective (LR 38–39, 157). And there being no pleasure for John but "his" own, he will, insofar as pleasure is his primary end, pursue Jean's pleasure also only because this has as a further effect his experiencing pleasure as well—either because it happens to give him pleasure to see her experiencing pleasure, or because he calculates that if he give her pleasure she will choose to reciprocate. Her pursuit of his pleasure will be similarly accidental. Each partner will be giving only to receive. This remains use, if bilateral use (LR 39; cf. 87–88). It is therefore necessary for the partners to subordinate pleasure to the good of the person—for each to pursue pleasure only for the good of the other.

But an action that is objectively primarily the pursuit of even another's pleasure for its own sake is still not pursuit of personal good. Pleasure may certainly be appreciated and welcomed as a sign of such a good, and indeed it is of great psychological importance, but it is nonetheless "essentially incidental [and] contingent" (LR 36). Pursuit of a personal good will not necessarily give pleasure, and many things that may give pleasure are not good for the person. Therefore pursuit of pleasure does not suffice to justify intercourse as an act of love.[59] It is necessary to turn to an evaluation of the natural and personal significance of intercourse to see how it might be an act of love.

The "sexual urge," and the behaviors to which it gives rise, culminating in intercourse, have a natural purpose or end: procreation. To describe this purpose as natural is to say that sexuality has this purpose independent of personal acts of will (LR 51; cf. 49).[60] Importantly, the natural end of intercourse belongs to every act of intercourse, not only to all the acts of a marriage somehow considered as a "totality." An act of intercourse implicates procreation in an irreducible way (cf. LR 226)—such acts do not give rise to procreation by cumulative effect.[61] It remains only for acting persons to choose whether to accept or reject this potentiality. And procreation represents not only a biological finality, but an existential one (LR 51–52, 56–57, 62–63, 226; cf. 230). Each human person exists because of the sexual urge. Because of our sexuality, we can participate in the order of existence in a trans-personal way. Insofar as existence, of the species as well as of ourselves as individuals, is the "first and most basic good" (LR 52), procreation is not a humanly indifferent purpose. The natural end of intercourse is normative for the acting person.[62] Without respect for it, there can be no love of the person who is one's partner in intercourse, only use (LR 226–27), since the nature of the person is integral (LR 229–30).[63]

But the problem of the "rigorist" interpretation of sexuality illustrates that respect for nature, in the sense of this purpose, is, while necessary, still insufficient for love. Rigorism respects the finality of sexuality as such, but uses the person as a means to sexuality's end of procreation (LR 57–61; cf. 233–34). For rigorism does not respect the nature of the person as such. In fact, in view of the integrity of the person, the sexual urge itself must be understood as being directed to a person (LR 49, 76–82, 107–10, 122–24, 128–30, 132–34, 150, 160, 178), and this rules out the rigorist interpretation of the urge just as it rules out the (more common) "libidinistic" one (LR 61–66).[64] Thus, "the norm that emerges from an understanding of the nature and purpose of the sexual urge must be supplemented with the personalistic norm. The necessity of combining these two norms into one ... is *indispensable for preserving the order of nature.* ... [T]he aims of nature must always come together with the value of the person. Otherwise the reasoning will be *incomplete, or even one-sided and partially flawed.* "[65] Indeed, in view of the integral nature of the person, one can even say: "To realize merely the ends of the urge without realizing the personalistic norm would not satisfy the normative principle of the order of nature."[66] Only given the understanding that "'[n]atural-ness' ... is an expression of harmony not just with nature but also with the person" can one conclude: "In sexual activity... a person is not an object of use to the extent that the act is in harmony with nature and, therefore, basically subordinated to its purpose."[67]

Sexual love is not something superadded to the natural purpose of intercourse, but rather a way of choosing that purpose in partnership with another person. Procreation, as the natural end of sexuality, makes it possible for sexual intercourse to be an act of love (LR 30). Thus nature supplies, as it were, the "material" for love in the natural purpose of sexuality (LR 53, 226). Persons recognize this material and by acts of will "form" it into love (cf. LR 49–50). And because the good shared in this love is such an intimate good of the person, the love in which sexuality finds its place has, like no other kind of love, as "[i]ts decisive character ... the giving of one's own person (to another)," even though other loves "are all ways by which one person goes out towards another" (LR 96; cf. 125–26).[68] The union that results from mutual self-donation of this kind gives rise to an ecstasy (*ekstasis*) that is more than a psychological phenomenon; indeed, subjectively important as the psychological component of love is, it must be integrated into objective love to be itself really love (LR 119–20, 127–28).

Objective love requires the choice of certain kinds of actions, and it is now possible to inquire into how specific actions bear upon the above principles. Let us consider first the use of naturally infertile times to regulate procreation. Now even those acts of intercourse that we tend to describe as naturally infertile are nonetheless rightly said to have procreation as a natural end, since such acts still engage a system whose full function would make them fertile but is lacking for reasons independent of human intention.[69] Certainly, then, marital intercourse during naturally infertile times is not *ipso facto* immoral. It is still the kind of intended act (moral object) that is compatible with love. Such intercourse is an expression of tenderness, and this is a part of love, so long as it is not isolated from the good of the person, which it is not so long as the act itself is natural (see LR 200–208) since it then retains its natural end. But the question still arises whether it is illicit to reserve intercourse for infertile times with the intention of excluding procreation. Does this intention make intercourse an act of use for the sake of pleasure only? One can, in fact, broaden the question. Does not the lack of desire to procreate transform even naturally fertile intercourse into "use"?

To answer these questions requires the introduction of some distinctions.

First, a positive (subjective) desire to procreate is never necessary. On the contrary: "Marital intercourse is in itself an interpersonal act, an act of betrothed love, so that the intentions and the attention of each partner must be fixed upon the other, upon his or her true good. They must not be concentrated upon the possible consequences of the act, especially if that would mean a diversion of attention from the partner. It is certainly not necessary always to resolve that 'we are performing this act in order to become parents.' It is sufficient to say that 'in performing this act we know that we may become parents and we are willing for that to happen.' That approach alone is compatible with love..." (LR 233–34; cf. 229).

Second, a positive desire not to procreate at a given time can be just or unjust. Acceptance of procreation does need to characterize the marital relationship as a whole (LR 242–43).[70] Furthermore, to the extent that a marital act is naturally fertile, this must be accepted along with the possibility of procreation that follows, even if there is a desire that this possibility not be actualized (LR 227–29, 231, 243–44). "There are, however, circumstances in which [the] disposition [to procreate] itself demands renunciation of procreation, [because] any further increase in the size of the family would be incompatible with parental duty" (LR 243).[71] Now if a couple have a just reason to avoid procreation, they need not have intercourse at the times when it might be fertile. And this does not transform any acts of intercourse during infertile times into acts of use. It entails no objective rejection of the natural end of any act of intercourse (LR 236). And the just (subjective) intention to avoid procreation cannot change what we have seen to be an objectively moral choice of action into an immoral one.[72] Hence, in both its avoidance of intercourse during fertile times and its use of intercourse during infertile times, NFP is morally licit and compatible with love.

Contraception, however, is morally different from NFP. Contraception alters the moral object "intercourse," the choice to have intercourse. For unlike NFP, contraception alters the acting persons *vis-à-vis* inter-course—specifically, in such a way as objectively to entail rejection of the natural structure of intercourse with its finality. Therefore, contracep-ted intercourse (unlike naturally infertile intercourse) is no longer the kind of intended action that is ordered to procreation. Consequently, contracepted intercourse is no longer the kind of action that can be chosen as an act of love. As a rejection of nature, contraception is a rejection of the integrity of the person.[73] But furthermore, it leaves nothing to serve as the basis for unification in love by intercourse. Objectively, "[t]he very fact of deliberately [artificially] excluding the possibility of parenthood from marital intercourse makes 'enjoyment' the intention of the act" (LR 235; cf. 228, 234). Enjoyment or pleasure, as we have seen, of its nature cannot found love.[74] And since love is the only morally adequate way in which to treat a person, one cannot simply redefine marriage to allow contraception. "Marriage" so redefined would not only not be something other than marriage, it would be an immoral situation for a human person.

Now insofar as contracepted sex is as such an act of use, it forms the acting person to be disposed to use other persons. Presumably this disposition will manifest itself especially in sexual matters, since contraception is specifically sexual use (unchastity). However, the principle allowing one to make another an instrument for sexual pleasure must be broad enough to encompass other kinds of use as well. Either one is objectively required to respect the good of the person, or one is not. If one is not required to respect the good of the person in one kind of action (sexual intercourse), then there is no objective reason to regard oneself as required to respect the good of the person in other kinds of actions. A disposition toward this false principle will be a disposition contrary to the good of the person as such and will probably come to manifest itself in ways other than contraception and other subspecies of unchastity. At most, subjective qualms will inhibit such use. But strong though they may be, subjective qualms are not reliable. We all face situations of grave temptation, especially when many others are using people in some way.[75] Eventually people will find themselves in situations in which their subjective affection for another is weak, or in which the gain from use would be very great and is therefore very attractive, and use will follow if they have admitted its possibility. Only true marital love is likely to guarantee familial love and even social justice.[76]

Finally, contraception affects cultural dispositions, not only individual ones. And when contraception becomes culturally widespread and, finally, typical, it becomes more difficult to encourage chastity or other forms of love on the part of individuals. Furthermore, societies are more than sums of individuals, and cultural acceptance of contraception affects the way in which our common life is organized. As an obvious example, public funding for contraception has become a major component of our political response to certain situations both foreign and domestic. Consider only the role contraception plays in domestic social policy. Few proposals or programs to address the problem of childbearing by unmarried women, especially teenagers, do not have a contraceptive component. And this "squeezes" out willingness to encourage chastity, not only because limited availability of time and money usually sets up something close to a zero-sum game, but more importantly because contracepted intercourse is use and unchaste *qua* contracepted. To teach that contraception is acceptable, even if not best, is therefore *ipso facto* to teach that unchastity is acceptable. Any accompanying message that "abstinence is best" can then only be a calculation, and one that is dubious insofar as it prescinds from the value of pleasure. Those who formulate or administer programs know this, if only inchoately, even if they are not already ideologically committed to the proposition that fornication is *per se* desirable, and social policy is set on a downward spiral. And again, sociopolitical acceptance of contraception and of other forms of use are mutually reinforcing dispositions.[77]

IV. CONSEQUENCES FOR LIFE ISSUES

The meaning and significance of Pope John Paul's statements in *Evangelium Vitae* characterizing contraception as unchaste and, as such, contrary to "true love" have now been explained. To complete the argument concerning the relationship between contraception and abortion requires that I show why it is true that, in the pope's words, "[o]nly a true love is able to protect life." Given an understanding of the meaning of "love" as opposed to "use," one can explain the need for love to protect life—and thus also the relationship between unchastity and contraception on the one hand, and life issues on the other—with reference to *Evangelium Vitae*'s discussion of the meaning of a "culture of life."

The idea of a culture of life is introduced by implication when John Paul's initial diagnosis of today's problematic situation finds that the opposite of such a culture now prevails. The pope says that "while the climate of widespread moral uncertainty can in some way be explained by... today's social problems, ...it is no less true that we are confronted by an even larger reality, which can be described as a veritable *structure of sin.* This reality is characterized by the emergence of a culture which... in many cases takes the form of a veritable 'culture of death.' This culture is actively fostered by powerful... currents which encourage an idea of society excessively concerned with efficiency" (EV #12).

Now such a culture is precisely a culture of use of persons (cf. esp. EV #19, 23). For efficiency looks only to predetermined ends and to the potential usefulness of things and persons for achieving those ends, not to whether the ends in question are good for other persons and things, nor, *a fortiori,* whether other persons are willing or able to pursue the same ends. Other persons become at best tools. Moreover, they become at worst, and often, obstacles and enemies. The extreme but logically inexorable manifestation of use is the taking of innocent life when the killing itself would serve a chosen end or when an end would be more easily attained were some person not alive. This is what is meant by the statement that the disposition toward oneself and one's spouse embodied by contraception is related to the disposition embodied by disrespect for life. While the unchastity of contracepted intercourse and the injustice of immoral homicide are specifically different insofar as they use persons in different ways, or insofar as they contravene different natural goods of persons under different kinds of circumstances, they do have in common the objective, false principle that persons may be used.

We may turn next to John Paul's positive description of a culture of life. *Evangelium Vitae*'s third chapter, "You Shall Not Kill: God's Holy Law," concludes with a section explaining that the law's negative precepts, proscribing irredeemable actions, are a "minimum" (#75), and that to "promote" life "is not only a personal but a social concern which we must all foster... so that our time... may at last witness the establishment of a new culture of life, the fruit of the culture of truth and of love" (#77). The fourth chapter then proceeds to describe in more detail people's responsibilities toward the end of building such a culture.

There *Evangelium Vitae* speaks of the need, in a culture of life and love, for *"a contemplative outlook"*: "the outlook of those who see life in its deeper meaning, who grasp its utter gratuitousness, its beauty and its invitation to freedom and responsibility... of those who do not presume to take possession of reality but instead accept it as a gift" (#83).

Consistent with my analysis thus far, this attitude is precisely the opposite of the "excessive concern with efficiency" that underlies use. Indeed, it requires *"a new life-style,* consisting in making practical choices ... on the basis of a correct scale of values: the primacy ... of the person over things" (#98).[78] Such a primacy cannot allow use of persons. It therefore gives rise to the "true love" that alone protects life, which is mentioned by John Paul in very close connection with the "correct scale of values."

In *Evangelium Vitae,* the basis for and content of this love are elaborated especially in theological terms, with reference to God not only as creator but also as the end of the life of each human person.[79] This theological anthropology does not contradict the primarily philosophical approach of *Love and Responsibility,* but rather further explains it by revealing its meaning most completely.[80] Indeed *Love and Responsibility* (41) mentions that the personalistic norm is presupposed by the New Testament commandment to love, and even that "we can, taking a broader view, say that the commandment to love *is* the personalistic norm."

Now abortion in particular is a manifestation of the culture of death's use of persons. In fact our culture's attitude to new life in general reflects a tremendous ignorance of the meaning of procreation, in which a new person comes to be from the love, the mutual personal self-giving, of his or her mother and father, and comes to maturity, fullness of personal being, from that same love.[81] A child is seen as something which can and may be acquired to make adults' lives fulfilling independent of spousal love.

One sees, for example, single persons or members of homosexual "couples" (couples constituted as such by another form of unchastity) bearing children (often with "surrogate" arrangements, and/or aided by artificial reproductive technology, all of which reflects and compounds the moral evil) or adopting them. One should hasten to add that altruistic desires to give an already-existing and suffering child a better home are likely at work in the case of many such adoptions. But there seems to be no shortage of married couples waiting to adopt, so that the choice need not be between leaving a child in a situation of suffering and allowing his or her adoption into an irregular situation. And in the frequent cases of childbearing outside marital contexts, altruistic motives to rescue an existing child are irrelevant. The conclusion that children are being treated as means to an end seems inescapable. Such treatment is becoming increasingly culturally acceptable, and is allowed and facilitated by the law. Given this general cultural disposition, when a child who has been conceived is seen as an obstacle to the ends of the mother or father, abortion will often be the response; and laws will and do allow and promote abortion (cf. EV #23).

The argument that contracepted intercourse embodies and reinforces a disposition of use of persons that is the same disposition that defines the culture of death in which abortion is acceptable has strategic implications for those who seek to minimize or end abortions. Most obviously, encouraging and facilitating contraceptive use will not minimize abortions, especially over the long term. Certainly babies conceived in cases of contraceptive failure will be especially likely to be aborted. Here the objective disposition of use promoted by contraception will be joined with (and indeed make more selfish, more "contralife") the subjective desire to avoid bearing a child. However, not all abortions follow contraceptive failure. In some cases, couples want to conceive and bear children, but change their minds for reasons of many kinds, ranging from trivial to serious. In these cases, the probability of recourse to abortion is likely to be proportionate to, *inter alia,* the acceptability of abortion, which will be a function of a more general acceptability of use as opposed to love, which will in turn be greater where contraception is acceptable.

In other cases, couples (often unmarried) do not want to conceive, but, either unrealistically denying the possibility of conception or just carelessly, choose to have intercourse but not to use contraception. No campaign encouraging or facilitating contraception will ever convince everyone in such circumstances to use contraception. Some babies will be conceived, and the acceptability of contraception will increase the acceptability of recourse to abortion. Perhaps even more seriously, however, the acceptability of abortion that is finally of a piece with acceptability of contraception will undermine the promotion of contraception itself. For to the extent that abortion is acceptable, to that extent is the incentive to use contraception diminished.[82] Indeed this may be a root of the invariably (and, my argument implies, inevitably) limited effectiveness of promotion of contraception even at bringing about actual recourse to contraception, let alone at reducing abortions.

When contraception is promoted as a matter of public policy, it becomes an element of the political component of culture, and here, too, it makes abortion more intractable. A politics that actively encourages contraception will be a politics oriented toward use, not love, of persons, and therefore not toward justice. It will be more likely to allow and even encourage forms of injustice including abortion and other unjust homicide (cf. EV #20, 68–72).[83]

Most segments of the pro-life movement have not, as such, promoted contraception, although many legislators and administrators who at least support pro-life measures also support at least some promotion of contraception. However, the implications of the argument I have offered bear upon pro-life groups' common stratagem of neutrality toward contraception as well. An effective campaign against abortion cannot rest content with demonstrating the humanity of the unborn child and pointing to the injustice of killing innocent human persons. Acceptance of the ethos of use of persons is a very great obstacle to acceptance of arguments about justice. It is the very foundation and reality of justice that is in question. Only a culture of life, devoting renewed attention to the good represented by the person, will move people to be just. An unapologetic and clearly explained rejection of contraception is necessary to make that good visible.[84]

To translate this into strategic practice, some distinctions are necessary. First, it is appropriate and prudent for groups to concentrate on fighting the injustice of abortion (and issues very similar in kind, such as euthanasia), and to take no positions on other moral issues. This is all the more the case since a necessary component of a just resolution of the abortion issue must be political: not merely an end to state promotion and funding of abortion, but also legal protection of innocent life through proscription of abortion, is necessary. It is of the very essence of politics to proscribe injustices like abortion. It is only necessary to ensure that groups' specialization is not confused with indifference. When groups dedicated to educational, political, and other efforts specifically against abortion are asked about contraception, their answers should direct attention back to abortion as the issue around which the groups are constituted, explaining that abortion is unjust but not suggesting that contraception is unimportant—merely that it is different.

Such groups cannot, however, represent pro-life strategy in its entirety. Those who would end abortion must also work in other ways, individually and together, against contraception. At this time (and for the foreseeable future), such efforts will not have the political component that efforts directly against abortion will. State promotion of contraception should be fought as much as individual use of contraception. But contraception does not touch upon the common good of the political community as directly as does abortion, and it would be most imprudent to seek laws against it. (Indeed, it would almost certainly be imprudent to campaign at this time for laws against even some abortions—perhaps most notably, those brought about by abortifacient "contraceptives.")[85] But even prudential legal toleration of contraception should be explained, when it needs to be explained, in moral terms, so as not to suggest indifference. That is, it should not be suggested that contraception is not a grave evil; rather the harm that could result from laws against something so widely accepted and consensually employed should be stressed.[86] The conjunction of this explanation with visible efforts to end political promotion of contraception will help to clarify that no indifference is intended.

Finally, the necessary moral campaign against contraception should have a primarily positive focus. It should begin by proclaiming, celebrating, and serving the Gospel of life—the good news concerning and represented by the human person. It should therefore include, as appropriate, evangelization (cf. EV #78, 80).[87] It should include also more specific reference to the meaning of sexuality and the value of spousal love. In the context of this teaching concerning love, NFP, a way for spouses to practice true love, should be taught (EV #88, 97). By such promotion of love and chastity, not only can situations in which abortion might be a temptation be minimized, but dispositions toward the person can be fostered which will make the rejection of abortion more likely.

CONCLUSIONS

In *Evangelium Vitae,* written to be "a precise and vigorous reaffirmation of the value of human life and its inviolability" (#5, emphasis deleted), Pope John Paul II teaches that contracepted intercourse is unchaste and that contraception must be therefore be rejected if life is to be protected. This reflects the argument he has developed concerning precisely the good of the person and the inadequacy of unchaste actions and contracepted intercourse in particular as responses to this good. Contraception transforms intercourse into an action that can objectively be no more than use of another person, not the love that persons deserve. Abortion is a manifestation of the same use. In view of these arguments, the notion that promoting contraception will lower the abortion rate should be decisively rejected. In fact, the pro-life movement must clarify the meaning of love and the evil of contraception if individuals and society are to recover pro-life dispositions.

In general, fidelity to the moral law is often difficult. It becomes more so when commandments are seen as extrinsic and unconnected obligations. But the Holy Spirit renews our hearts and enables us to fulfill the law by making loving gifts of our hearts and our whole selves. The law can then be seen as a unified framework signifying the very purpose of human life, "good news" rather than a burden (EV #48–49).[88] Contraception, as an obstacle to love, is an obstacle to this renewal, and therefore also to our obedience to the commandment, "You shall not kill." And contraception is now deeply rooted in our culture. Yet there is room for hope that the problem is not intractable. The Lord always speaks through the value of the human person, and conscience can always awaken to this voice (EV #24–25). Signs of the Lord's victory over sin and death, of recognition of the transcendent value of the human person, are not lacking even in our culture of death (EV #26–27). In company with and inspired by the Mother of God, who alone among humans cooperated without reservation with the Spirit and was associated fully with Christ's love even through suffering (EV #103), let us in hope offer the world even the most countercultural challenges of the Law and Gospel of life, especially by our example, and build upon the signs of hope already present (among them, I might add, the ministry of Pope John Paul II).[89]

NOTES

1. "Contraception" in this essay denotes *actions or methods chosen to render (marital) intercourse infertile*—that is, to prevent either ovulation, or (using a barrier or spermicide, or, more rarely, withdrawal) fertilization of a released egg.

One can rightly call contraception of this sort "artificial," at least since the infertility is imposed or ensured by human "artifice," not by the natural absence of an egg or failure of sperm to meet egg. The meaning and implications of this artificiality will be explored in some depth below.

"Contraceptives" that prevent implantation of a fertilized egg, such as "morning-after pills," are evil and should be rejected primarily because their use is homicidal; homicide, that is, is the means to the end of "contraception." (The term "abortifacient" is accurate as a moral assessment, but is also controversial because "abortion" is generally defined relative to "pregnancy," which in turn is defined relative to the mother's responses to and support of the implanted embryo and later the fetus.) Of course, someone genuinely ignorant of this might use them with only a contraceptive intent, and so only "commit" contraception. (See the references in n. 19 concerning the moral importance of the "intended" action.) My analysis applies to such cases by extension. But education concerning the homicidal nature of these methods is urgently necessary. Responsibility to the good of life requires that we promote knowledge of what is necessary to avoid its destruction, especially as end or means.

Many "oral contraceptives" that act primarily by suppressing ovulation do not do so with 100% efficacy—a woman taking such a pill may rarely have an ovulatory cycle. For example, the formulations manufactured and sold as the combination (estrogen plus progestin) pills Loestrin 1/20 and 1.5/30 (Parke-Davis) have been reported to allow ovulation in 4.2% of 378 cycles and 0.6% of 629 cycles, respectively (Joseph W. Goldzieher, Armando de la Peña, C. Brandon Chenault, and T. B. Woutersz, "Comparative Studies of the Ethynyl Estrogens Used in Oral Contraceptives: II. Antiovulatory Potency," *American Journal of Obstetrics and Gynecology* 122 [1975] p.621). (Interestingly, this study found that the formulation in the pill Lo/Ovral [Wyeth-Ayerst] allowed ovulation in none of 266 cycles.) "Minipills," which contain progestins only, allow ovulation much more frequently. As examples, I. Aref, F. Hefnawi, O. Kandl, and T. Abdel Aziz ("Effect of Minipills on Physiologic Responses of Human Cervical Mucus, Endometrium, and Ovary," *Fertility and Sterility* 24 [1973] pp.578–83) cite other studies that found ovulation in 66–81% of cycles in women using various progestins, and report results of their own indicating ovulation in, respectively, three out of four cycles, one out of three cycles, two out of three cycles, and three out of four cycles in women using four different progestins; and according to *Physicians' Desk Reference* (51st ed. [1997] p.1903), the minipill Micronor (Ortho) "prevent[s] conception by suppressing ovulation in approximately half of users...." Both combination pills and minipills also have at least two other modes of action, however: they thicken cervical mucus, decreasing the likelihood that a sperm will reach an egg, *and they alter the endometrium, preventing implantation of a fertilized egg.* As examples, *Physicians' Desk Reference* (p.1914) says of the combination pills Ortho-Cyclen and Ortho Tri-Cyclen (Ortho), using language typical of its descriptions of combination pills:

"Although the primary mechanism of action is inhibition of ovulation, other alterations include changes in the cervical mucus... and the endometrium...." Micronor, in addition to "suppressing ovulation in approximately half of users," is described as acting also by "thickening the cervical mucus ... and altering the endometrium" (p.1903). (See also Leon Speroff and Philip D. Darney, *A Clinical Guide for Contraception* [Baltimore: Williams & Wilkins, 1992] p.40, concerning combination pills; Aref et al., "Effect of Minipills," concerning minipills; and concerning both combination pills and minipills, David D. Baird and Anna F. Glasier, "Hormonal Contraception," *New England Journal of Medicine* 328 [1993] p.1543.) If a woman using a pill has intercourse during an ovulatory cycle (of which she will be unaware), and the mucus-thickening and other genuinely contraceptive modes of action do not suffice, intercourse will be fertile (again, the woman will be unaware of this), but the embryo will likely die. This is a morally unacceptable risk (all the more so since [1] if it happens, it happens as a means to the contraceptive end, not as a side effect; and [2] the intended end, contraception, is itself morally unacceptable, as I shall show, and so could not justify any evil even as a side effect). (Cf. Nicholas Tonti-Filipini, "The Pill: Abortifacient or Contraceptive? A Literature Review," *Linacre Quarterly* 62, no. 1 [1995] pp.5–28.) However the risk is sufficiently low for combination pills (which are more commonly used than minipills) that I think it more helpful to concentrate moral analysis on the truly contraceptive nature of such pills, this alone making them unacceptable. (I am grateful to James Linn, M.D., for providing me with most of the materials cited in this paragraph.)

2. I assume it is unnecessary to document this extensively. One needs only to read regularly the editorial and op-ed pages of any major newspaper to observe examples. To cite but one, consider the article by Naomi Wolf, "Pro-Choice *and* Pro-Life," on the *New York Times* 3 April 1997 op-ed page, which I quickly found online and is available in full at http://search.nytimes.com/search/daily/bin/fastweb?getdoc+site+site+61+0++. Wolf writes that:

> a full-fledged campaign for cheap and easily accessible contraception is the best antidote to our shamefully high abortion rate.... If we asked Americans to send checks to Planned Parenthood to help save hundreds of thousands of women a year from having to face abortions, our support would rise exponentially....
>
> To those who oppose access to contraceptives, yet hold up images of dead fetuses, we should say: This disaster might have been prevented by a few cents' worth of nonoxynol-9; this blood is on your hands.
>
> For whatever the millions of pro-lifers think about birth control, abortion must surely be worse.
>
> A challenge to pro-choicers to abandon a dogmatic approach must be met with a challenge to pro-lifers to separate from the demagogues in their ranks and join us in a drive to prevent unwanted pregnancy.

> The Common Ground Network for Life and Choice has brought activists together from both sides.... The network has even found that half of the pro-lifers in some of its groups would support a campaign to improve access to birth control....
>
> ...Congress and the Administration should champion the "common ground" approach, and add to it bipartisan support for financing far more research, development and distribution of contraceptives.
>
> We have all lived with the human cost of our hypocrisies for too long. It is time to abandon symbolic debates on Capitol Hill in favor of policies that can give women—who have been so ill-served by the rigid views on both sides—real help and real choice.

3. Cf. the comments—which bracket a chapter consisting of a generally negative discussion of contraception—of Dr. and Mrs. J. C. Willke (*Abortion: Questions and Answers* [Cincinnati: Hayes, 1985]): "The [Right to Life] movement limits itself to the protection of life from conception until natural death. It takes no position on the 'preliminaries.' Therefore it has no opinion on contraception or sterilization" (p.225); "To the extent that [Planned Parenthood's activities] help married couples use contraceptives to plan their families, Right to Life has no opinion" (p.232). Perhaps indicating that the Willkes and others in the pro-life movement have begun to reconsider the wisdom of this neutrality, neither these nor similar comments were included in the corresponding chapter (on contraception) of the new, updated version of the Willkes' book (*Why Can't We Love Them Both: Questions and Answers about Abortion* [Cincinnati: Hayes, 1997], ch. 35).

4. This correlation is established with only with some difficulty, especially when one attempts an historical inquiry. In the U.S., there were probably 150,000 to 200,000 abortions annually before legalization (Brian W. Clowes, "The Role of Maternal Deaths in the Abortion Debate," *St. Louis University Public Law Review* 13 [1993] p.332), or 10–13% as many as there came to be within a few years of *Roe v. Wade.* This (rapid) increase obviously reflects the availability that came with legalization.

Some conclusions about acceptance can be drawn from survey data. While the results of public opinion polls about abortion vary greatly with the exact question asked (probably because many people's opinions are not firm), we are fortunate to have results from identically-worded survey questions asked repeatedly over a period of years, enabling us to measure changes in opinion. These surveys asked: "Please tell me whether or not you think it should be possible for a pregnant woman to obtain a legal abortion (a) if there is a strong chance of serious defect in the baby; (b) if she is married and does not want any more children; (c) if the woman's own health is seriously endangered by the pregnancy; (d) if the family has a very low income and cannot afford any more children; (e) if she became pregnant as a result of rape; (f) if she is not married and does not want to marry the man?"

I present here, and discuss briefly in the following paragraph of this note, selected data from these surveys, namely, the percentage answering yes to each question (a)–(f) above (with 95% confidence intervals), in each of the years 1965, 1972, 1973, and 1982: question (a), 1965: 54.6 ± 2.5; 1972: 74.3 ± 2.1; 1973: 82.2 ± 1.9; 1982: 81.1 ± 2.0; question (b), 1965: 15.4 ± 1.8; 1972: 37.6 ± 2.4; 1973: 46.1 ± 2.5; 1982: 46.3 ± 2.5; question (c), 1965: 70.3 ± 2.3; 1972: 83.0 ± 1.8; 1973: 90.6 ± 1.5; 1982: 89.4 ± 1.6; question (d), 1965: 21.2 ± 2.1; 1972: 45.6 ± 2.4; 1973: 51.7 ± 2.5; 1982: 49.7 ± 2.5; question (e), 1965: 55.7 ± 2.5; 1972: 74.1 ± 2.1; 1973: 80.6 ± 2.0; 1982: 83.1 ± 1.9; question (f), 1965: 17.4 ± 1.9; 1972: 40.5 ± 2.4; 1973: 47.3 ± 2.5; 1982: 46.7 ± 2.5. (These data were collected by the National Opinion Research Center, University of Chicago. The 1965 data are from Study 870, conducted for the NBC Study of Honesty and Ethics. The 1972–82 data are published in James A. Davis, *General Social Science Survey Cumulative File, 1972–1982* [machine-readable data file], 1st ICPSR ed. [Ann Arbor, MI: Inter-university Consortium for Political and Social Research, 1983]. I thank Professor John McAdams for providing me with these sources.)

In summary, the data indicate that acceptability of abortion increased primarily in the years prior to legalization (even though the majority of Americans have never come to accept the virtually unlimited abortion license under *Roe*). There were statistically significant increases in the fraction responding yes to each question between the 1965 and 1972 surveys (I have no data prior to 1965 or for 1966–71). The smallest such increase was for question (c) (danger to woman's health, which produced the largest yes result to begin with in 1965). Considerably smaller, but still significant, increases were observed between 1972 and 1973. Between 1973 and 1982 there were no significant net increases (I have not analyzed the data from the 1974–81 surveys to determine whether any fluctuations were significant). Thus, not only has abortion become more acceptable, but this has not been primarily the result of legalization. (It might be suggested that the conviction indicated by a yes answer to the question, "Do you think it should be possible for a pregnant woman to obtain a *legal* abortion if..." is not necessarily that such abortions are morally acceptable, nor even that they, in themselves, benefit society in some non-moral way, but perhaps only that most of them will take place anyway but at lesser cost if they are legal than if not. This hypothesis would not seem, however, to account for the very different numbers of people who approve of legalized abortion under different circumstances—in particular, for the much higher levels of approval in what are generally regarded as the "hardest" cases.)

Now the use of contraception, even as a means to postpone and/or limit marital fertility, clearly increased at around the same time as did the acceptability (though not yet availability and therefore not yet frequency) of abortion. This surely reflects, to some degree, the development of oral contraceptives. However, to what degree it also reflects increased acceptance is unclear. It is doubtful that such figures as Margaret Sanger ever appealed solely to an elite; and the very development of "birth-control pills" reflected some demand. Thus, the circumstances *vis-à-vis* contraception in which abortion became more acceptable are somewhat ambiguous. One might not know what to expect from a situation of demand but not availability.

Furthermore, an increase in acceptability will reflect some combination of persuasion and disposition to be persuaded. Prior to legalization of abortion, attempts to persuade people to accept it did increase (while attempts to persuade people to the contrary lagged). One does not know whether this alone explains the pre-*Roe* increase in acceptance of abortion, or to what degree an increased disposition to be persuaded, perhaps resulting in part from contraception, contributed.

Somewhat more conclusive are studies of the effects of introduction of "family-planning services" to populations whose abortion rates can be predicted. One such study considered data from all 50 states plus the District of Columbia over the period 1976–1982. With controls for other variables, it was found that per 1000 teen-aged "family-planning service" clients, there were, consistently, 40 more pregnancies and 120 more abortions than would otherwise have been expected (Stan E. Weed and Joseph A. Olsen, "Policy and Program Considerations for Teenage Pregnancy Prevention: A Summary for Policymakers," *International Review* 13 [1989] pp.273–74).

5. See especially John Paul II, Encyclical Letter *Evangelium Vitae* (1995; hereafter cited parenthetically as EV), ch. 4, and the contrasting "culture of death" described in #10–24.

6. For an excellent introduction to this topic that is more extensive (monograph-length) than is necessary for, or possible within the scope of, this essay, see Andrew N. Woznicki, *A Christian Humanism: Karol Wojtyla's Existential Personalism* (New Britain, CT: Mariel Publications, 1980). For further discussion of John Paul's sources and method, see Kenneth L. Schmitz, *At the Center of the Human Drama: The Philosophical Anthropology of Karol Wojtyla/Pope John Paul II* (Washington, DC: Catholic University of America, 1993). Finally, see Rocco Buttiglione, *Karol Wojtyla: The Thought of the Man Who Became Pope John Paul II,* trans. Paolo Guietti and Francesca Murphy (Grand Rapids, MI: Eerdmans, 1997), esp. ch. 4 on *Love and Responsibility,* my most important source (see n. 33).

7. One of the most recent formulations of this argument is elaborated in Germain Grisez, Joseph Boyle, John Finnis, and William E. May, "'Every Marital Act Ought to Be Open to New Life': Toward a Clearer Understanding," *The Thomist* 52 (1988) pp.365–426.

8. Grisez *et al.*, "'Every Marital Act'," p.370.

9. Grisez *et al.*, "'Every Marital Act'," pp.372–74.

10. Grisez *et al.*, "'Every Marital Act'," p.374.

11. Grisez *et al.*, "'Every Marital Act'," p.378.

12. Grisez *et al.*, "'Every Marital Act'," p.380.

13. See Grisez, *Christian Moral Principles,* vol. 1 of *The Way of the Lord Jesus* (Chicago: Franciscan Herald Press, 1983), ch. 5 and pp.180–83.

14. Grisez repeats virtually the same argument with explicit reference to his "basic goods"/"modes of responsibility" theory (see n. 15) in *Living a Christian Life,* vol. 2 of *The Way of the Lord Jesus* (Quincy: Franciscan Herald Press, 1993) pp.506–15.

15. More specifically, reason imposes "modes of responsibility"—also *per se nota*—which distinguish between moral and immoral pursuit of goods. Among these are prohibitions of willing against any of the goods. See Grisez, *Christian Moral Principles,* ch. 8, esp. pp.215–22; also pp.189–92.

16. Grisez *et al.*, "'Every Marital Act'," p.385. The authors also say that contraception is unjustly contralife because in the event that it fails and a baby is conceived, this baby begins life objectively unwanted (pp.385–86). While more persuasive, this fails adequately to account for the difference between willing that something not come to be and willing not to accept something if it has come to be. Additionally and paradoxically, this argument would no longer apply if a method of contraception guaranteed 100% effective could be developed!

Martin Rhonheimer, in contrast to Grisez *et al.*, says that "to explain the connection between contraception and abortion, there is no need to interpret contraception as being essentially contralife or even in analogy with 'homicide.' ... The connection between contraception and abortion is sufficiently explained by the fact that abortion, insofar as it is promoted by spreading contraception, is characterized by a contraceptive mentality, that is, by a mentality which excludes the responsibility for the procreative consequences of one's sexual behavior. The *basic* problem is not that people do not want to have children; the basic and first problem is that they want to have sex without children" ("Contraception, Sexual Behavior, and Natural Law—Philosophical Foundation of the Norm of 'Humanae Vitae'," *Linacre Quarterly* 56, no. 2 [1989] p.56, n. 39). This explanation too is undermined by its exploitation of an ambiguity in the meaning of "want[ing] to have sex without children." There is a difference between wanting to have sex without conceiving children and wanting children conceived not to go on living. It is not clear why the former must objectively entail the latter. Now *insofar as* the two do sometimes in fact coincide in the form of a generalized wanting to have sex while avoiding childbearing at all other costs, even at the cost of childrens' lives, Rhonheimer is right, and his explanation corresponds to the "subjective" connection between abortion and contraception envisaged in *Evangelium Vitae* and discussed below. However, as I go on to explain, Pope John Paul has reason to think that there is also a deeper, "objective" connection.

17. While Grisez insists that the basic goods are constitutive of the person (*Christian Moral Principles*, p.121), they clearly function abstractly at least at the beginning of practical reasoning as he envisages them in his moral theory— only in an abstract sense of "life" can both the intentional taking of a life and the intentional prevention of a new life's genesis be called "contralife." In fact, notwithstanding Grisez's criticism of proportionalists' treatment of human goods as "premoral" (pp.144–45), there seems no way to avoid the conclusion that his basic goods are, by the very nature of his theory, premoral. Only goods considered from the beginning in relation to the person could be moral goods, goods whose pursuit is *ipso facto* moral.

Grisez's position concerning what count in practical reason as "goods" appears first in his idiosyncratic exegesis of St. Thomas Aquinas's discussion of the principles of the natural law ("The First Principle of Practical Reason: A Commentary on the *Summa Theologiae* 1-2, Question 94, Article 2," *Natural Law Forum* 10 [1965] pp.168–201), which attributes to Thomas a premoral conception of practical reason and human goods. According to Robert P. George's explanation and defense of Grisez's theory ("Recent Criticism of Natural Law Theory," *University of Chicago Law Review* 55 [1988] p.1382), Grisez "retain[s] Aquinas's fundamental theory of practical rationality as he understands it."

For more on the problems with the relationship between person and goods in Grisez, see Russell Hittinger, *A Critique of the New Natural Law Theory* (Notre Dame: University of Notre Dame Press, 1987) pp.66–74.

Martin Rhonheimer rightly denies not only that abstract consideration of goods can "lead to a morally qualifying judgment," but also that a "practical" or willed relation to a good can be non-moral ("'Intrinsically Evil Acts' and the Moral Viewpoint: Clarifying a Central Teaching of *Veritatis Splendor*," *The Thomist* 58 [1994] pp.6–11). Unfortunately, Rhonheimer's understanding of how goods are known [pp.13–16] is problematic in a way reminiscent of the way in which Grisez's is (giving rise to a confused description of the moral object in [just] capital punishment [p.19, n. 20; cf. my discussion in n. 20, below]).

It is precisely because his goods are not moral goods that Grisez must deny that practical reason is moral from the outset in its pursuit of his goods: "The principles of practical reasoning considered so far [*viz.*, that good is to be done and pursued and evil avoided, *and the basic goods' specifications of this first principle*] do not tell us what is morally good" (*Christian Moral Principles*, p.183). Further acts of reason beyond cognizance of the goods are necessary, for Grisez, to place them in relation to the moral good of the acting person.

It should be noted an account of the relationship between practical reason and morality very different from Grisez's is presented in the discussion of conscience in John Paul II, Encyclical Letter *Veritatis Splendor* (1993; hereafter, VS) #59: "The judgment of conscience... is a judgment which applies to a concrete situation the rational conviction that *one must love and do good and avoid evil. This first principle of practical reason is part of the natural law* [emphasis added]; indeed it constitutes the very foundation of the natural law, inasmuch as it expresses that primordial insight about good and evil... which... shines in the heart of every man. But whereas *the natural law discloses the objective and universal demands of the moral good* [emphasis added], conscience is the application of the law to a particular case.... Conscience thus formulates *moral obligation* in the light of the natural law: it is the obligation to do what the individual, through the workings of his conscience, *knows* to be a good he is called to do *here and now.*"

18. See also Hittinger (*A Critique*, pp.47-48), who argues that Grisez's conclusions presuppose that the goods have more moral content than Grisez wants them to (or, I would add, than they actually do when they are conceived so abstractly as in Grisez's theory).

Cf. the description of a certain morality of freedom in VS #48: "A freedom which claims to be absolute ends up treating the human body as a raw datum, devoid of any meaning and moral values until freedom has shaped it in accordance with its design. Consequently, human nature and the body appear as *presuppositions or preambles,* materially *necessary,* for freedom to make its choice, yet extrinsic to the person, the subject of the act. Their functions would not be able to constitute reference points for moral decisions, because the finalities of these inclinations would be merely *'physical'* goods, called by some 'pre-moral.' To refer to them, in order to find in them rational indications with regard to the order of morality, would be to expose oneself to the accusation of physicalism or biologism." Grisez's clear intention to the contrary notwithstanding, his theory seems to accept too much of the starting point of this logic to avoid its conclusion.

19. Cf. VS: "[T]he *primordial* moral requirement of loving and respecting the person... also *implies...* respect for certain fundamental goods" (#48, emphasis added); "To give an example, the origin and foundation of the duty of absolute respect for human life are to be found in the dignity proper to the person and not simply in the natural inclination to preserve one's own physical life. Human life, even though it is a fundamental good of man, thus acquires a moral significance in reference to the good of the person, who must always be affirmed for his own sake.... [N]atural inclinations take on moral relevance only insofar as they refer

to the human person and his authentic fulfillment" (#50).

This does not subvert the pope's critique of proportionalism's insistence that reference to subjective intention (beyond the intention or choice of the action itself) and/or circumstances is always necessary for (negative) moral evaluation of an object. The contrary is true; moral absolutes are grounded in (personal) being as good. This good (and not basic goods in the abstract) always forbids the choice of certain kinds of actions; thus, moral goodness is never compatible with the direct taking of an innocent human life, nor, as will become clear, with contraception. No further reference to intention or circumstances is necessary to evaluate murder or contraception (except as bearing on their gravity). But reference to "basic goods" alone could not ground such evaluations. (For further, helpful discussion of what is needed to describe a morally relevant object, see Mark Lowery, "A New Proposal for the Proportionalist/Traditionalist Discussion," *Irish Theological Quarterly* 61 [1995] pp.115–24. For the role of intention specifically, see Steven J. Jensen, "A Defense of Physicalism," *The Thomist* 61 [1997] pp.377–404; Rhonheimer, "'Intrinsically Evil Acts'," pp.11–13; and Martin Rhonheimer, "Intentional Actions and the Meaning of Object: A Reply to Richard McCormick," *The Thomist* 59 [1995] pp.279–311, with the caveat that Rhonheimer's application of his principles can be faulty, as in his untenable distinction, in the form of a putative exegesis of the *Catechism of the Catholic Church,* between masturbation and "the same behavior pattern... to get semen for fertility analysis" [p.296]—untenable since sexual pleasure is a necessary [and still impermissible] means to the end of ejaculation.)

20. Perhaps the clearest illustration of the distinction between morally licit and illicit actions against such "goods" is provided by the issue of just punishment. Why may political authorities treat someone convicted of a crime (assuming a just criminal code and fair trial) in ways in which one may not treat someone who has not? Either the requirements of the good of the person underlie "retributive justice," or all punishment is merely utilitarian. Grisez rightly accepts the former position (*Living a Christian Life,* p.891). If acting against any "basic good" is always contrary to the good of the person, however, then a just punishment could never act against such a good. But at least one kind of punishment—capital punishment—does act against such a good, and does so in a more obviously morally relevant way than does contraception, since capital punishment takes the life of an existing person. And capital punishment (while not as in accord with Christian morality, and so to be avoided when protection of society does not demand it as other means; see the end of n. 80, below) is just, since it may be used against those who have committed heinous crimes when nothing else would accomplish punishment's secondary end of protecting society (EV #56). (Grisez himself would rule out capital punishment in principle, though, strangely, seems to find it necessary to appeal to distinctively Christian principle [*Living a Christian Life,* pp.891–94]. Even given this appeal, incidentally, his argument is

problematic. An argument from Christian love could not preclude in principle an act of retributive justice for the reason John Paul suggests: protection of society, so long as it is not accomplished in a way that transgresses the bounds of retributive justice, is itself a matter of justice, a dimension of the common good, for which political authorities are responsible and which is indeed presupposed by Christian love.)

21. See also Hittinger, *A Critique,* pp.62–63.

22. Grisez *et al.,* "'Every Marital Act'," p.369.

23. Grisez *et al.,* "'Every Marital Act'," p.371.

24. Grisez *et al.,* "'Every Marital Act'," p.370.

25. Cf. Rhonheimer ("Contraception," p.30, emphasis deleted): "A contraceptive choice is the choice of an act that prevents... sexual intercourse... foreseen to have procreative consequences, from having these consequence, and which is a choice made just for this reason."

26. Cf. Grisez and his co-authors' reference to suicide as the kind of homicide most similar to contraception: "Although contraception intervenes before any new person emerges, still it is a choice to interfere with existing human life. For... those who chose to contracept attack their own lives as they tend to become one through their sexual act. By contracepting, they as it were commit limited suicide...." ("'Every Marital Act'," pp.388–89). In fact those using contraception do seem to attack themselves and each other, though they attack their "lives" only in a very broad sense. Yet the attack on their sexual natures bearing on intercourse is of possible moral relevance. Cf. also the example that Grisez *et al.* employ to illustrate the distinction between contraception and sexual acts: "A dictator who wanted to control population might contracept by having a fertility-reducing additive put in the public water supply. He would engage in no sexual behavior whatsoever, and might not will any such behavior. He might also exhort people to abstain, but reason that if they did not, the additive in the water would prevent the coming to be of some of the possible persons he did not want" (pp.369–70). This dictator would affect those people who engage in sexual behavior more immediately than the potential future generation. This should raise the most immediate moral questions. Finally, that contraception modifies the sexual act is implied by the authors' argument that rape victims "are morally justified in trying to prevent the ultimate completion— namely, conception itself—of the wrongful intimate bodily union" (p.390). If contraception prevents completion of bodily union when intercourse is a wrongful violation, this is because it does so to intercourse as such. In the case of non-violative intercourse, this again raises moral questions.

27. NFP is most broadly defined as the determination, through observation of such variables as cervical mucus or body temperature, of the times when a woman is fertile, and the use of these data to time intercourse to maximize *or* minimize fertility. In this essay "NFP" will have the narrower meaning of the use of the above methods to avoid pregnancy.

28. Grisez *et al.*, "'Every Marital Act'," p.368.

29. Grisez *et al.*, "'Every Marital Act'," p.402.

30. For more on the difficulties with Grisez's position, see Janet E. Smith, Humanae Vitae: *A Generation Later* (Washington, DC: Catholic University of America Press, 1991) pp.340–70.

31. It might be objected that my exegesis of the teaching that "only a true love is able to protect life" introduces unwarranted complexity. That is, John Paul might mean, simply (and, it would seem, tautologically), that a departure from "true love" or "chastity" will endanger life *qua* (immediately) unreceptive to new life, rather than, as I shall argue, *qua* promoting dispositions contrary to respect for life in an indirect manner. In reply, I would offer the observation, which the remainder of this essay will elaborate and, I hope, bear out, that between John Paul's description in *Evangelium Vitae* of the dispositions toward the unborn underlying abortion, and his pre-papal descriptions (as contrary to love) of the dispositions toward one's spouse underlying contraception, there is such striking similarity that I think the teaching in *Evangelium Vitae* about "true love" must be an allusion to the pre-papal work.

32. One could also examine in more detail the general meaning of chastity, and the particular threats to love posed by other forms of unchastity besides contracepted intercourse. These matters are beyond my scope. However it should be mentioned that other forms of unchastity (genital acts of themselves not oriented toward spousal love as I shall explain it, intercourse itself between persons not married to each other, and lack of respect for the indissolubility of marriage) will also undermine respect for life, even while many of them give rise to an increasing number of pregnancies in situations themselves representing temptations to have recourse to abortion.

33. Karol Wojtyla, *Love and Responsibility,* trans. H. T. Willetts (San Francisco: Ignatius Press, 1993); hereafter cited parenthetically as LR.

34. Grisez *et al.*, "'Every Marital Act'," esp. pp.394–99, 408, 414–15; cf. also Rhonheimer, "Contraception," pp.47–48.

35. Grisez *et al.*, "'Every Marital Act'," p.416.

36. On the latter see Grisez, "A New Formulation of a Natural-Law Argument against Contraception," *The Thomist* 30 (1966) p.343.

37. See Karol Wojtyla, "Subjectivity and the Irreducible in the Human Being," in *Person and Community: Selected Essays,* trans. Theresa Sandok, ed. Andrew N. Woznicki, Catholic Thought from Lublin, vol. 4 (New York: Peter Lang, 1993) pp.209–17. Cf. also the description of the rational soul as the "form" of the body, *e.g.,* Thomas Aquinas, *Summa Theologiae,* I, q. 76, aa. 1, 3, 4, 5; *Catechism of the Catholic Church* #365.

38. See Thomas Aquinas, *Summa Theologiae,* I, q. 5, aa. 1, 3.

39. See Wojtyla, "The Problem of the Theory of Morality" in *Person and Community,* pp.142–50, 154–157; also, esp. on the resulting self-determination of the acting person, Wojtyla, "Human Nature as the Basis of Ethical Formation" in *Person and Community,* pp.95–99; "The Personal Structure of Self-Determination," in *Person and Community,* pp.187–95. For further discussion see John F. Crosby, "The Personalism of John Paul II as the Basis of His Approach to the Teaching of *Humanae Vitae"* in *Why Humanae Vitae was Right: A Reader,* ed. Janet E. Smith (San Francisco: Ignatius, 1993) pp.208–10; and Smith, Humanae Vitae: *A Generation Later,* pp.232–37.

40. Cf. the discussion of wrongs specifically against persons in the Second Vatican Council's Pastoral Constitution *Gaudium et Spes* (1965) #27: "[W]hatever is opposed to life itself, such as any type of murder, genocide, abortion, euthanasia or willful self-destruction, whatever violates the integrity of the human person, such as mutilation, torments inflicted on body or mind, attempts to coerce the will itself; whatever insults human dignity, such as subhuman living conditions, arbitrary imprisonment, deportation, slavery, prostitution, the selling of women and children; as well as disgraceful working conditions, where men are treated as mere tools for profit, rather than as free and responsible persons; all these things and others of their like are infamies indeed. They poison human society, but *they do more harm to those who practice them than those who suffer from the injury"* (emphasis added; quoted also in EV #3).

41. Wojtyla, "The Problem of Catholic Sexual Ethics" in *Person and Community,* p.287; cf. p.280; cf. also Wojtyla, "The Human Person and Natural Law" in *Person and Community,* pp.181–85.

42. For further comments on the subject of the following paragraphs, see John Grondelski, "Nature and Natural Law in the Pre-Pontifical Thought of John Paul II," *Angelicum* 72 (1995) pp.519–39.

43. Cf. Thomas Aquinas, *Summa Theologiae,* I-II, q. 1, a. 1.

44. Cf. also VS #48; EV #19, 57, 76, 99.

45. Wojtyla, "The Problem of Catholic Sexual Ethics," p.284.

46. Wojtyla, "The Problem of Catholic Sexual Ethics," p.287.

47. Cf. Crosby, "The Personalism of John Paul II," pp.220–21. Crosby refers more specifically to the "love" that, I shall explain, is the substantive requirement of the personalistic norm.

48. Note also LR 57: "[T]he 'order of nature'... means the totality of the cosmic relationships that arise among really existing entities."

49. None of this implies that it is never appropriate to act toward another person in a manner contrary to his or her will. One should note the qualified formulation quoted above: "remember... that he or she too has, *or at least should have,* distinct personal ends" (LR 28, emphasis added). The qualification reflects recognition that "we must demand from a person... that his or her ends should be genuinely good, since the pursuit of evil ends is contrary to the rational nature of the person. This is also the purpose of education, both the education of children, and the mutual education of adults; it is just that—a matter of seeking true ends, *i.e.* real goods as the ends of our actions, and of finding and showing to others the ways to realize them. But in this educational activity, especially when we have to do with the upbringing of young children, we must never treat a person as the means to an end" (p.27). The latter is avoided precisely in an education that directs children to what is genuinely good for them, as opposed to merely what it would be useful to others for them to believe and do. (For an illuminating discussion, see C. S. Lewis, *The Abolition of Man; or, Reflections on Education with Special Reference to the Teaching of English in the Upper Forms of Schools,* U. of Durham Riddell Memorial Lectures, 15th series [New York: MacMillan, 1947], esp. pp.13–16.) The degree to which one is morally required to respect the willingness, or lack thereof, of the one being educated will depend on that person's maturity. Additionally, insofar as the actions of even an adult bear upon the requirements for the common good in society as these are codified in law by the competent authorities, the representatives of the political community may justly punish people for choosing to violate these laws, unwilling as they may be to accept punishment. We may say that someone who consents to an action thereby also consents to the requirements of retributive justice. Fully to explain this, however, would require more detailed moral analysis of authority and consent, a much-needed project but beyond the scope of this essay.

50. See also John S. Grabowski, "Person: Substance and Relation," *Communio: International Catholic Review* 22 (1995) pp.154–56.

51. In view of the interpersonal communion to which it gives rise, the person's relational being is called *communio*. See Wojtyla, "The Family as a Community of Persons" in *Person and Community,* pp.320–23.

52. See also, for this in relation to personal self-determination (cf. the works referred to in n. 39), Wojtyla, "The Person: Subject and Community" in *Person and Community,* pp.219–261. For further discussion see Crosby, "The Personalism of John Paul II," *passim.*

53. See VS #73, 78; cf. n. 19.

54. See Aristotle, *Categories,* 8b26–35; *Nicomachean Ethics,* 1105b19–7a8; Thomas Aquinas, *Summa Theologiae,* I-II, qq. 49–55; and q. 71, aa. 1–3; cf. Wojtyla, "Human Nature as the Basis of Ethical Formation," pp.98–99.

55. This is because such dispositions are grounded in the (moral) self-determination of the acting person (see again the references in n. 39).

56. John Paul II, Encyclical Letter *Centesimus Annus* (1991) #13; Letter to Families *Gratissimam sane* (1994) #17.

57. Cf. VS #98–101.

58. Cf. *Catechism of the Catholic Church* #1869.

59. For the importance of "justification" of the concrete act, see esp. LR 225.

60. Thus, while it is true that every human act, *qua* intentional, is in one sense not "natural," one can still speak of intentions and intentional acts as being more or less harmonious with nature.

Rhonheimer shares Grisez's reluctance to speak of nature and his dichotomy between nature and intention ("Contraception," pp.25–26), yet he appeals to "procreative meaning" or "dimension" (pp.33–36), and refers to intercourse (even naturally infertile intercourse) as "an act... which by its very nature serves procreation" (p.36).

61. This situation differs from that of, for example, eating and nutrition. It has been objected that the claim that it is morally illegitimate to frustrate the natural end of intercourse by contraception would imply that it is morally illegitimate to frustrate the natural end of eating by chewing gum, since chewing seems naturally to belong to the process of eating as the beginning of digestion to the end of nutrition and eventual health and growth (cf. Rhonheimer, "Contraception," p.26, and Grisez, *Christian Moral Principles,* p.105). What precludes this analogy and the *reductio ad absurdum* is that in general, no one act of eating puts the health and existence of a human person at stake (and if a

situation arose in which this were the case, it would indeed be morally wrong to choose to chew gum instead of eating!).

62. One should note the difference between this appeal to the good of existence and Grisez's appeal to the "good" of life (see n. 17). Here, existence, even insofar as it is trans-personal, is nonetheless clearly treated not abstractly but insofar as it is a good in which the existing person participates, and so is a moral good. And precisely because of the difference between the manner in which the person participates in it in sexuality and the manner in which another person participates in it by living, no analogy is drawn between contraception and homicide.

63. Also Wojtyla, "The Problem of Catholic Sexual Ethics," pp.289–90.

64. It is chastity that disposes us to an integral view of the human person *qua* sexual; see LR 143–73. By virtue of its "transparency" to the person, chastity "is above all the 'yes' of which certain 'no's' are the consequence" (p.170). As will be seen, contraception is one of these "no's."

65. Wojtyla, "The Problem of Catholic Sexual Ethics," p.288, emphasis added.

66. Wojtyla, "The Problem of Catholic Sexual Ethics," p.289.

67. Wojtyla, "The Problem of Catholic Sexual Ethics," p.295.

68. This is the philosophical basis for the "nuptial meaning of the body," which has become very important for John Paul. The scope of this essay precludes full explanation. Briefly, the "nuptial meaning of the body" refers to the "potential of the masculinity and the femininity of the human body to serve the supreme self-donation of persons" (Crosby, "The Personalism of John Paul II," p.221). This is a strikingly anti-dualist anthropology (cf. LR 107). See Smith (Humanae Vitae: *A Generation Later*, pp.243–55) for explanation of the theological dimension of this anthropology; this is elaborated in John Paul's 1979–84 Wednesday addresses, which have been published as the following four volumes by the Daughters of St. Paul (Boston): *Original Unity of Man and Woman: Catechesis on the Book of Genesis* (1981), *Blessed are the Pure of Heart: Catechesis on the Sermon on the Mount and Writings of St. Paul* (1983), *Reflections on Humanae Vitae* (1984), and *The Theology of Marriage and Celibacy* (1986).

69. In cases in which a man or woman suffers from a condition that prevents fertility by preventing full function of the reproductive system, we all recognize that the infertility leaves the system's purpose unrealizable, not irrelevant. In cases in which a woman's age or the time of her cycle do not allow for fertility, we recognize that this natural infertility results from mechanisms that facilitate the functioning of the system as a whole, ordered as it is to fertility. Most relevant

for a discussion of NFP, the infertile times during the cycle make possible the fertile times because they are necessary for preparation for ovulation and for the implantation of a fertilized egg (the cycle itself is necessary because an unfertilized egg cannot survive indefinitely after ovulation). Infertility after menopause happens to correspond, first, to the aging of the oocytes in a woman's ovaries. Before a woman's own birth, the DNA in these cells has undergone its final replication and the cells have undergone the first of their two meiotic divisions (in which a "polar body," containing little except one of each pair of replicated chromosomes, is ejected). Only the final cellular fission (ejection of a second polar body containing little except a copy of each replicated chromosome) remains to be completed prior to ovulation. With the aging of a woman and therefore of these cells and the DNA within them, there is some increase in the frequency of abnormalities in that DNA. But more importantly, infertility after menopause corresponds to the appropriateness that a woman giving birth be sufficiently young that she will be able to be an active mother for years to come, given a normal life-span — this maternal role in children's formation, as well as the corresponding paternal role, being part of procreation (LR 260; cf. also John Paul II, Apostolic Exhortation *Familiaris Consortio* [1981] #36).

70. Since sexual expressions of love are distinctive to marriage, the requirements for loving sexuality give rise to the Church's understanding of the ends of marriage. This has been the subject of much confusion in recent decades. Historically the primary end of marriage has been understood to be procreation; mutual assistance (*mutuum adiutorium*) has been considered a secondary end, and relief of concupiscence (*remedium concupiscentiae*), a tertiary end (cf. LR 66). Prior to the Second Vatican Council, personalist considerations about the importance of love had led to the calling into question of the primacy of procreation. Then, the Council's Pastoral Constitution on the Church in the Modern World *Gaudium et Spes* seemed not to repeat the teaching concerning the hierarchy of ends: "Marriage and conjugal love are by their nature ordained toward the begetting and educating of children.... Hence, *while not making the other purposes of matrimony of less account,* the true practice of conjugal love... ha[s] this aim: that the couple be ready with stout hearts to cooperate with the love of the Creator and Savior, Who through them will enlarge and enrich His own family..." (#50, emphasis added). Likewise, *Humanae Vitae* speaks of "the inseparable connection... between the two meanings of the conjugal act: the unitive meaning and the procreative meaning (*ratio*)" (#12). Closely linked with questioning of the hierarchy was a confusion of the personalist good of love with the secondary end in the traditional hierarchy, mutual assistance.

John Paul responded to this confusion, denying that the teaching concerning the hierarchy of ends could be revoked, both before (LR [originally published in 1960], pp.66–69; cf. pp.217–18) and after (Wojtyla, "The Problem of Catholic

Sexual Ethics" [originally published in 1965], p.291) the Council (in which he took an active part, including in the composition of *Gaudium et Spes*). In brief, love in the personalist sense is emphatically not to be identified with mutual assistance, and furthermore it is rather a formal principle than an end. For this reason it can be said to be of neither more nor less importance than procreation; comparing the importance of principles of different kinds seems dubiously meaningful. But in pointing to the way in which all the ends should be realized, love requires the preservation of the objective hierarchy of those ends. In particular, mutual assistance serves loving procreation (understood as entailing cooperation in family life), which gives procreation a certain priority over mutual assistance.

71. Such circumstances include most prominently those in which the effects of a larger family would harm all the children—any already existing as well as those whose conception is at issue. Additionally, when it is foreseen that pregnancy would put a mother's health in grave jeopardy, this not only involves the risk of serious harm to her children, but also threatens the good of fertility for her, so for this reason too she could legitimately seek to avoid use of the reproductive faculty. The most obvious such cases are those in which a woman's reproductive system itself can be adjudged to be probably incapable of supporting pregnancy to the point of viability, whether or not the mother's health would be gravely endangered in other ways by a pregnancy. In such cases, it seems to me, it would be entirely licit to perform a hysterectomy. The express purpose of the operation would be to remove an organ that is irreversibly diseased and indeed dangerous in its inability to function normally. The "contraceptive" effect of the operation would be tolerated as inseparable from the removal of the organ, not intended as either a means or an end. When a condition not related to the reproductive system itself (*e.g.*, a heart condition) would make pregnancy dangerous for the mother, NFP would seem the proper recourse.

72. In fact when this intention leads to practices such as NFP, practices involving temporarily abstaining from intercourse, the intention is being used in accordance with continence. Insofar as continence is willing to forego intercourse for the good and specifically for the good of the person, it is a virtue and it promotes love (LR 241). This is because continence is part of chastity (LR 173); it is a response to "the superiority of the value of the person to that of sex" (LR 197).

Studies of NFP users indicate that the moral health brought by NFP to relationships bears psychological and spiritual fruit. See J. Marshall and B. Rowe, "Psychologic Aspects of the Basal Body Temperature Method of Regulating Births," *Fertility and Sterility* 21 (1970) pp.14–19; Joseph Tortorici, "Conception Regulation, Self-Esteem, and Marital Satisfaction among Catholic Couples: Michigan State University Study," *International Review of Natural Family Planning* 3 (1979) pp.191–205; Thomasina Borkman and Mary

Shivanandan, "The Impact of Natural Family Planning on Selected Aspects of the Couple Relationship," *International Review of Natural Family Planning* 8 (1984) pp.58–66; Richard J. Fehring, Donna M. Lawrence, and Catherine Sauvage, "Self-Esteem, Spiritual Well-Being, and Intimacy: A Comparison Among Couples Using NFP and Oral Contraceptives," *International Review of Natural Family Planning* 13 (1989) pp.227–36; Richard J. Fehring and Donna M. Lawrence, "Spiritual Well-Being, Self-Esteem and Intimacy Among Couples Using Natural Family Planning," *Linacre Quarterly* 61/3 (1994) pp.18–29. Results of these and related studies are reviewed and further discussed in Richard J. Fehring, "Reflections on the Spirituality of Natural Family Planning," *Chicago Studies* 33 (1994) pp.179–87; and Richard J. Fehring, "Toward a Model of Fertility Integration," in *Life and Learning IV: Proceedings of the Fourth University Faculty for Life Conference,* ed. Joseph W. Koterski (Washington, DC: University Faculty for Life, 1995) pp.216–29.

Additionally, there is some evidence that NFP-using couples become more receptive to pregnancy over time: see Richard J. Fehring, "Contraception and Abortion: Fruits of the Same Tree," in *Life and Learning VI: Proceedings of the Sixth University Faculty for Life Conference,* ed. Joseph W. Koterski (Washington, DC: University Faculty for Life, 1997) pp.155–57, 160. This, too, would be a result of the dispositions characteristic of (embodied and promoted by) NFP use, dispositions which deepen spousal love, since openness to fertility as appropriate is (partially) constitutive of spousal love.

(I thank Richard Fehring for providing me with these studies.)

73. Rhonheimer's argument ("Contraception") concerning the morally relevant difference between NFP and contraception bears some similarities to John Paul's on this point. Briefly, Rhonheimer contends that self-giving *human* love must have as its subject the body-soul unity; for actions to express such unity they must be chaste, with bodily goods (procreation) integrated; contraception is opposed to such integration (while periodic continence is compatible with it). However, this integration is evidently regarded by Rhonheimer as existing solely or at least primarily on the level of disposition (see esp. pp.40–44); concrete actions are prescribed or proscribed solely or primarily insofar as they contribute to good or bad dispositions. This stands in contrast to the view I am elaborating that intentional actions as such already embody dispositions; that is, they may, *qua* actions, be evaluated as compatible or incompatible with love (so that the evaluation of actions is prior to, or at least coeval with, the evaluation of dispositions). Additionally, Rhonheimer leaves unclear how self-giving is morally required by the personhood of the other.

74. Pope John Paul has expressed these considerations in terms of the meaning and language of the body, introduced in n. 68: "[T]he innate language that expresses the total reciprocal self-giving of husband and wife is overlaid, through

contraception, by an objectively contradictory language, namely, that of not giving oneself totally to the other. This leads not only to a positive refusal to be open to life but also a falsification of the inner truth of conjugal love, which is called upon to give itself in personal totality" (*Familiaris Consortio* #32). See Smith, Humanae Vitae: *A Generation Later*, pp.110–18; and Cormac Burke, "Marriage and Contraception" in *Why Humanae Vitae was Right*, pp.160–64.

75. As an example specifically different from sexual matters (or life issues, to be treated in the section below), economic behavior very easily becomes use of others for profit. This is all the more likely to be the case when "capitalism" or the "free market" is conceived as a "value-neutral" mechanism for maximizing economic growth by harnessing avarice. It may often be true that rational behavior in such a market economy will require treating consumers and workers well (see, e.g., Michael Novak, *Free Persons and the Common Good* [Lanham: Madison Books, 1989] pp.55–69). But this will not always be the case. More importantly, the very priority given to profit already embodies use of persons (see David L. Schindler, *Heart of the World, Center of the Church:* Communio *Ecclesiology, Liberalism, and Liberation* [Grand Rapids: Eerdmans; Edinburgh: T&T Clark, 1996], ch. 2–3). Calculated beneficence does not cease to be use in economic matters any more than in sexual matters; if either possessions or pleasure is understood as the supreme purpose of an action, the action will *ipso facto* be use. Of course, the economic principles rejected by Catholic social teaching were proposed long before modern contraception became generally acceptable and widespread, so if one helped to pave the way for the other it was probably economic use that fostered dispositions expressed today as sexual use.

76. This is all the more so since marriage is such an important experience for most people—most people marry (and children all experience the importance of marital love, either by its presence or its absence from the environment in which they are formed), and much of one's life is spent interacting with one's spouse or parent(s). See Wojtyla, "Parenthood as a Community of Persons" in *Person and Community*, pp.338–42; cf. *Familiaris Consortio* #42–43; *Gratissimam sane* #13, 17; see for discussion Mary F. Rousseau, "Fairest Love: Pope John Paul II on the Family," *Anthropotes* 11 (1995) pp.160–65.

77. Contraception itself becomes a form of use on the part of political authorities when it is offered (frequently with some degree of compulsion) to women on welfare and to poor or developing countries, as an alternative to genuine social and economic assistance (besides as an alternative to promotion of chastity).

78. Cf. Wojtyla, "The Problem of the Constitution of Culture Through Human Praxis" in *Person and Community*, pp.263–75.

79. In brief, Jesus Christ reveals human life as a call to receive a share in God's love, a share in the Trinitarian communion (EV #1–2, 29–30, 37–38). The commandment to love and protect human persons and human life, even by self-giving to the point of death, is part of this share (#25, 41, 49, 51, 76). Thus, the anthropological teaching concerning the person's capacity for love, and the ethical requirement that the person therefore be loved, are seen to have a theological and specifically Trinitarian/Christological dimension.

80. The theological dimension of anthropology and ethics reflects not a superadded perfection, not even a necessary yet extrinsic support, but their intrinsic integrating principle, typical neo-Scholastic (but not authentically Thomistic) dualistic theories of nature and grace to the contrary notwithstanding. See esp. Henri de Lubac, *The Mystery of the Supernatural,* trans. Rosemary Sheed (New York: Herder and Herder, 1967); John Paul II, Encyclical Letter *Redemptor Hominis* (1979), esp. #10; and for discussion and elaboration, David L. Schindler, "Christology and the *Imago Dei:* Interpreting *Gaudium et Spes,"* *Communio: International Catholic Review* 23 (1996) pp.156–184; "Christological aesthetics and *Evangelium Vitae:* Toward a definition of liberalism," *Communio: International Catholic Review* 22 (1995) pp.193–224; *Heart of the World,* Introduction; pp. 77–79; ch. 10; and *passim;* "Reorienting the Church on the Eve of the Millenium: John Paul II's 'New Evangelization,'" *Communio: International Catholic Review* 24 (1997) pp.728–773; and Lawrence J. Welch, *"Gaudium et spes,* the Divine Image, and the Synthesis of *Veritatis splendor,"* *Communio: International Catholic Review* 24 (1997) pp.794–814.

The relationship between nature and grace is in fact analogous to the relationship between the distinctively personal dimension of human nature and its other dimensions that was posited in Part II of this essay. Grace and the love in which it gives us a share "bind natural human goods together and make them perfect," just as personhood *qua* natural binds together and transforms from within other natural goods. To fail to respect the human person—to fail to live out the share grace gives us through Christ in the Trinitarian communion—is to fail to live in accordance with this finality in ourselves, essential as this finality is, and so it is profoundly disintegrating, just as to fail to respect the person *qua* person is to fail in our own personhood and is disintegrating. And not only is respect for the person's supernatural finality necessary, and not only does it provide a new reason for respect for the person and for all dimensions of human nature, but it also compels us to respect all dimensions of personhood precisely *qua* integrated and transformed by this finality, just as we must respect all of human nature *qua* personal.

Respect for the person that is "informed" by grace will not always "look" different in practice from respect for the person that considers only nature. Because nature remains real in the theological anthropology I am discussing, we can still know apart from theology that contraception and abortion are wrong and even, in some measure, why they are wrong (as I hope to have shown in the case of contraception!; concerning abortion, cf. EV #29: The Gospel of life *"can... be known in its essential traits by human reason,"* and #101), and pre-theological considerations are indeed essential to understanding their wrongness and are presupposed by the theological argument. In some cases, however, there will be a "practical" difference (as, for example, in the case of capital punishment, as I understand John Paul's teaching on the subject [EV #9, 27, 40, 56]).

81. See Wojtya, "Parenthood," pp.332–34.

82. The results of the study cited in the last paragraph of n. 4 are consistent with this hypothesis.

83. See also my earlier essay, "The Politics of a Culture of Life" in *Life and Learning VI,* pp.245–66.

84. It might be asked why *this* particular form of use should be of especial concern to the pro-life movement. In fact, other forms (economic, for example) should also be of concern. However, many other issues are already linked in people's minds with the abortion issue (cf. the "consistent ethic of life" or "seamless garment"). (Futhermore, disputes about these issues are often purely prudential; *e.g.,* they concern how to form an economy that will serve persons.) Contraception, far from being generally so linked, is, as I have indicated (see n. 2), in fact seen by many people as a solution to the problem of a high abortion rate, as well as to that of a high rate of pregnancies in (subjectively or objectively) undesirable circumstances. But additionally, contraception is especially important because of its impact on marital/familial love, perhaps the most significant love in our lives (see n. 76). Finally, although this essay has considered contraception objectively, it is relevant for the importance of the issue that the objective connection between contraception and abortion can cause a subjective connection between these two to arise more easily than one could arise between most other forms of use and abortion, since abortion can come to be seen specifically as a "backup" or even primary "contraceptive."

85. There is an unfortunate tendency within some segments of the pro-life movement to oppose any form (even tactical, let alone strategic) of political compromise. See, e.g., Mary H. Sadik, "Legislating Pro-Life Principle: Victory Without Compromise," *Linacre Quarterly* 59, no. 2 (1992) pp.27–36. It must be remembered that while abortion is not a *merely* political issue, it is a political issue *insofar as* its resolution must have a political dimension; and in pursuing that dimension one cannot prescind from the limits of politics. Thus, when the only choices in practice would allow one to protect either more or fewer, but not all, lives, one should do what will protect more. "This does not in fact represent an illicit cooperation with an unjust law, but rather a legitimate and proper

attempt to limit its evil aspects" (EV #73; cf. also #90 which speaks of "political leaders... taking into account what is realistically attainable"). Someone, that is, whose goal is to prohibit one subset of abortions—a just goal—may tolerate that the civil law will not prohibit all others. And neither magisterial teaching nor reason require a narrow understanding of this principle. Its prudent application will be informed by a mature understanding of the political process. For an excellent discussion, see Christopher Wolfe, "Abortion and Political Compromise," *First Things* no. 24 (1992) pp.22–29. (Furthermore, the problems faced by voters in deciding between candidates, when some or all candidates are not fully pro-life, and/or when some are pro-life but unlikely to be electable or to be effective if elected, are analogous to the problems faced by legislators who cannot accomplish total protection of innocent human life. While the pope only addresses the legislator, he does not deny that what he says should apply to the analogous case of the voter, and it is reasonable to extend such an application, especially since voting in a democracy really is a sharing in the legislative role.)

86. Contraception's relationship to marital intimacy does not necessarily render laws against contraceptive use wrong in principle, *pace* Justice Douglas (*Griswold v. Conn.*, 381 U.S. 479, 482, 484–86 [1965])—though one suspects he was being cynical—and popular perception. First, as has been noted, contraception is an action separate from intercourse, even though its primary effect is on intercourse. Second, laws could be formulated specifically to proscribe the sale (and perhaps the manufacture) of contraceptive devices and drugs (indeed, *Griswold* arose only when a seller of contraceptives was charged as an accessory to violation of the Connecticut statute). (Compare laws against [dangerous] drugs used to heighten sexual drive and pleasure.)

87. This is true especially because the of the intrinsic role within anthropology and ethics of their theological (Trinitarian/Christological, as indicated in n. 79, and, I now add, ecclesiological) dimension (see n. 80). Again, the personal capability to recognize and live in accordance with truth and goodness finds its integrity only within the person's supernatural finality, not in a still-independent end supported by grace merely extrinsically. In view of this we may conclude that, even when received in cooperation with grace, purely philosophical persuasion will not finally avail. It is necessary that the person come to live in accordance with the fullness of the Gospel.

88. For the importance of the Holy Spirit, see again nn. 79 and 80. To the discussions therein I add that it is the Spirit who conforms our hearts and persons to Christ's and so gives us our share in the Trinitarian communion. In sum, we come to receive and return the love of the Father, through the Son, in the Spirit.

MOURNFUL NUMBERS: QUANTITATIVE TOOLS FOR COMBATING THE OVERPOPULATION MYTH

J. T. Maloy

Tell me not, in mournful numbers,
Life is but an empty dream! —
For the soul is dead that slumbers,
And things are not what they may seem.

Henry Wadsworth Longfellow
A Psalm of Life

NURSERY RHYMES NOTWITHSTANDING, these are the only lines of verse I can recall my father reciting to me more than fifty years ago. Little did I realize then how pertinent they would be today, living here in the Culture of Death. Each day we are confronted by mournful numbers telling us that Life is but an empty dream. (After all, those who find it advantageous to promote this Culture have the wherewithal to provide the statistics that seem to support their position.) So many of us have succumbed to these mournful numbers that we, perhaps unwittingly, continue to propagate the agenda of those who wish to enjoy the benefits of the Culture here and now. It is my intent in this essay to provide some sound demographic data to dispel some foolish notions regarding overpopulation that have crept into the national dialogue as a result of these ubiquitous statistics. Truly, these things are not what they may seem.

As a chemistry professor I seldom employ these mournful statistics in my research or in my teaching of graduate or upper division courses. Instead, I encounter them when I am called upon to teach lower division chemistry courses to non-majors. These science appreciation courses for non-scientists appear as a part of the required curriculum at our institution and, I suspect, at most colleges and universities in the nation. They provide fertile ground for the promotion of these ideas to an unsuspecting audience.

The last time I taught this course I used the well-established text *Chemistry for Changing Times* by John W. Hill and Doris K. Kolb.[1] Its content is similar to that of other texts that are available for this course, but I prefer it because of its depth of coverage. Like all of the others that I have examined, *Chemistry for Changing Times* has the Culture's agenda concerning overpopulation. The tip-off appears in the first five pages of text as the cast of characters is introduced, in order of appearance: Aristotle, Francis Bacon, Rachel Carson, Thomas Malthus, and Robert Boyle. Thus students read Carson's *Silent Spring* and Malthus's "Essay upon the Principles of Population" before they learn of *The Sceptical Chymist,* Boyle's chemistry text published nearly two centuries before Malthus's essay.[2]

Some three hundred pages later when the question "How Crowded is Our Spaceship?" is posed,[3] the following response is given:

Every day people die and other people are born, but the number born is about 250,000 more than the number that die. Every four days our world population goes up by a million people. In 1992 world population was 5.4 billion. It should reach 6.4 billion by the year 2000. A billion more people in just 8 years!
... At the present rate of growth, world population should be 10 billion by 2025, and one century from now it could reach 40 billion!

A plot showing the world population as a function of time is then displayed; Figure 1 is adapted from this graph. To their credit, the authors do point out that advances in the chemical sciences (pharmaceuticals, petrochemicals, agriculture and medicine) are responsible for the increase in population growth observed during the nineteenth and twentieth centuries. They conclude, however, with this admonition:

... One thing is sure. That curve cannot keep rising indefinitely. It must bend sooner or later. If we don't make that happen by curbing our uncontrolled birth rate, then nature will take care of the problem by increasing our death rate. Let's hope it doesn't come to that. Nature's methods are not always kind.

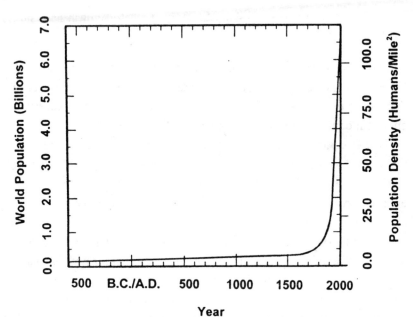

Year

Figure 1. World Population Data as a Function of Time. Total population (left ordinate) is adapted from *Chemistry for Changing Times*.[3] Population density data (right ordinate) was computed using data taken from the *1997 Almanac*.[5]

Malthus is revisited in a subsequent chapter on agricultural chemistry. The following text[4] (apearing in a section entitled "Some Malthusian Mathematics") is accompanied by a graph that shows geometric growth as looking remarkably like Figure 1 over the last two centuries:

In 1830, Thomas Malthus, an English clergyman and political economist, made the statement that population increases faster than the food supply. Unless the birthrate was controlled, he said, poverty and war would have to serve as restrictions on the increase.

Malthus's predictions were based on simple mathematics. Population, he said, grows geometrically, while the food supply increases arithmetically....

Growth Period	0	1	2	3	4	5	6	7
Arithmetic	1	2	3	4	5	6	7	8
Geometric	1	2	4	8	16	32	64	128

...Note that arithmetic growth is slow and steady; geometric growth starts slowly and then shoots up like a rocket.

Clearly, readers come away from this exercise with the understanding that the Malthusian skyrocket has already taken off. It is little wonder that they are so ready to accept the inevitability of chemical abortifacients and chemical contraceptives that is presented later in the text.

It is at this point that I remind my students that some of the skepticism that Robert Boyle directed towards the alchemists of his time might well be directed towards those of ours. How much do you have to go over in order to have overpopulation? Six billion human beings seems like a lot, but six billion atoms are barely ten femtomoles, and with ordinary instrumentation, it's quite difficult even to detect ten femtomoles of atoms. Are ten femtomoles of humans enough to overcrowd our planet? That all depends upon how large this spaceship is.

Here is the relevant spaceship data taken from the *1997 Information Please Almanac.*[5] (It won't change much no matter when you read this.) The land area of the surface of the earth is 57.50×10^6 mile^2. The water area is 139.43×10^6 miles^2, almost three times as much. The sum of these two areas gives the total surface area of 196.93×10^6 mile^2. The *1997 Almanac* also gives the world population as 5.790×10^9 humans. (This will change from year to year.) From this and the total land area one can compute the 1997 world population density as (5.790×10^9 humans) / (57.50×10^6 mile^2) = 100.7 humans/mile^2. Thus, while there are nearly six billion of us living on this planet, only one hundred of us, on the average, occupy each square mile of land.

Consider what this means. Figure 2 shows a cartoon depicting 100 human beings occupying one square mile of land area. Since 1 mile = 1,760 yd, each cartoon character is 176 yd from the nearest neighbor (who may be a relative). Each occupies a lot that is 176 yd x 176 yd;

that's 30,976 yard^2/person. Since there are 4,840 yd^2 in 1.0 acre, a population density of 100 humans/mile^2 implies that there are 6.4 acre of land for every man, woman, and child living on this planet.

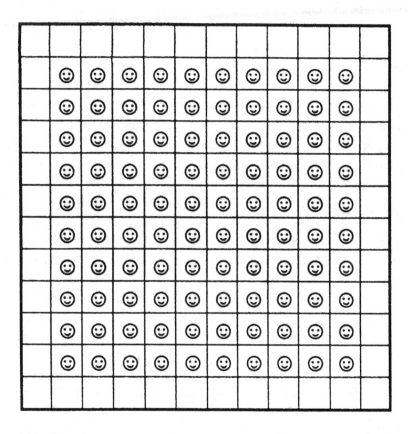

Figure 2. Cartoon Representation of a Population Density of 100 humans/mile^2. Each character occupies a plot that is 176 yd x 176 yd or 6.4 acre/person; *ca.* two such characters would inhabit the land area that is occupied by Giants Stadium in Rutherford, New Jersey.

It is possibly more relevant to view this from a football perspective. The playing surface of a football field is 120 yd x 160 ft; that's 6,400 yd². A scale drawing[6] of the field and the seating area of Giants Stadium in Rutherford, New Jersey appears in Figure 3. The footprint of the entire stadium (excluding external entrance ramps) occupies less than nine football fields; that is, the footprint of Giant Stadium occupies less than 57,600 yd². At the current global population density of 100 humans per mile², only two people could inhabit Giant Stadium if they were allotted this piece of real estate as their fair share of our planet.

What happens in this model when the population increases? Obviously, the area available to each person decreases. Note, however, that there is *not* a simple inverse relationship between population and the interpersonal distance. Should the population increase by a factor of four, the cartoon characters occupying the 1 mile² area in Figure 2 would have to be arranged in a 20 x 20 array. At this point, the interpersonal distance would be 88 yards, exactly half of the interpersonal distance illustrated in Figure 2. Thus, multiplying the population by four causes the interpersonal distance within the population to be divided by two. Here, the Malthusian concept of geometric growth works to the advantage of the denser population.

All of the above examples employ a two dimensional area in the computation of the population density. As implied by the Giant Stadium example, however, it is possible to build three dimensional structures that allow for much higher occupancies. Should the world population increase by a factor of ten over the next 100 years, this three dimensional structure the size of Giant Stadium would then be occupied by less than twenty inhabitants.

These two examples have been presented merely to illustrate the concept of population density and to point out the vast land area of our planet. Of course, they do not account for local terrain, climate, or infrastructure. For a more realistic assessment of the concept, though, consider the actual population densities of some of the representative states and nations of the world shown in Table I. This Table gives the actual population density as reported in the *1997 Almanac* for each of these states and shows the nearest neighbor distance and Giant Stadium occupancy as computed using the two methods discussed previously.

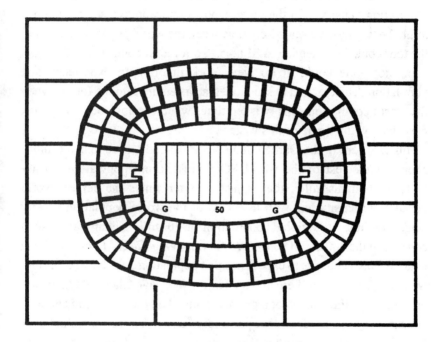

Figure 3. A Scale Drawing of the Footprint of Giants Stadium. The playing area of a regulation football field is 6,400 yd². The footprint of the entire stadium (excluding egress ramps) occupies less than nine field areas. At the current world population density, two persons would occupy Giants Stadium.

While the trends in Table I are somewhat informative, these data are most useful because they provide a convenient listing of locations where one can experience what it is like to live at a given population density. For example, the tour through time that is illustrated in Figure 1 might be taken today by beginning in Alaska, and proceeding through Wyoming, Nevada, Nebraska, Arizona, Maine, Iowa, Texas, and West Virginia until reaching Louisiana, the state whose 1990 population density (as reported in the *1997 Almanac)* is approximately equal to the current world population density. On the other hand, if one wants to see how things might be twenty-five years from now when the world population doubles, the tour could be extended to Illinois. To forecast conditions fifty years from now one could go to New York in order to experience that population density. And to see more than a century into the future, when the world population density is ten times what it is now, one could visit New Jersey, the home of this writer.

You see, here in the Garden State we are already more than a century ahead of the rest of the world. Our most recent population density is 1,035 humans/mile^2; that is just over ten times the current world population density and well in excess of the world population density corresponding to a global population of 40 billion that was of such concern to the authors of *Chemistry for Changing Times.* (You only have to go to Massachusetts to experience that population density.) To be sure, we have our problems here in New Jersey. We have Giants Stadium, and on some days there are a lot more occupants than the 20 person average. We have two toll roads and we pay a lot of taxes. We're not rioting over food, but it must be admitted that there are more fools per inch^2 in New Jersey than there are in any other state. Other than that, we're getting along just fine, thank you. If you want to see for yourself, come on by; there's plenty of room for visitors.

Table I. Population Density Data for Some Representative States of the World[7]

Country or State	Population Density (humans per mile^2)	Nearest Neighbor Distance (yards)	Number of Occupants of Giants Stadium (humans)
Vatican City	4883	25	90.80
New Jersey	1035	55	19.25
Rhode Island	951	57	17.68
Japan	861	60	16.01
India	774	63	14.39
Massachusetts	769	63	14.30
New York	380	90	7.06
China	328	97	6.10
Illinois	205	123	3.81
Georgia	110	168	2.04
World	101	175	1.90
Example	*100*	*176*	1.86
Louisiana	95	181	1.77
United States	75	203	1.39
West Virginia	74	205	1.38
Texas	65	218	1.21
Iowa	50	249	0.93
Maine	40	278	0.74
Arizona	32	310	0.60
Nebraska	21	388	0.38
Nevada	11	531	0.20
Australia	6	718	0.11
Wyoming	5	787	0.09
Alaska	1	1760	0.02

The data in Table I also allows one to compare the population density of some of the nations of the world with those of more familiar states in the United States. Thus, the population density of China is slightly less than that of New York. The population density of India is not unlike that of Massachusetts, while the population density of Rhode Island exceeds that of Japan. All of the countries reported in Table I except Vatican City have a lower population density than New Jersey, our most densely populated state. We do not impose population control measures on the citizens of our country. How, then, could someone try to justify population control measures on the citizens of other nations on the basis that they are overpopulated?

In this regard, it is useful to identify those countries that exhibit a greater population density than the state of New Jersey. Only 18 of the 224 countries appearing in the *1997 Almanac* have a population density higher than that of New Jersey. These are listed in Table II along with their population densities and their actual populations. There is a grand total of 203×10^6 humans living in these 18 countries. These 203×10^6 human beings comprise roughly 3.5% of the total world population of $5,790 \times 10^6$ humans. Therefore, more than 96% of the current world population lives with less overpopulation than the people of the state of New Jersey. Surely, there is no way to justify global population control measures on the basis of overpopulation.

A clear understanding of the meaning of population density, combined with a cognizance of the actual demographic data can go a long way toward dispelling the concerns regarding overpopulation that are presented in the literature of the Culture. For example, by merely changing the scale of the ordinate of Figure 1 to include the population density of New Jersey one can easily show that the old the Malthusian skyrocket is more fizzle than fire. Those who buy into the overpopulation myth should note this well: you are being offered solutions for which there is no problem.

Table II. World Countries Having Population Density Exceeding That of New Jersey[8]

Country	Population Density (humans/mile^2)	Population (millions)
Bahrain	2,459	0.6
Bangladesh	2,213	123.1
Barbados	1,548	0.3
Bermuda	3,105	0.06
Gibraltar	14,252	0.03
Guadeloupe	1,247	0.4
South Korea	1,195	45.5
Maldives	2,354	0.3
Malta	3,051	0.4
Mauritius	1,447	1.1
Monaco	43,450	0.03
Nauru	1,252	0.01
Macao	82,806	0.5
San Marino	1,039	0.02
Singapore	13,769	3.4
Taiwan	1,533	21.3
Hong Kong	15,158	6.3
Vatican City	4,883	0.0008
Total	----	203.4

NOTES

1. John W. Hill and Doris K. Kolb, *Chemistry for Changing Times*, 7th edition (Englewood Cliffs: Prentice Hall, 1995).

2. *Ibid.*, pp. 1-5.

3. *Ibid.*, pp. 333-34.

4. *Ibid.*, p. 549.

5. *Information Please Almanac* (Boston: Houghton Mifflin, 1997), p. 129.

6. The maximum width and length of the outside stadium walls are 610 feet and 780 feet, respectively.   This information was obtained in a personal communication with Fred Clements at the Meadowlands Sports Authority.

7. *Almanac*, pp. 143-297 and p. 831.

8. *Ibid.*, pp. 143-297.

ABORTION, BREAST CANCER, AND IDEOLOGY

Joel Brind

IN INNUMERABLE NEWSPAPER and television stories shortly after New Year's, the reassuring news was passed to the American people: Science—in the form of the *New England Journal of Medicine*—had spoken on the question of abortion and breast cancer. A supposedly definitive study from Denmark, prepared by Dr. Mads Melbye and his colleagues in Copenhagen, had concluded, "Induced abortions have no overall effect on the risk of breast cancer."

There was perhaps something disingenuous in the reassurance, for the prior evidence of abortion's contribution to breast cancer was news that had been assiduously suppressed by much of the mainstream medical and popular press. But now, with the publication of the Danish study, all doubts were put to rest. The debate about abortion is now rightly restricted to "abortion itself—a debate that is ethical and political in its essence," declared Dr. Patricia Hartge of the National Cancer Institute in an editorial that accompanied the publication of the study in the January *New England Journal of Medicine*. Women need no longer "worry about the risk of breast cancer when facing the difficult decision of whether to terminate a pregnancy."

It was ususual for such advice—and such canonization of a study as "definitive"—to come only three months after a comprehensive review of the literature, published in the British Medical Association's *Journal of Epidemiology and Community Health*, reached essentially the opposite conclusion. Written by myself and colleagues at Penn State's College of Medicine in Hershey, the review compiled the data from all twenty-three available studies, dating back to 1957. Even with the most conservative statistical averaging method, we found a significant 30% increase in the risk of breast cancer attributable to a woman's having had one or more induced abortions.

Having arrived at this finding about what is in the vast majority of cases an elective surgical procedure, we urged the opposite of Dr. Hartge's reassurance that women need not worry—pointing out the "present need for those in clinical practice to inform their patients fully about what is already known." There now stands an impressive total of thirty studies worldwide, twenty-four of which show increased breast cancer risk among women who have chosen abortion, seventeen of which are statistically significant on their own. Such an overwhelming preponderance of the evidence is usually more than enough to convict any risk factor in the eyes of the medical establishment, particularly when the connection makes biological sense, with the marked overexposure to estrogen (the female hormone implicated in most breast cancer risk factors) experienced by women who elect to terminate a normal pregnancy.

But the problem is, of course, that abortion is a medical procedure whose political and social significance sets it outside normal public health concerns—even, or perhaps especially, for the public health professionals who overwhelmingly support legalized abortion and who have proved willing to set aside their medical scruples whenever legalized abortion appears threatened. The U. S. Department of Health and Human Services has been conspicuously active whenever the link between abortion and breast cancer has received any notice. In November 1994, when Dr. Janet Daling of the Fred Hutchinson Cancer Research Center in Seattle reported a significant 50% increased risk of breast cancer with induced abortion, the *Journal of the National Cancer Institute* printed the study with an accompanying editorial that impugned Daling's findings. And from the *Washington Post* to *Elle* magazine, the popular press reported explanations and denials from government experts. In the February 1995 issue of *Elle*, for example, Assistant Surgeon General Susan Blumenthal criticized Daling for failing to take into account the effect of birth control pills, a patent falsehood that Dr. Blumenthal's office has declined to retract.

In January 1996, convinced by Daling's study and other work, a pro-life group rented advertising space in rapid-transit stations in Washington, Philadelphia, and other major cities, putting up posters warning about the increased risk of breast cancer that accompanies abortion. Within days after the signs went up, the order came from then-Assistant Secretary of Health, Dr. Philip Lee, to remove them. The case is presently on appeal in the federal courts.

More recently, in December 1996, another study in the *Journal of the National Cancer Institute* described a 90% increase in the risk of breast cancer in Dutch women who had had abortions. But this time even the authors impugned their study, calling their own findings flawed, an artifact likely due to something called "reporting bias." In an accompanying article, the National Cancer Institute editorialists—taking the opportunity to attack the review my colleagues and I had published two months earlier—developed the theme, blaming any significant link between abortion and breast cancer on "a systematic bias" that "may affect all (or nearly all) studies."

"Reporting bias" is the sort of statistical artifact that must always be considered a possibility in any epidemiological study that depends on subjects' recollections. In any study—especially of a subject as sensitive as abortion—inaccuracies may exist in the reports of the women interviewed. If, for example, the women with breast cancer are more honest in reporting abortions than the women without breast cancer, then there will appear, as a result of this reporting bias, an apparent but false increase in the risk of breast cancer. Researchers must be vigilant about reporting bias, not only because the exposure in question is particularly sensitive, but also because such risk elevations as 30, 50 or even 90% are relatively small in epidemiological terms—and even a little bias can go a long way in producing a false result.

The trouble is that, despite the certainty at the National Cancer Institute that this bias exists in breast cancer research, the only credible evidence ever produced is against it. Thus, for example, Dr. Daling and her colleagues tested for its presence in their 1994 study by looking at cervical cancer incidence (which is known *not* to be associated with abortion) and found no apparent risk elevation and no evidence of reporting bias. In defense of the reliability of the same 50% risk elevation for breast cancer Daling had found, a 1995 study on women in Greece noted the "widespread social acceptance" of induced abortion in Greece and reviewed other studies on Greek women to support the conclusion "that healthy women in Greece report reliably their history of induced abortion." In 1989, a study of New York women based on *prospective* computer-registry data (as opposed to the usual retrospective data based on subject recall, and therefore automatically free of the possibility of reporting bias) found a significant 90% breast cancer risk increase with induced abortion.

The notion of abortion reporting bias in connection with breast cancer has its source in a 1989 study and a 1991 paper by a Swedish group that compared two studies on the same population of Swedish women, one based on patient recall and the other on prospective computerized records. Seven Swedish breast cancer patients reporting having had abortions for which there was no computer record, and were thus declared to have "over-reported" their abortions (*i.e.*, made them up). Relying upon this apparent phenomenon, the authors of the 1996 study of Dutch women ascribed to reporting bias the risk increase among women from a more religious, conservative region of Holland, when compared to women from a more secular, liberal region. One ought to be suspicious of the inexplicable nature of this claimed bias, which on any straightforward reading ought to run the other way—religious women claiming *fewer* abortions than they really had, not *more*. But even with this problem set aside, the Dutch study's dismissal of its own findings of a 90% risk increase turns out to be false to its own method, which found no evidence of bias between case and control subjects who had been matched by region. In order to create the claimed bias, the Dutch researchers were compelled to mismatch results with regions until they found their desired evidence of difference in reporting.

The lack of credible evidence for reporting bias notwithstanding, conclusive proof about the abortion-breast cancer link—as nearly all researchers agree—can come only from studies using prospective data like the 1989 New York study that found a 90% increased risk of breast cancer attributable to induced abortion. This was the importance of the "definitive" Danish computer-registry study led by Dr. Mads Melbye and published in the January 1998 *New England Journal of Medicine*. The Melbye study claims to be definitive not only because of the prospective nature of the data, but also because of its size, encompassing all 1.5

million women born in Denmark between 1935 and 1978, over 280,000 of whom have had legal abortions, and over 10,000 of whom have had breast cancer. The study concludes that "Induced abortions have no overall effect on the risk of breast cancer," having found an overall risk increase associated with abortion of exactly 0%.

The study falls apart, however, upon the close scrutiny made possible by the substantial body of published data concerning the same population of Danish women. Although abortions have been legal in Denmark since 1939, the Melbye study used computerized abortion records beginning only with 1973. The authors understate this weakness of the study, acknowledging only that "we might have obtained an incomplete history of induced abortions for some of the oldest women in the cohort." But a check of pre-1973 abortions shows that they misclassified some 60,000 women who had abortions as not having had any.

Yet even this egregious misclassification is not the most significant flaw in the study. The generally long latency of breast cancer means that the study largely compared younger women (with more abortions and fewer incidents of breast cancer) to older women (with more incidents of breast cancer and fewer abortions). The authors are aware of this potential source of error. But in correcting for it by adjusting for a "cohort effect," they made an astonishing blunder. The "cohort effect" is the acknowledged fact that the incidence of breast cancer has been generally rising for most of this century. The problem, however, is that the causes of this rising incidence are unknown, and since the frequency of induced abortion has similarly risen through most of this century, abortion may well be a cause of the cohort effect. And if abortion is indeed a factor in the risk of breast cancer, the cohort adjustment the Melbye study performs necessarily eliminates its effect—making the 0% increased risk a virtually guaranteed result.

And there is plenty of evidence that induced abortion is indeed the missing cohort factor. First, Melbye and his colleagues show enough data to compute the unadjusted relative risk, and this calculation shows a 44% risk increase (it is extremely disturbing, from a scientific point of view, that this number did not appear in the paper). Second, a 1988 study of part of the same cohort of Danish women found a 191% increased risk among childless women (the only women reported on) who had any induced abortions. Third, a close examination of the legal abortion rate in Denmark since 1939 shows a striking parallel with the rates of breast cancer incidence. The abortion rate peaked in 1975 and the average age at which a Dutch woman had an abortion is twenty-seven, which means that the greatest number of abortions were performed on women born around 1948. But the latest age-specific data in Denmark show that the incidence of breast cancer is maximal for women born between 1945 and 1950, and is on the decline for women born more recently. A proper analysis would likely show a significant breast cancer increase in the neighborhood of 100% for induced abortion.

Abortion is not a controversial subject in Denmark and Dr. Melbye seems a sincere and competent man. But his study reveals the entrenched bias in favor of the view that abortion is harmless to women, a bias that is decades old. One in every six Danish women has had at least one abortion, which means that complicity in abortion decisions is pervasive in the society. How willing can members of such a society be to acknowledge that they have put themselves and those they love at risk of one of the most dreaded, life-threatening diseases that a woman can get? What hope is there in such a society for scientific integrity to overcome a witting or unwitting wall of denial?

Fortunately, abortion is still a controversial subject in America, but denial from high places of its harmfulness to women is hard to miss—even in the partial funding for the Melbye study provided by the U. S. Department of Defense. If we are to maintain scientific integrity in medical research, we must denounce, wherever it appears, the manipulation of studies to provide socially desired results. The point of maintaining scientific integrity in medicine, of course, is not just to preserve the abstract notion of truth, but to save the lives of both women and their babies.

THE "MORNING-AFTER PILL": ANOTHER STEP TOWARDS DEPERSONALIZATION?

Hanna Klaus

WHEN CONDOMS WERE FIRST INTRODUCED, they were meant to prevent sexually transmitted disease. Either they were designed for single men, or for married men to use when visiting a brothel. It took several decades to persuade people to use condoms for birth control purposes. But the "memory" of their initial use has never quite gone away. And now, according to Dr. Malcolm Potts, one-time Medical Director of the International Planned Parenthood Federation and later the Director of Family Health International: "The health care community is trying to persuade men to try to go back to the original purposes, namely, the prevention of STDs." Many people have feelings of discomfort about using contraceptives, and this is not restricted to those who were brought up to believe that using contraception was against their faith. Today, one often finds unmarried couples who consider using a condom to be a sign of distrust: the presumption is that those who need to use a condom have been promiscuous. This is a particular problem for those who are using condoms to prevent the spread of AIDS. To add to the distress of the health care community, in spite of assiduous counseling, clients at highest risk for AIDS generally use no "protection." Any contraceptive, not only the condom, is designed to prevent conception while engaging in the sexual act.

When the so-called sexual revolution began, particularly in the late 50's and early 60's, it was heralded as the reversal of the Victorian culture. A Victorian woman was supposedly a prude and never really said "yes" to sex. Now the woman on the pill can never give a good reason for saying "no." While sexual mores have deteriorated enormously in the last forty years, the resulting sexual freedom has not brought the happiness that was expected. Already German magazines like *Der Spiegel* write about the total sexual satiety of unmarried youth. They have tried everything and found it wanting, and they are now reluctantly embracing celibacy because they are totally disappointed with sex. As if this were not enough, one-third of young American females are alleged to be clinically depressed. Curiously this figure parallels the rate of depression of contraceptive pill users, which is thought to be due to the progestin in the pill, which builds up the endorphen which generally heightens the mood and is responsible for the feeling of well-being. But America is a country in love with technology and control, and so in spite of the fact that women have many reservations about many forms of contraception, the medical profession has chosen to ignore all hesitations and to introduce yet another step in separating sex from procreation. Post-coital contraception, whether by an increased dose of so-called birth control pills, or methotrexate and misoprostol (prostaglandin) or mifepriston (RU486) and misoprostol, all lead to the same goal—the altering of the endometrium so that any embryo which had been conceived can no longer embed in the endometrium. This is interoception, or early abortion.

The early reports of recipients of so-called medical termination of pregnancy are mixed, many women preferring the certainty of the surgical abortion to the delay, the wondering, the discomfort or pain or nausea of the agents used, and the uncertainty of whether or not the abortion will be complete. To date, no one has asked about the women's deeper feelings, and to date, in spite of the recommendations for the use of these agents within 72 hours of "unprotected intercourse," no one has ever asked women how they feel about this, so we are free to speculate.

Helene Deutsch, a Freudian analyst from Austria, who later taught at Massachusetts General Hospital and Harvard Medical School, wrote in her classic *The Psychology of Women*: "For the feminine woman at the unconscious level, every coital act contains within it the psychic germs of a child." Dr. Deutsch wrote this in 1945 and had many followers. But once the pill came in, Deutsch was disavowed. A whole generation of women's physicians were now devoting up to a third of their practice time to the prescription of contraceptives. Psychological studies of the effect of contraception have been scarce, and when they confirm depression, they have generally been ignored. One might think that women might not want to know whether they have conceived or not, but on a much deeper level they do want to know that they have actually achieved something with their coital act, other than the moment of union which, in the cases where post-coital contraception is most vigorously promoted, is most likely to be somewhat ephemeral anyway because couples who are married generally plan their families a little bit more painstakingly.

Why should there be hesitation about not knowing? It is a question of not knowing whether anything one does has an effect. If nothing I do has an effect, then nothing I do matters. If I can have no effect, then I am not an agent, I am certainly not a moral agent, and persons are meant to be moral agents. Loss of moral agency then equates with non-personhood and that, to say the least, is depressing. The reaction to this realization can be either frank depression or impotent rage. Biochemically, women are more likely to react with depression, which is anger turned inward, while men are more likely to express their rage externally.

I was overseas in the beginning of the 60's and returned to the U.S. in 1968 shortly after the riots of the summer. Discussing possible causes with Msgr. John Shocklee, an experienced inner city pastor in St. Louis, confirmed my intuition. Until contraception became easily available, the black man could be told where he could live, where he could work, where he could become educated, but at least he could be a man; he could have children. With contraception—and five years later with abortion—anything a man could do could be made void by the woman. This may have been part of the driving anger of the summer of 1968. If nothing one does is of any value, one is nobody. Jesse Jackson sensed this with his "I am somebody" approach to young people. He may not have had the sexual act in mind, but he understood the principle.

Certainly, when abortion is easy, it is easy to exploit women. A man needs to take no responsibility for a child if he can persuade the woman to abort. With the morning-after pill, it should be even easier and certainly less expensive. The difficulty is, if one exploits people, one is an exploiter, and exploiters ultimately begin to despise themselves. Sometimes this takes the form of highly aggressive acting-out behavior. But it still comes from the same psychological root. What then can we offer to counter this trend in our society. I return to the Theology of the Body, a doctrine which has been taught by the Holy Father almost from the beginning of his Pontificate and one whose philosophical foundations were laid much earlier while he was a professor at Lublin. He is well aware that only an acting person is a person, in other words, a moral agent. He is also deeply aware that we are embodied individuals, that our bodies are a sign of the person, and that they are a gift of God. Our bodies are sexed: either male or female. Everything that we do is a result of either a male's or a female's action. I suggest, therefore, that we re-emphasize the reality of the body in our teaching as well as in our informal interaction with students, and that we include teaching not only about the physiology but also about sexuality and relationships, and that we invite young people to consider these matters in great depth. College freshmen especially need assistance in these areas. Statistics show that generally 50% of females are already sexually experienced when they begin their freshmen college year. At the end of the first year, this figure has risen to 80%. If it is possible to prevent the increase with education, we will have done a worthwhile thing because many young women begin sexual liaisons in college simply because of peer pressure. Many become pregnant and far too many of them abort because they have no other choices open to them, or at least they think that they do not.

Our group has originated a program called Holistic Sexuality which has already found good acceptance in several universities, and it is one model which can be recommended. There are many groups which have discussions about sex, but the Holistic Sexuality program, as far as I am aware, is the only one which includes the experience of the body's fertility signs, in the case of the woman, and a discussion of these signs in considerable depth with both male and female participants. When one includes the experience of cyclic fertility, it is like a two-handed piano piece: the left hand is fertility and the right hand is sexuality in its emotional, intellectual, social, and spiritual aspects. The two-handed piece is far richer than either the melody or the harmony alone. When this program has been offered, it has shown excellent outcomes in supporting chastity among its users.

The most recent group of participants is eager to help incoming freshmen walk the same path and also to reach out as facilitators to the community. Some colleges offer community credit for community service; this opens up a new direction. It is possible that some may be wondering about the appropriateness of teaching unmarried persons about fertility: how to recognize it, when it begins and ends, and what rules couples follow. In my experience, when unmarried persons are engaging in sexual intercourse and they choose to plan to delay pregnancy by using natural methods, their relationship changes. If they have more than a genital relationship, they find that they need to give themselves fully to one another and they marry. On the other hand, if their relationship is merely physical, it usually ends. The reason for this, I believe, is that it is impossible to respect someone's body without respecting the person since they are one as long as they are living. And in doing so, the need for total commitment becomes evident.

REFERENCES

Billings, E.L. and J.J. *Teaching the Billings Ovulation Method*, Melbourne, Australia: Ovulation Method Reference and Research Centre, 1997.

Deutsch, Helen. *The Psychology of Women.* Vol. 2: *Motherhood.* Chapter 4: "The Psychology of the Sexual Act. New York: Grune and Stratton, 1945.

Hogan, R. and LeVoir, J.M. *Covenant of Love.* Garden City: Image, 1986.

Klaus, Hanna. "Positive Woman or Negative Man?" *Linacre Quarterly* 43/4 (1976) 244-48. Awarded the Thomas Linacre Award for 1976.

Klaus, Hanna. "The Existential Isolation of Contraception," *Linacre Quarterly* 59 (1992) 329-32.

CATHOLIC RETREAT FOR POST-ABORTION WOMEN AND MEN: RESULTS AND THEOLOGICAL REFLECTIONS

William S. Kurz, S.J.

INTRODUCTION

As part of a Catholic response to healing, reconciling, and offering new spiritual life to those suffering from the grief and guilt of abortion, a Milwaukee-based team, of which this author is a member, has for over three years provided a semi-annual retreat for people who have had abortions.[1] These retreats arose as a response by a director of a Milwaukee crisis pregnancy center to needs manifested by women who had had previous abortions. As the director, who was Catholic, listened to woman after woman struggling with her past and present situations, she sensed that for at least some of the Catholic women, a spiritual remedy beyond sacramental reconciliation, one which originated from within their own religious beliefs and experiences, was needed, and not only material and psychological solutions to their problems. At least in the Milwaukee area, most of the popular ministries to post-abortion women, such as Bible studies like PACE, were Protestant. She had read about a Catholic retreat, "Raphael (God Heals)," offered in Texas to women who had had abortions, and she sent for information.[2] She concluded that a similar retreat would provide one important avenue of recovery from abortion aftermath, and she formed a team to plan and give such retreats.

After eight successful retreats, in which this team continuously adapted and improved the format to respond to observed deficiencies and needs, people who knew of the good results of these retreats requested that the team present their results at prolife and academic conferences and publish the results. To present these results would not only supply important confirmation of the routinely denied harmful effects of abortion on many who have had them but also provide some very promising avenues for

150

reaching out to those who had aborted their babies and for helping them come to full spiritual as well as psychological and physical wholeness afterwards. It was hoped that such a report might prompt others in other parts of the country and world to provide similar retreats.

Two previous reports based on earlier retreats have been given at "Healing Vision: An International Conference on Post-Abortion Aftermath and Its Resolution," where they were very well received by the conference participants, who included some of the world's leading experts in post-abortion aftermath.[3] But in one sense, these reports were "speaking to the saved," in that those participants already had considerable expertise in understanding, appreciating, and trying to ameliorate the harmful aftereffects of abortions even on the living. The academic establishment has for eleven years been ignoring the results of the Healing Vision conferences, because it is not politically correct to draw so much attention to suffering by women from the abortions they chose to have. Therefore many who knew about our retreat expressed the view that this information needed to reach a wider academic audience. This article provides a description and theological evaluation of our retreats, arguing that these retreats provide important evidence about the traumatic aftermath of abortion for many, and about what is important for their full reintegration into the Church as Body of Christ.

DEVELOPMENT OF POST-ABORTION RETREATS

The first team which was assembled to plan and give these retreats included the director of the crisis pregnancy center, one of her volunteer helpers (who was also a veteran volunteer counselor for Pregnancy Aftermath Helpline), a Catholic woman who had recovered from traumatic abortion aftermath, and two Catholic priests. The team gathered to plan the retreat in a prayerful atmosphere and manner, not simply as if they were some kind of secular committee.

One of their first decisions was to modify the format of the Texas retreats to include more explicit ministry concerning the abortions that the women had had. The Texas arrangement, because the program also included support groups and follow-up, was often to send individual women anonymously to generic Ignatian silent retreats, that is, retreats based on the *Spiritual Exercises* of St. Ignatius promoted especially by the

Jesuits.

The team agreed that the weekend would remain primarily a traditional "generic" Catholic retreat without the primary focus being placed on abortion itself, which was the genius of the Texas experiences. There are other programs for explicit ministry to women who have had abortions for their psychological and spiritual healing. But such women cannot go through the rest of their lives identifying themselves primarily with their abortion as a "post-abortion woman." We believed that God calls these women, as converted and healed sinners, to true wholeness, full Christian living, to sanctity itself.

But the team did consider it important to deal explicitly with abortion in a supportive context with others who were suffering from similar grief and guilt, and to do some direct ministry facilitating recovery of the retreatants from the effects of the abortion itself. The result remains basically an Ignatian retreat, based primarily on traditional topics and focuses from the *Spiritual Exercises* (for example, God's love and mercy, Creation, Sin and Reconciliation, Incarnation, Eucharist, the Passion of Jesus, Mary and saints, and prayer). But the retreat also includes explicit witness to post-abortion trauma and recovery, opportunity for retreatants to talk about their abortions among themselves and with the retreat team members, private counseling and confessions (the Catholic sacrament of reconciliation), some brief input on chastity and purity, and an explicit but brief and limited memorial at the Eucharist for the retreatants' lost children.

The team also met briefly at times during the retreat and returned afterwards for debriefing and looking prayerfully at the results of the retreat just given. One of the very first modifications was to change the name of the retreat. The primary title remained the same: "The Love and Mercy of God." But our initial descriptive subtitle had been "A Retreat for Post-Abortion Catholic Women." We changed this to express better what the retreat actually is: "A Catholic Retreat for Post-Abortion Women." This would open the retreat to non-Catholic women, as long as they were at peace with unapologetically Catholic teachings, spirituality, worship, devotions, etc. Experience, including that at the crisis pregnancy center, had alerted us to the intense need of most women who have had abortions to learn the basics of their Catholic faith, worship, and sacraments. We could not afford to miss the opportunity to provide this basic grounding in their Catholicism under the strictures of a "least-common-denominator ecumenism."

Before one of our very first retreats, after it had been advertised and most of the women had signed up for it, a man asked if he also could be allowed to make the retreat. The team called every woman who had signed up for the retreat and got their permission to make this modification, so that the current subtitle reads, "A Catholic Retreat for Post-Abortion Women and Men." This has been a happy modification. Most of our retreats have included at least one male retreatant, and the women retreatants (without any exceptions of which I am aware) expressed appreciation for and benefited from seeing the suffering and concern which some men also had over aborted babies, since so many of these women had been abandoned or pressured into the abortion by irresponsible males who had impregnated them. In turn, several of the men were quite stunned by the depth of the women's pain and the reality of what they had done, as when one man saw the booties a mother kept to remember her two aborted babies. Although the male retreatants have always been a small minority, the masculine presence of the two priests has helped them also be comfortable as part of the retreat group.

FORMAT AND CONTENT OF RETREATS

The retreat is structured around talks which set the tone, instruct, and prepare for private prayer and use of the sacraments. It includes two Masses, the first on Saturday at 3 p.m., and the second on Sunday at 10:30 a.m., which ends the retreat. There is a simple memorial for the retreatants' aborted babies at the Saturday Mass. Counseling from the staff and confessions with the priests are available throughout. Quiet times for prayer, rest, and walking are important. So is the sharing among the retreatants and staff members, both in the formal group sessions as well as over meals and evening relaxation with snacks.

At the opening of the retreat on Friday evening, a welcoming hospitality is extremely important in order to overcome the anxiety and awkwardness many if not most of the retreatants experience initially. It is a time for greeting, for quiet and undemanding repetitious prayer (the rosary) while waiting for other retreatants to arrive, for a strong proclamation of the gospel of God's mercy and love followed by a witness given by a post-abortion staff member of that mercy, for explanation of the memorial for their lost babies, and for informal conversation as the retreatants wish.

Saturday is very full, with morning talks and prayer, afternoon time for personal ministry as well as talks and the Mass with the memorial service, and evening talks, quiet adoration and prayer in a eucharistic chapel, and finally optional relaxation together. Sunday ends the retreat with a morning talk on how to pray, followed by the closing Mass and blessing, and a brief session of farewells, debriefing, and feedback.

The team generally meets for lunch afterwards for further immediate debriefing, and some weeks later for a prayerful overview of the previous retreat and first steps toward planning the next one. In these debriefing sessions the team reflects on the written evaluations of the retreatants, as well as on recollections of their oral remarks and the team's own observations of the retreat dynamics, to make suitable adjustments.

TOPICS OF RETREAT TALKS

The focal points of the retreat talks come primarily from the *Spiritual Exercises* of St. Ignatius, with some special attention to distinctive requirements with respect to the retreatants' moral and spiritual lives in general and their abortions in particular. The retreat team was convinced that most prospective post-abortion retreatants would have additional needs beyond just the potential for basic conversion for which the process promoted by the *Spiritual Exercises* is appropriately distinguished. Most of these retreatants would also require a lot of basic catechesis in their Catholic faith, practices, and moral principles, as well as, of course, healing from the traumatic effects of their abortions.

Therefore the talks were to have these three dimensions: (1) the fundamental conversion processes from the *Spiritual Exercises,* (2) remedial basic Catholic catechesis in topics such as God, creation, sin, redemption, the incarnation, birth, suffering, and death of Jesus, the sacraments of reconciliation and Eucharist, devotion to Mary and the saints, the virtue of purity or chastity, and the importance and methods of prayer, plus (3) healing and ministry specifically dealing with the aftermath of their abortions.

Talk 1: The Love and Mercy of God. Many if not most of the retreatants enter the retreat Friday evening with some mixture of anxiety, guilt, fear, and yearning for healing and relief. It is important from the very beginning that the speaker set a tone of acceptance, hope, and God's love and mercy, which is therefore the primary aim of the opening talk. After a welcome and some introductory procedural suggestions for the retreat, the talk focuses on who this God is with whom we are about to spend the weekend. The retreatants learn that (1) God created each of our souls out of love for us and with a plan for each of our lives; (2) it is important to come to realize that God loves me, since that is the beginning of a new freedom and dynamic life; (3) as our hearts spontaneously go out to a sick or injured child, so God's love for us is compassionate love. At the culmination of the introduction, the speaker reads and unpacks some implications from Isaiah 43:1-7 ("you are precious in my eyes") and compares God's love and mercy to the sun which is always shining, even when we do not see it.

The body of the talk is based primarily on biblical passages that emphasize God's mercy. The speaker continues by reading and explicating the mercy of God as a Father who knows his children's frailty in Psalm 103. Then Romans 8:28-39 provides the assurance that nothing can separate us from God's love. Finally, the three parables of the lost sheep, the lost coin, and the prodigal son in Luke 15 emphasize that there is more joy in heaven over one sinner who repents than over ninety-nine who have no need for repentance and that with unconditional acceptance the Father takes joy over the returning prodigal: "My son was dead and is alive again, was lost and is found." The speaker concludes by urging the retreatants to ground their retreat in an awareness of God's love and mercy for them and to "let God tell you that he loves you."

Retreatants in this situation are not well served by downplaying the gravity of the wrong and harm of abortion, for they would not be making this retreat if they were not already at least implicitly aware that something was seriously wrong with their abortion choice and action. Most retreatants have had years to live with the consequences of their abortion. In our early retreats most of the abortions had occurred 14-20 years previously, and in later retreats, when some women came whose abortions were only 6-10 years old, their wounds were often conspicuously more raw and, as it were, still "bleeding." Almost all of the retreatants have suffered severely after their abortions. Some have struggled terribly and for years with guilt and self-hatred.

Therefore, it is important to be forthright about the seriousness of the wrong of abortion, lest one appear to be either condescending to the retreatant or ignorant of the depth of her suffering. First, however, one must lay a foundation that enables retreatants to face their sin by focusing on God's love as a compassionate love which reaches out to us even more tenderly in our sinfulness and wrongdoing. The words of the Scriptures themselves provide perhaps the most eloquent witness to God's merciful love, along with the personal testimony of staff people who have been forgiven their own abortions.

Talk 2: Personal Witness of Post-abortion Reconciliation and Healing. Therefore, immediately after the opening topical talk on God's mercy, a staff member who had suffered after her abortion and been healed would share her experiences with the retreatants. Most retreats also featured a second witness by a former retreatant from one of our previous retreats, who was now healed enough to be able to function as a kind of adjunct member of our retreat team. This second talk builds added hope in the retreatants by testifying specifically to the effectiveness of this particular form of retreat for others who have made it before them.

Talk 3: God the Creator and Creation ("The First Principle and Foundation" of the Ignatian Spiritual Exercises). Saturday morning's opening talk focuses on who God is and who we are as created by God. Since a major element in serious human sin is "wanting to be like gods" (cf. Gen 3:5) and to determine for ourselves what is right and what is wrong, the *Spiritual Exercises* of St. Ignatius focus initially on the reality and implications of God as our Creator and we as creatures, who are not ourselves God.

An important treatment of the concept of creation is "The First Principle and Foundation" of the *Spiritual Exercises.* Its preamble states that we humans were created to praise, reverence, and serve God, with whom we thus reach eternal happiness.[4] On the first evening, the team provides copies of this principle for private reflection and for review after the retreat.

This notion of ourselves as created by a loving God, to whom we are responsible for our lives and for everything about ourselves, is quite alien to the reigning secularist contemporary mindset. It is an essential prerequisite for attaining a reasonable sense of the horror of all sin. Since it is important not to focus so exclusively on the sin of abortion in isolation from other serious sins that one reinforces many retreatants' false sense of being uniquely unforgivable and unlovable, the traditional elements of the retreat continually contextualize the sinfulness of abortion within the general biblical concept of the gravity of all forms of seriously sinful wrongdoing against our Creator God. When the retreatants can see (for example, from Scripture) how common and how many are the kinds of serious sins that humans commit, they can overcome the false but typical notion that by their abortion they have committed the only terrible wrongdoing and a sin that is uniquely unforgivable.

Talk 4: Sin and Confession (Sacrament of Reconciliation). After these foundational talks on God's love, mercy, and majesty as our Creator, the retreatants are more prepared to hear a straightforward presentation of the meaning and gravity of sin, and of the beauty and power of God's remedy in the Church's Sacrament of Reconciliation. Even this talk, however, has an introductory focus on God's mercy, as manifested in the account of the sinful woman anointing and weeping over Jesus's feet in Luke 7:36-50. Especially important is its conclusion in the mouth of Jesus, which links forgiveness and love: "Therefore I tell you, her sins, which are many, are forgiven for she loved much; but whoever is forgiven little, loves little." The speaker emphasizes that not only does their sin not make them unworthy of being loved and loving, but both the gospel and the experience of members of the retreat staff emphasize how the experience of God's forgiveness can lead to an extraordinarily profound love of God.

The body of the talk is organized around some key biblical passages. Genesis 3 illustrates what sin is, from which the speaker further explains the classical (and pastorally still very helpful) distinction, on which St. Ignatius constantly insisted, the distinction between mortal and venial sin.[5]

Psalm 32 provides a powerful biblical witness to the need to admit and confess one's guilt lest one suffer serious psychological and even physical consequences. On this biblical foundation, the speaker can provide some key elements of traditional Catholic catechesis on the Sacrament of

Reconciliation: (1) The priest within this sacrament is functioning "in the person of Christ" when judging and forgiving the penitent's sins. (2) The biblical fact that Christians are not isolated individuals but members of the Body of Christ explains why sins have social consequences, since they affect other members of the Body and not just the sinner. Such social consequences require the social remedy of confession to a representative of Christ's Body, the priest-confessor. (3) The context of private confession of sins in this sacrament provides an excellent opportunity for a skilled confessor to counsel, encourage, and minister to the penitent.

Talk 5: Incarnation and Birth of Jesus. This talk is a straightforward combination of the two corresponding Ignatian contemplations in the "Second Week" (that is, the second section) of his *Spiritual Exercises.* Concerning the incarnation, the retreatants are invited to use their imaginations and faith to contemplate the Trinity determining to rescue sinful humans from their hopeless slide toward hell by sending the Second Person, the Son, to become human in order to save our race. They are also to imagine the angel inviting Mary to cooperate by becoming mother of the Incarnate Son of God.

In the contemplation on the birth of Jesus, the retreatants are invited to enter personally into the events through their faith imagination and to be present with Mary and Joseph as they travel to Bethlehem, to be told that there is no room for them in the inn, and to find a place for animals where Jesus is born and laid in a feeding trough, and then to respond or to worship Jesus as they find themselves drawn.

The emphasis on faith imagination rather than on rational processing of the abstract doctrines of the incarnation provides a way for the retreatants to become participants in this mystery of faith and thus to experience and appreciate its significance for them.[6] Four centuries of experience in offering this form of prayer to retreatants confirm that retreatants come to quite personal appreciations of what it means that God became man to save them from the eternal consequences of their sins. This is no less true of this particular retreat population of people who have had abortions, and the contemplation is very healing for many of them. It focuses on divine and human love, rather than on commandments, sins, and punishments, but it effectively shows both the magnificent generosity of God for us and the seriousness of sin against such a loving God as well as the presence among us of a divine and human savior as a helpless baby. Because of their abortions, some retreatants might be afraid of God or of Jesus as judge. They are not likely to be afraid of Jesus as a newborn baby.

Talk 6 (as Homily): The Eucharist. The next talk utilizes the occasion of the sermon or homily at the Catholic Mass to provide catechesis on the meaning and practice of the Eucharistic Liturgy (as Jesus's Sacrifice, as Meal, as Sacrament, and as Memorial) and on receiving Holy Communion appropriately, as well as to explain the biblical liturgical readings for the day and to provide at least remote preparation for the memorial of the retreatants' aborted and miscarried babies during the offertory and communion portions of the Mass. Because the Eucharist is at the heart of Catholic worship and devotional life and yet is becoming so routinely misunderstood, eucharistic catechesis seems especially imperative. Although it is not explicitly related to abortion aftermath as such, frequent and reverent reception of the Eucharist is an important element of the retreatant's overall healing and growth as a Catholic disciple of Christ.[7]

Talk 7: Passion and Death of Jesus. Like the contemplation on the incarnation and birth of Jesus, the talk on the suffering and death of Jesus invites the retreatants to enter imaginatively with Jesus into what he suffered for their sake. It appeals not to reasoning about abstract doctrines like atonement, but to faith-filled imagination of what our salvation actually cost Jesus and to the desire to be somehow present with him as he undergoes his suffering for us. Willingness by the retreatants to share with Jesus in his sufferings on their behalf helps to deepen their awareness of the incredible depth of Jesus's love for them and to strengthen their resolve not to hurt him by any additional sins.

The retreatants are invited to imagine themselves at the foot of the cross with Jesus, his mother Mary, the beloved disciple, and Mary Magdalen (as portrayed especially by John's Gospel). They are to ask for "sorrow with Jesus in sorrow, tears and deep grief because of the great suffering Jesus endures for me."[8] Very helpful scriptures for appreciating what Jesus suffered for sinners are the seven biblical words of Jesus on the cross (see below), Psalms 69 and 22, and Isaiah 52:13-53:12, 42:1-9, 49:1-26, and 50:1-11.

As they enter into this contemplation by imagining themselves at Christ's cross, many retreatants find especially moving the seven words of Jesus on the cross: (1) "Father, forgive them, for they know not what they do" (Luke 23:34); (2) "Woman, behold your son... behold your mother" (John 19:26-27); (3) "I thirst" (John 19:28); (4) "This day you shall be with me in paradise" (Luke 23:43); (5) "My God, my God, why have you forsaken me?" (Matthew 27:46 and Mark 15:34); (6) "It is finished" (John 19:30); (7) "Father, into your hands I commend my spirit" (Luke 23:46).

In the contemplation itself, retreatants are first invited to see in their imaginations what is happening among all the people at the cross, the mockery, etc. They are to listen to what everyone is saying, to those jeering, to Jesus, to the disciples, and so on. Psalm 69 provides many powerful insights into these things in the psalmist's urgent petition to God to save him from those who surround him and hate him, how he is suffering for our sake, how there is no one to comfort him.

Retreatants are to consider what Jesus suffers and try to share his sorrow. The psalmist's cry to God in Psalm 22—"why have you abandoned me?"—is followed by his sense that he is a "worm and no man, scorned by men and despised by the people," surrounded by bulls and ravenous lions, poured out like water, with his hands and feet pierced and his bones numbered, his garments divided by lots.

Retreatants are to consider further "how Jesus suffers all this for my sins" and how they can respond to Jesus. Isaiah 52:13-53:12 is very well-suited for this consideration: "There was no comeliness in him; he was despised; he has borne our griefs; we have esteemed him smitten by God; yet he was wounded for our iniquities; upon him was laid the chastisement that makes us whole, and by his wounds we are healed. Though oppressed he opened not his mouth, like a lamb led to the slaughter. They gave him a grave among the wicked, though he had done no violence. He bore the sin of many, and made intercession for the sinners."

The final focus of this contemplation is to ask for an awareness of the horror for the retreatants' personal sins which caused such agony in God's own Son dying to save them from those sins; to appreciate more fully the depth of God's love for each of them personally in undergoing all this suffering for them; and to take hope that if God was willing to do all this to save them from their sins, they can have assurance that God wants to bring them to himself in heaven. This kind of selfless looking at the suffering of Jesus for us implies a certain level of maturity in retreatants. But it also fosters such maturity, so that even most spiritual beginners are touched in some way by this presentation.

Talk 8: Devotion to Mary and the Saints. Saturday evening begins with a cheerful change of pace. Experience with many converted and healed post-abortion Catholics attests to the important influence which Catholic devotion to Mary and saints can have on their healing and growth. This talk also signals to the retreatants that the retreat's goal is not simply reconciliation and healing from their past abortions but to challenge them to lead holy lives in the future, as Mary and the saints did. Focus on Mary also offers the retreatants a mother-figure whom they can trust.[9]

Talk 9: Purity (Chastity). Because so often abortion is a consequence of unchaste behavior (including unchaste uses of contraception within marriage, which imply antecedent rejection of any child "accidentally" conceived), catechesis on chastity to counter the omnipresent propaganda of the sexual revolution seems particularly relevant in this retreat. Besides, unchastity fosters dispositions toward others (such as "using" them) that themselves lead to disrespect for human life. Most retreatants have not been taught to recognize God's authority over their sexual behavior, nor the value and importance of the virtue of chastity, nor the true meaning of and divine purposes for marriage, nor the exclusive relationship in God's plan between sexual intercourse and committed marriage which is open to having and educating children. In one sense, this is a pro-active approach to help forestall future problems with abortion rather than just a reaction to crises produced by unchaste behavior. After healing from past abortions, retreatants need to live their future lives on the sound footing of this virtue of chastity. Most retreatants respond favorably to this talk, though some, whose tiredness or headache may be mostly an excuse, simply do not come to it.

Talk 10: Importance of Prayer and How to Pray. This is another important talk in preparing retreatants for the future. If it had not been clear to them before this point that God desires not only their healing and reconciliation but their love and intimate friendship (and consequently sanctity), this talk demonstrates it plainly.

The context for this instruction on prayer is a comparison to any love relationship between persons. The introduction acknowledges what they all know from their experience to be true—that all humans, even those in a happy marriage, have some loneliness and a hunger for love which can never be satisfied. As the well-known saying of Augustine puts it, "You have made us for yourself, O Lord, and our hearts are restless until they rest in you."[10] The only solution for this fundamental aloneness is to know the love of Jesus and of God his Father. But one cannot grow in love of any person if one does not spend time communicating with that person. The same is true for one's relationship with God. Nor in communication can one person do all the talking. To get to know someone else, one must listen to that person. To get to know God, one must listen to God.

The speaker can point out further experiential incentives to daily prayer from the retreatants' struggles to live peaceful, upright lives without discouragement. It is most helpful for the speaker to provide his or her personal witness to the necessity and practice of daily prayer in the speaker's life. When I give this talk, I describe my practices of a daily extended prayer time: what I do and how I pray and what I use for prayer. I also describe my practices of frequent short prayers interjected throughout my whole day.

From this concrete personal example, the speaker then describes what prayer is—conversation with God and a sharing of one's life with "the God who loves me." The speaker underlines the importance of prayer: (1) for awareness of God's presence and love in one's life, (2) for God's guidance and peace in one's daily living, (3) for protection against delusion and temptation, (4) to repent of sin and begin anew.

The basic catechesis then describes four simple kinds of prayer: (1) set prayers (liturgical prayer, the rosary, devotions), (2) brief prayers throughout the day, often referred to as "practicing God's presence,"[11] (3) prayerful reading of Scripture, listening to God speak to one's own life and situation, (4) extended quiet listening prayer (often called "meditation") such as the retreatants learned in meditating on the birth and sufferings of Jesus.

The heart of the catechesis is actually to show the retreatants some simple methods of meditative prayer. The speaker speaks from a handout which the retreatants can use as a guide after the retreat. He or she gives basic instructions such as the following steps, which are adaptations of various forms of prayer taught in St. Ignatius's *Spiritual Exercises.* (1) Prepare a place where one can pray regularly with some privacy. (2) Prepare one's heart, trying to quiet oneself, giving one's cares to God. Do a short examination of conscience, asking and thanking God for his forgiveness. (3) Begin meditation by asking that everything that happens be for God's praise and service. (4) Read the scripture passage slowly (e.g., Luke 10:38-42 on Mary and Martha, or Matthew 6:7-15—the Our Father in context) and really to listen to it. (5) See in one's imagination the setting (perhaps re-reading the passage), trying to enter the scene oneself. (6) Ask the Lord for what one desires, such as intimate knowledge and love of Jesus. (7) In imagination *see* what is happening, (8) *listen* to what is said, and (9) *imagine oneself in the scene,* especially listening to what Jesus shares with oneself. Once one has entered into the passage, one should remain there in silence even if it feels uncomfortable, letting God do what he wills in one's heart. At the end, thank God for whatever happened and close with an Our Father.

This catechesis and instruction in how to pray, for which many retreatants are particularly grateful, provides important means for the retreatants to continue to grow in their knowledge and love of God and to find ever more peace and meaning in their lives.

MEMORIAL AT MASS FOR ABORTED, MISCARRIED, STILLBORN BABIES

This memorial in the Saturday afternoon Mass is typically an especially powerful moment in the retreat. In preparation for it, the team gives instructions after the first talks of the retreat on Friday evening. Most of the retreatants have a deep sense of whether their aborted baby was a boy or girl. The memorial gives them an opportunity to remember them individually and to offer them to Jesus. Friday night the team provides vigil candles which the retreatants decorate in any way they choose with items like ribbons, pictures, and flowers provided by the staff. The retreatants are invited to name their babies if they have not already done so, which treats them as the persons they are. Before the Saturday Mass the retreatants place the vigil lights on the altar. During the prayers of the faithful these children are mentioned by name and offered to the Lord. The retreatants find this an especially healing prayer. Many find great relief when they name their babies and acknowledge their identity. As they recognize the dignity of these babies, they do what they failed to do at the time of the abortion. Now they can offer them to Jesus and his mercy.

SUMMARY THEOLOGICAL REFLECTIONS ON RETREAT RESULTS
Forgiveness of past sins brings genuine healing and change in the present. So often people remain depressed over past wrongdoing because they have refused to face openly what they have done. This retreat preaches the full gospel message, both its pleasant and uncomfortable aspects. It preaches the goodness and forgiveness of God, but also the evil and horror of sin. Forgiveness is not just that God overlooks what we have done. Forgiveness looks squarely at the evil one has done and not only forgives it but empowers the penitent to reject and turn away from that sinful behavior and live a newly whole and holy life.

In this way the adult human dignity of the retreatants is respected. One does not "enable" their denials nor gloss over what they have done wrong and what they instinctively know to be quite wrong. It is the basest form of condescension not to treat persons as adults who are accountable for what they have done in the past nor to call them to a reformed and responsible way of living in the present.

An important (and characteristically Catholic) aspect of the retreat is that it invites the retreatants to enter into the concrete realities of how the human race was created and saved. Faith is not just abstract doctrines assented to by reason. The retreatants enter into the concrete realities of the life of Jesus in the first century as narrated in Scripture in order to appreciate who he was on earth and who he is in his risen life today. Not only do they enter into humanly responsible life but into the life of the Body of Christ today as made present to them in the sacraments, especially of Eucharist and Reconciliation.

Finally, they concretize and recognize the identity and dignity of their aborted children, living in the truth about the dignity of every human person from conception to natural death, and rejecting the lies and denials of the personhood of the "fetus" that contribute to the present "culture of death." But the retreat is not primarily for focusing on past wrongs—it is a call for the retreatants' present renewal and change and their new freedom as beloved daughters or sons of God. It is a call to accept God's forgiveness and invitation to intimate friendship and holiness of life that overflows into generous love toward others.

The retreat team hopes that this retreat is a concrete way of expressing to women who have had abortions the consoling message of the Church to them, as expressed by Pope John Paul II in *Evangelium Vitae* #99:

I would now like to say a special word to *women who have had an abortion.* The Church is aware of the many factors which may have influenced your decision, and she does not doubt that in many cases it was a painful and even shattering decision. The wound in your heart may not yet have healed. Certainly what happened was and remains terribly wrong. But do not give in to discouragement and do not lose hope. Try rather to understand what happened and face it honestly. If you have not already done so, give yourselves over with humility and trust to repentance. The Father of mercies is ready to give you his forgiveness and his peace in the Sacrament of Reconciliation. You will come to understand that nothing is definitively lost and you will also be able to ask forgiveness from your child, who is now living in the Lord. With the friendly and expert help and advice of other people, and as a result of your own painful experience, you can be among the most eloquent defenders of everyone's right to life. Through your commitment to life, whether by accepting the birth of other children or by welcoming and caring for those most in need of someone to be close to them, you will become promoters of a new way of looking at human life.

NOTES

1. On post-abortion suffering, treatment, and ministry, see Susan Stanford-Rue, "Healing Post-Abortion Trauma" in *Life and Learning V: Proceedings of the Fifth University Faculty for Life Conference, June 1995 at Marquette University,* ed. Joseph W. Koterski, S.J. (Washington, D.C.: University Faculty for Life, 1996) pp. 177-90; Susan M. Stanford-Rue, *Will I Cry Tomorrow? Healing Post-Abortion Trauma* (Grand Rapids: Fleming H. Revell [Baker], 1990 [1986]); Wanda Franz and David Reardon, "Differential Impact of Abortion on Adolescents and Adults," in *Life and Learning: Proceedings of the Second University Faculty for Life Conference,* ed. Joseph Koterski, S.J. (Washington, DC: University Faculty for Life, 1993) pp. 60-70, with good bibliography; David C. Reardon, *Aborted Women: Silent No More* (Westchester: Crossway Books [Good News Publishers]/Chicago: Loyola Univ. Press, 1987); Michael T. Mannion, *Abortion and Healing: A Cry to be Whole,* 2nd ed. (Kansas City: Sheed and Ward, 1986); *Post Abortion Aftermath,* ed. Michael Mannion (Kansas City: Sheed and Ward, 1994), papers at international conference of post-abortion

experts convened by James Cardinal Hickey in Washington, D.C.; Linda Cochrane, *Women in Ramah: A Post-Abortion Bible Study Group* (self-published for the PACE program by Christian Action Council Education and Ministries Fund, Falls Church, Va., 1987); Ken Freeman, *Healing the Hurts of Abortion* (self-published: Last Harvest Ministries, Inc., 2734 W. Kingsley Road, Garland, TX 75041, telephone 972-840-3553); The Elliot Institute, *The Post Abortion Review* (Spring 1993-); Jeanette Vought, *Post Abortion Trauma: Nine Steps to Recovery* (Grand Rapids: Zondervan, 1991); Terry Selby, *The Mourning After: Help for the Post-Abortion Syndrome* (Grand Rapids: Baker, 1990); John J. Dillon, *A Path to Hope: For Parents of Aborted Children and Those Who Minister to Them* (Mineola: Resurrection, 1990); Douglas R. Crawford and Michael T. Mannion, *Psycho-Spiritual Healing after Abortion* (Kansas City: Sheed and Ward, 1989).

2. The name and address are: *Raphael (God Heals) of North Texas,* 3704 Myrtle Springs Rd., Fort Worth, TX 76116, telephone: 817-738-1086. The phases of the Raphael program are five: (1) Application, (2) Silent Spiritual Retreat, (3) Group Counseling, (4) Celebration of Mass of Christian Burial for children who die without baptism, (5) Days of Recollection.

3. Healing Vision international conferences are held annually in middle or late June at Marquette University in Milwaukee. This year's "Healing Vision XI" took place from Saturday to Monday, June 21-23, 1997, with a day-long pre-conference introductory workshop primarily for helping professionals and clergy unfamiliar with post-abortion aftermath and healing on Friday, June 20. "Healing Vision XII" is scheduled for Friday to Sunday, June 26-28, 1998. These conferences are sponsored by The National Office of Post-Abortion Reconciliation and Healing (NOPARH), P.O. Box 07477, Milwaukee, WI 53207-0477, business telephone: 414-483-4141, referral line: 800-5WE-CARE, Fax: 414-483-7376, Email: noparh@juno.com, Web site: www.mu.edu/dept/comm/rachels.

4. As a classic among many translations, see Louis J. Puhl, S.J., *The Spiritual Exercises of St. Ignatius* (Chicago: Loyola Univ. Press, 1951) #23, "First Principle and Foundation."

5. *Pace* some theologians, theories of the so-called "fundamental option" have not eliminated the practical truth and usefulness of this distinction. To deny the common usefulness of this distinction between mortal and venial sin can have consequences that border on implying that the vast majority of human beings are moral cripples incapable of either serious sin or genuine sanctity and love of God and others. Cf. Pope John Paul II, *Veritatis Splendor (The Splendor of Truth;* St. Paul Books and Media, 1993) #65-70; Pope John Paul II, *Reconciliatio et Paenitentia (On Reconciliation and Penance in the Mission of the Church Today;*

St. Paul Editions, 1984) #17. See also the recent summary in *Catechism of the Catholic Church* (Libreria Editrice Vaticana [several US publishers], 1994) #1854-64, #1874-76, "The Gravity of Sin: Mortal and Venial Sin."

6. Christian faith is not ultimately grounded in "abstract" doctrines, for these are themselves grounded in actual historical events and persons. To appreciate this faith, it makes sense to try to come to a deeper comprehension of the actual persons and events that have brought salvation. Cf. Aidan Nichols, *The Shape of Catholic Theology* (Collegeville: Liturgical Press, 1991) p. 79; Pontifical Biblical Commission, *The Interpretation of the Bible in the Church* (Boston: St. Paul Books and Media, 1993), esp. "Conclusion"; Ignace de la Potterie, "The spiritual sense of Scripture," *Communio: International Catholic Review* 23 (Winter 1996) 738-56, with special reference to Henri de Lubac's notions of spirit and history; and Henri de Lubac, *Catholicism: A Study of Dogma in Relation to the Corporate Destiny of Mankind,* trans. Lancelot C. Sheppard (New York: Longmans, Green and Co., 1950), chaps. 5-6.

7. Cf. John Paul II, *Evangelium Vitae* #84: "We are called to express wonder and gratitude for the gift of life and to welcome, savor and share the *Gospel of life* not only in our personal and community prayer, but above all in the *celebrations of the liturgical year*. Particularly important in this regard are the *Sacraments,* the efficacious signs of the presence and saving action of the Lord Jesus in Christian life. The Sacraments make us sharers in divine life and provide the spiritual strength necessary to experience life, suffering, and death in their fullest meaning. Thanks to a genuine rediscovery and a better appreciation of the significance of these rites, our liturgical celebrations, especially celebrations of the Sacraments, will be ever more capable of expressing the full truth about birth, life, suffering, and death, and will help us to live these moments as a participation in the Paschal Mystery of the Crucified and Risen Christ."

8. St. Ignatius, *Spiritual Exercises* #203.

9. See the powerful symbolism in John 19:25-27, where Jesus on the cross gives Mary as mother to his beloved disciple (which all Christians are invited to become).

10. Augustine, *Confessions* 1.1.

11. Cf. the helpful and very readable classic (of which there are many translations and editions), Brother Lawrence of the Resurrection, *The Practice of the Presence of God,* trans. John J. Delaney (New York: Doubleday Image Books, 1977).

FAITH, SUFFERING,
AND THE PROLIFE MOVEMENT

Sidney Callahan

MANY OF THE CURRENT ethical conflicts in the prolife movement turn on the question of suffering. Must one be a religious believer in order to see that some forms of suffering, whether in problem pregnancies or in death and dying are preferable to extinguishing human life? Can we convince our fellow citizens of moral truths by moral reasoning which is not based upon revelation? I think this effort at moral consensus can be successful but its success rests on confronting and arguing certain basic questions. Believers and nonbelievers must ask themselves: (1) Is Christian ethics distinctive? (2) Do Christians have a special and distinct ethical perspective on suffering? and (3) Can Christians and others share a perspective on morally necessary suffering?

IS CHRISTIAN ETHICS DISTINCTIVE?
If we hold with certain Christian ethicists that Christian believers must live by a morality and ethics completely distinct from nonbelievers and 'secular bioethics,' then a pluralistic society must remain divided on questions of abortion and death and dying.[1] Believers can hardly impose their morality and ethical attitudes toward suffering and dying upon others who do not share their faith commitments. Nor can they expect religious conversion. The best that the faithful can hope for is to segregate themselves from a secularized culture and concentrate on creating their own enclaves and exemplary religous institutions. At the very least believers who are facing problem pregnancies or are ill or dying in mainstream medical settings should be able to have access to care-givers and spiritual counselors who share the unique moral and ethical convictions.[2]

Christians who affirm that a great moral and ethical divide exists between those who stand beneath the cross of Christ and those who do not make claims of uniqueness because they view their morality and ethics as directly founded and uniquely shaped by Divine revelation in Scripture and the tradition of their Church. They may even go so far as to describe nonbelievers without their own faith-commitments as "moral strangers."[3] Since such believers have little hope of persuading their fellow citizens to adopt their moral and ethical convictions, they can only ask that a pluralistic society allow religious persons to follow their conscience and practise their faith in separate communities. Yes, believers can state their faith perspectives in the public square, but without much hope for reaching moral consensus and affecting public policy. The divide between believers and unbelievers will be seen as most unbridgeable when life and death issues are at stake; in these questions of humankind's ultimate destiny believers will affirm that it is crucial to take into account the fact that human beings will have a future with a Divine Creator beyond the limits of this life.

Happily, other Christian ethicists with whom I take my stand do not argue for a separatist strategy based upon unbridgeable ethical and moral divisions. Instead, the claim is made that in morality and ethics there can never be a conflict between what can be discerned and accepted by all persons of good will as authentically human and the Christian faith.[4] This humanistic view has been the position of many prominent Roman Catholic ethicists who further affirm that believers and unbelievers of good will can morally reason together to reach moral consensus on basic ethical requirements of society.[5] This hopeful affirmation of "integral humanism" rests on the belief that all human beings everywhere are created in the image of God and are endowed by God with reason and conscience. Even those who have never heard the Gospel good news can have God's moral law written in their hearts. Therefore there can never be any moral strangers; there may be evildoers but not strangers. Even Cain did not have his conscience destroyed nor did God allow him to be killed after his transgression. All humankind and every society, even those without explicit Christian faith-commitments, can possess the moral resources to seek and respond to the good and thereby accept essential moral truths.

Pope John Paul II voices this universality when he does not hesitate to address and instruct the whole world on disputed moral and ethical matters concerning life and death or justice and peace. While specific religious and Church obligations will be required only of those committed to faith in Christ and the Church, moral truths about good and evil can be known by all persons of good will through the gift of human reasoning; and universal moral truths impose moral obligations upon all competent persons and all societies. Statements of universal human rights, for instance, can justifiably be articulated by the United Nations and must be respected always and everywhere.

When such a universalist moral position, based upon an affirmation of the rational moral nature of humankind made in the image of God, is taken as a foundation for ethics, then it follows that Christians in American society should never withdraw from mainstream civic and ethical debate. Believers need never give up their hopes of rationally persuading others of basic moral truths. Whether it is a matter of war, welfare, sexuality, or any other challenging bioethical question of life and death, the claim is made that persons who share a common human nature can reach a moral consensus.

In an optimistic Christian approach to ethics, God's role as Creator of a good creation is emphasized as well as God's self-revelation in Scripture and unique saving action in the Incarnation. Christ's redemptive work is viewed as restoring the creation and fulfilling the original blessing.[6] As it was in the beginning, is now in the present, and ever shall be, God's Spirit moves the world, constantly urging human hearts and minds Godward. In Christ the Author of creation becomes Incarnate as a human being, Divine and one of us, and through the Spirit initiates the final birthing of the new creation.[7] Truth, love, and justice are one; truth is great and will prevail. These faith-assumptions about God, the creation, and the goodness of rational human nature lead to beliefs that, despite setbacks and regressions, all of humankind can hope for moral progress in history. After all, while evil behavior still exists, no one today would morally defend the institution of slavery, witch trials, genocide, or torture of heretics.

The acknowledgment of dynamic historical processes of change within the world and also within the Church is an important new insight in Roman Catholic moral theology recognized since the Second Vatican Council. Change is no longer considered to be "synonomous with dissolution." As moral theologian John Mahoney, S.J. puts it in a chapter devoted to patterns in church renewal, "There cannot be any doubt that the Roman Catholic Church's teaching over the centuries and in recent decades has changed markedly in many respects...."[8] In Mahoney's assessment the process of reform in moral theology has been marked by an openness to new forms of social science such as anthropology and psychology, a drive to totality (especially interpersonal totality), a recognition of diversity and pluralism, and a recovery of mystery. When God is known as the God of love, then moral theology like all theology is an effort to make sense of divine reality. Human experience constantly questions the mystery of God and the meaning of the world.

Of course, when one focuses upon the mystery of God's love for the world, a believer must also confront the mysterious presence and power of evil. The woundedness and fallen, flawed condition of the world challenges the affirmation of a good creation filled with good human beings made in the image of God. Can moral progress really be affirmed? What of the terrible outbreaks of depravity and atrocities witnessed in our own century? It is the presence of so much cruelty and horror in history which convince Christian pessimists and separatists that human beings suffer from pervasive depravity. And with the power of sin over humankind acknowledged, they deduce that Christian ethics must be distinct from worldly wisdom. In the face of so much moral rejection of God and the good, so much deviousness in the innermost uses of the mind, moral truths can only be trusted that come from within the unique community created by God's unique revelation in the Word.

Pessimists doubt the power of human reasoning to discover truth and can also question the universality of moral striving for good conscience. They focus upon the negative evidence of human self-deception, selfishness, greed, lust, anger, cruelty and general sinfulness. Surely, they conclude, one can only take refuge in the new, unique, and saving effects of Christ's Incarnation as lived in the community of the Church as the body of Christ; only here can you find the final criteria of moral insight and truth. The role of Christian faith must be accorded its unique power to transform the mind and heart which will then "see" truths of morality. After all, even traditionally optimistic Catholic moral theology claims that human reason must be informed by faith. If persons without faith can through moral reasoning arrive at central moral and ethical truths, then what role is left for the Incarnation, for Divine revelation, for Scripture, for Church teaching?

My answer to this ancient tendency to doubt human rational capacities, to separate faith and reason, to oppose Jerusalem and Athens, is to affirm once again that the core *content* of ethical and moral truths always can be agreed upon by all competent persons of good will. Yet at the same time we can acknowledge that there can be some differences between Christians and others in the *ways* or *processes* which Christians use to go about the discovery and practice of moral truths. Ideally there should be a unique character to the lifestyle of Christians.[9] Moral discernment engaged in by Christians will employ more inclusive and extensive processes of truth seeking than unbelievers use in their search.

Christians who believe that the God of ethics is the God they worship in church will use their reasoning powers to reflect on their own experience and on the findings of secular inquiries. But at the same time they will seek moral insight through experiences of prayer, Scripture, liturgy, their Church's teaching tradition, and the study of theology. The range of human experience they will take into account will include their own and others' religious experiences of faith and revelation. The reasoned journey toward moral and ethical truth is thereby "informed by faith" because attention is explicitly focused upon God's Truth and Goodness as revealed within the faith. For instance, while all persons of good will can reasonably reach an understanding of the moral truth embodied in the golden rule, this command to treat others as one would wish to be treated has also been revealed in Scripture as God's word. A Christian believer, then, can have a double foundation for core moral and ethical insights into truths, one from reasoning about common human experience and one from focusing upon and reflecting upon God's revelation. And since the ground of both foundations is God, there can be no ultimate conflict.

By attending to revelation, Christians have often been the first to use reason to articulate moral insights which later become accepted as universal moral truths. Listening to the good news, Christians turned the world upside down when they affirmed the equality of all persons male and female, Jew and Greek, slave and free as members of one family. Today equal respect for all persons is the cornerstone of our ethics and concepts of justice. Unfortunately it must also be admitted that there have been instances when Christian communities have been blind or denied universal moral truths articulated by secular thinkers, or even occasionally, moral truths that once were part of an earlier Christian tradition but later became forgotten or ignored. A Church of sinners must be ever reforming, and moral progress in and out of the Church is not without its temporary regressions. Having learned humility, today's Christians can recognize that since the Spirit of God is always at work in the world inspiring other seekers of truth, the Church must read the signs of the times in order to benefit from other sources of truth in science and secular knowledge as well as in other religious communities.

Because of the double foundation of their moral insights and moral commitments, Christians may also speak in secular society with more assurance when they affirm the essential moral truths that they share with others. Perhaps a parable will help here. All human beings on earth find themselves taking part in an engrossing drama in which the plot-line seems unclear. But Christians in the play believe in a benevolent Author of the play who has even come to join the cast. And the good news brought from the Author to the participants in the drama is that the plot will move toward a superb finale with a triumphant happy ending; all will be well. In the meantime all members of the cast must struggle and help one another to construct and play their parts as well as they can—no matter how many more acts there will be.

When called upon to make decisions about challenging new problems, believers will join with their fellows in reasoned moral reflection using all common sources of knowledge. But Christians within their communities will also focus upon Christ the Word, through whom the universe is made, as a concrete norm and fulfillment of the moral life. As Hans Urs von Balthasar expresses this principle of moral guidance, Christ is both personal and universal, "This norm, therefore, embraces all men in their different ethical situations and unites all persons (with their uniqueness and freedom) in his Person. As the Holy Spirit of Freedom it also hovers over all men in order to bring them to the kingdom of the Father."[10]

As the fulfillment of creation, Christ assures humankind of God's presence and investment in human life. Christians do not have to wonder why to be moral. They are assured that God is on the side of morality; there is a reality to the universal call of conscience to pursue good and avoid evil. Our reasoning powers have not been given to us in vain. A sense of love and trust in God inspires and strengthens the rational moral quest. Reason is informed by faith, but faith in the Word as Logos makes us believe in reason and reasoning. Faith confirms reason and helps us trust in the moral meaningfulness of meaning and moral truth. God is the explanation of explanation who has given us the gift of reason in a wonder-filled good creation. Our experience with experience has been good. God grounds all moral seeking. Such a faith inspires moral reasoning and hope that we can cope with new challenges and reach moral consensus.

With the above foundation of integral humanism, it is possible to seek a moral consensus on the challenge of suffering. Here I will focus in particular on the ethical questions arising at the end of life.

WHAT IS A MORALLY GOOD APPROACH TO SUFFERING?

Developments in medicine and medical technology have produced new moral dilemmas and ethical complexities in decisions about the beginning and the end of life. Yet the very old question of suffering remains a part of the recent deliberations and conflicts over dying and a good death. What is the nature and meaning of suffering and what is an adequate response to it? Many in our society now claim that much suffering can be avoided by instituting and approving the practices of physician assisted suicide and euthanasia.[11] A traditional (and the currently held Roman Catholic) position is that it is morally wrong to approve of self-determined death or any form of mercy-killing for those who suffer. If this moral affirmation is valid and true, then it should be seen as the most authentically human position by all rational persons of good will. Christians should be able to mount convincing arguments that persuade the rest of society. I think that in order to succeed in this project of persuasion, believers first need to explore and articulate a more fully adequate perspective on suffering.

To try and articulate a Christian understanding of human suffering is a monumental task because many Christians, like the Jews before them, have struggled over the problem of the existence of human suffering in a world created and sustained by a good, loving, and omnipotent God. Indeed, all reflective human beings in every culture and in every religious tradition have had to confront the insistent and primordial challenge of the meaning of pain, suffering, and death.

Several points seem central to an adequate approach to suffering, for human suffering is a complex multidimensional phenomena. First, there can be suffering that comes from freely choosing wrongdoing and sin; this suffering is seen as incurring blame because it is voluntarily inflicted upon one's self.[12] Bad things happen to bad people. These bad things may include a host of physical losses as well as negative psychological experiences of guilt, shame, anger, self-contempt, disgust, sorrow, and remorse. In many cases suffering from negative emotions of self-blame may encourage repentance and reform. These instances have given rise to the ancient concept of suffering as leading to purification and moral growth.

The idea that suffering can lead to the growth of a better moral character has appeared in Jewish and Christian scriptures under the rubric of God's disciplining of His beloved children and chosen people. To accept this interpretation of suffering, however, you have to accede to the idea that God actively and directly visits suffering upon human beings. This idea is very similar to the idea that God intentionally sends suffering to test the innocent, as in the story of Job. Just as God is seen directly to send suffering to punish wrongdoers, so God disciplines and tests those whom He loves best. Today most theologians recoil at the view of a Loving God who would directly inflict suffering upon humankind.[13]

The explanation of suffering as directly sent by God appears to ignore secondary causes in the world and the independent integrity of creation. I think that theologians make more sense who affirm that the bad things that cause human suffering occur in our world as a consequence of the working out of the freely operating secondary causes of God's creation. Suffering that naturally arises from a human being's choosing evil is not ascribed to God's direct actions. Nor are acts of nature that inflict disasters upon persons to be viewed as sent by God to purify, test, or punish people. Evil in the world may be permitted but not actively inflicted by God. In other words God's omnipotence is somehow limited in our temporal world in order to give freely acting human beings in an independent creation the potentiality to develop and shape a new creation.

Unfortunately, no one can deny that human beings use their freedom to inflict suffering of all kinds upon other innocent victims. When the innocent suffer undeservedly, or disproportionately, blaming them is inappropriate. Blaming the victim may be a temptation, but lament is the only appropriate response when bad things happen to good people.[14] Other forms of innocent suffering are also found in our world. This misery does not arise from an individual's direct intention to inflict harm upon another individual or group. Today we understand that oppressive social structures and bureaucratic institutions can be built up over time and take on a life of their own, larger by far than any individual. These entrenched powers and institutions, such as forms of racial discrimination, caste systems, wars, or massive forces of poverty, can harm individuals caught up in the system. Some have described these unjust structural evils as "social sin."[15] Perhaps today we could see the forces that encourage abortion or the structures that work against the use of palliative medicine as entrenched structural evils.

Beyond social sin and large systemic forces there can be other suffering arising from random occurrences of disease, plague, drought, floods, earthquakes, volcanic eruptions, and genetic mutations and malfunctions. Here again no individual wrongdoer is to blame for the harm done to human life. These natural occurrences of suffering must also be responded to with lament rather than blame. We do not blame volcanos or viruses for the devastation they produce, nor do we blame the victims of these disasters. Among the natural processes which cause great suffering I would include the impairments of aging, illness, and dying. Everyone (good, bad, or in between) will eventually die. Becoming ill and impaired and dying is built into the human organism. Even when pain is absent or controlled by the good gifts of medicine, dying is almost always an occasion of suffering. A self-conscious person, even one who believes that they will rise again, must suffer loss. In dying there is an inevitable decline and loss of one's physical capacities to help others; usually there is also a sense of loss in leaving the world and those who remain behind. Then too the losses and grief of those one is leaving can become one's own.

Christian believers have always seen the jaws of death as the dread punishment of sin from which all have needed redemption; it is the ultimate affront to a living being created in the image of the living God to enjoy eternal life. We are made for life, love, and joy in the company of our beloved ones. Jesus joined his friends in their grief over the death of Lazarus, even though he would raise him again to life. Suffering is a natural and appropriate response to death, decline, and the losses that accompany dying.

Considering the reality of death's losses, I think it misguided to speak of "a good death" or "a natural death." What we mean is that some process of dying is a less awful process where there is no blame and less lament. Suffering may be lessened in certain deaths, but I do not think it can ever be removed. Perhaps to make this point more clearly we must delve more deeply into what suffering means.

There can be a distinction between experiences of pain and suffering, although pain usually produces suffering. This distinction is made by the physician Eric Cassell in his work on suffering. He say that "suffering can be defined as the state of severe distress associated with events that threaten the intactness of a person."[16] This definition means that sometimes pain will not be felt as suffering because it does not threaten the intactness of the self. For instance, pain accompanying superior athletic performance or pain felt in certain forms of medical therapies might not be experienced as suffering but as a welcome signal of success in the effort towards a desired goal. All too often, however, pain does attack and threaten the sense of personal integration and intactness, especially severe unremitting pain, or worse, pain inflicted as deliberate torture by hostile human beings.[17]

But there are also other dimensions of suffering. There can be vicarious empathetic suffering where one suffers for and with another's pain, sorrow, loss, or experiences of threat to their intactness as a person. Also important in the distress of suffering is the deep sense that such experiences of suffering should not be happening in a good world. Surely a Christian affirmation regarding suffering is that suffering may be undeserved and a mark of deep disorder in the world. This truth is several times made by Christ in the Gospel accounts. No one sinned and caused the blindness of the man born blind. The good and the innocent may experience undeserved suffering. Undeserved suffering is demonstrated by Christ's own suffering and death on the cross.

The Roman Catholic theologian Schillebeeckx has spoken of suffering as a "contrast experience."[18]   Suffering affronts us as being basically horrible because of its contrast with our experiences of life's goodness, joy, justice, and loving kindness.   Because of our human experiences of goodness, justice, love, and joy in a good world, we expect good things and become distressed by our experiences of pain, frustration, and the grievous wrongs and unjust inequalities oppressing human beings. The more we can be aware or conscious of the good that could be, the worse it is when we suffer. Therefore human beings with their developed and expanded awareness of self and others can suffer more than animals. The more experience of joy, goodness, and justice that one has known, the more one may suffer the contrasting condition.

Those who love others will vicariously suffer their sorrows as well. If it is true that those with the greatest experiences of joy and goodness and the greatest love for others will suffer more, then Christians can conclude that Christ on the cross suffered more intensely than any other human being. He as the sinless one who loved others most fully and absolutely also had the greatest experiences of joy and goodness in his intimacy with God to contrast with the experience of sin and disorder. Jesus would be a man of sorrows because he could suffer so intensely his own and other's distress. For Jesus there would be the greatest of contrasts, and therefore the greatest of sufferings in his experience of undeserved rejection, betrayal, disappointment, persecution, torture, and the pain of a shameful death on a cross between criminals. Yet Christians affirm that within and through this suffering of defeat and death on the cross, Christ wins for us the ultimate victory over death and the power of evil. The triumph of Christ's resurrection leads to the joy and triumph of the Kingdom now and to come.

But how is Christ's resurrection after suffering on the cross related to our suffering? While Christians have always looked upon our human suffering in the light of the Cross, the meaning of this relationship and the question of redemptive suffering has been interpreted differently. What do we make of the fact that human beings still suffer and die? Too often in the past there has been in Christianity what M. Shawn Copeland, a Black woman theologian, has called a "vulgar misuse" of the cross.[19] By this she means that the suffering of the poor, the enslaved, and those who are oppressed has been too much tolerated and dismissed. Sufferers have been seen as privileged to participate in the suffering of Christ and thereby gain salvation in the next world.

Following this logic, those who suffer unjust oppression, or any other illness or pain, have been counseled to be resigned, passive, and patient, to accept without question their share in the suffering of Christ. Those who suffer in this world should seek comfort in the opiate thought of their redemption in the next world, or pie in the sky when you die. Such advice to sufferers serves to co-opt the cross and human suffering; it can only confirm apathy and a detachment from the imperative to change this world. Such interpretations of Christian suffering excuse and thereby further the unjust *status quo* of a fallen and oppressed world. The poor you have with you always.

Yes, but in the total message of Christianity a different mandate is given: Love others, show mercy, relieve suffering, and eradicate injustice. Christians can never forget that Christ spent his life actively relieving physical and psychological suffering as he preached the kingdom, healed mental and physiological ills, raised the dead, and comforted the brokenhearted. He tenderly loved and relieved the suffering of fallen human beings and commanded his disciples to imitate his own works of love and mercy. Nor is apathy toward the *status quo* approved in the Gospel, because the new order of God's kingdom must come on earth. The active nonviolent stance of forgiving and turning the other cheek, along with the paradoxical twists of so many of Christ's parables are today interpreted as challenging the *status quo* and the powers that be.[20] Today Christ's revolutionary view of God's world as entailing a loving and healing ministry can hardly be used to counsel resignation in the face of pain and suffering. Love of neighbor means relief of his suffering.

But what of unavoidable suffering which we cannot relieve? We still must age, become ill, and die even if the sting of death is removed by a belief in the entrance into a new life with God. We may be like Christ in praying that the cup of suffering will pass from us, but unfortunately it does not. Christ's victory over death and his restoration and redemption of all creation does not keep us from pain. Ultimate despair and hopelessness is overcome by our faith that the victory of the Kingdom is already won, but we still live in an interim time of not yet. Much work remains to be done before the birthpangs of the new creation's childbirth is completely accomplished and every tear is wiped away. While we wait in joyful hope for the marriage of the lamb and the consummation of the Kingdom's coming, the final gladness has not yet come in its fullness.

In addition to unavoidable suffering, there can also be suffering which might be avoided but is freely inflicted upon others. Evil persons and oppressive unjust structures continue to do harm to persons. While Christians must struggle against these powers, they cannot do so violently or by doing evil themselves. Christ's disciples are enjoined to love God and neighbor and to do no evil. In following Christ his disciples must be ready to suffer for the sake of doing good and helping the kingdom to come. Christians must be prepared like their master for persecutions and other sacrifices that come upon them because they choose to obey God's will. Taking up one's cross will be necessary for all followers of God. Losing the old self in order to do God's work can exact a price. St.Paul speaks of disciples filling up the sufferings of Christ as they carry out the work of loving and redeeming the world.

An important Christian belief appears to be that suffering, even unjust dreadful lamentable suffering, can be used in the struggle for the new creation. Christ promised that his disciples would do greater work than he, even as they take up their cross to follow him. This union of effort and sharing in the work of love and creation can only be the case if all humankind is bound together into one body, one communion, one family. The crucial belief here is that the whole human race must be seen as interconnected with each member joined to all the others. The sense that the human species is one family and joined in a unity that transcends space and time is implicit in the Christian message that as all fall in Adam, so all are saved in Christ's redeeming act. Thus in the Kingdom the good actions and prayers and offerings of any one person affects many others. The life and death of each of us affects all. The belief in the communion of saints and the intercessions of the saints is a development of these beliefs in the intercommunion and uniting of effort possible to human beings.

In sum, for Christians part of the good news is that individual suffering need never be wasted. Time and space can be transcended so that suffering borne and offered up for the good of those not even present is seen to be effective in the work of redeeming the creation. Every kind of suffering can be offered as a part of the collective effort to bring a new creation to birth. Even blameworthy suffering can be offered up in repentance along with the more direct suffering that arises from loving others and doing good but painful actions for the sake of others. Even following the Christian mandate to relieve suffering may entail its own kinds of morally necessary sacrifice. Public witness and struggles for justice in the world almost always bring persecution from those with power and privilege who do not wish the *status quo* to change. As the old cynical saying has it, no good deed goes unpunished.

Some suffering, therefore, must (like Christ's) not be sought but be freely accepted, undertaken, and endured in order to do good, love others, and avoid evil. The more power at a person's disposal, the more temptation there can be to avoid suffering and the sacrifices necessary for loving others. When certain kinds of suffering are refused, harm can be done to the self, harm can be done to others directly, and harm can be done to the common good. The common good includes all the community, members of a family, a neighborhood, a society, a culture, or an ecological community. Increasingly, individual acts are recognized, just as many small effects, even microevents in a system change the course of the whole larger process. The "butterfly effect" that can operate to change physical systems of weather have their counterparts in the moral and psychosocial realm.

Christians therefore have to make prudential acts of judgment when it comes to suffering. Relieving suffering is part of love's mandate, but some suffering must be endured, even if avoidable, for the sake of the good of others. Redemptive suffering is morally necessary suffering. How can one know when suffering is morally necessary and serving love and the common good? There may be many forms of redemptive suffering, but it may be difficult to discern them. Perhaps a first guiding principle to be proposed is that any suffering which, if we were to avoid it, would do significant harm to others must be endured and not avoided. Another mark of morally worthwhile suffering will be that the particular suffering accepted can be seen to serve the greater intactness of the self in the long run, usually by serving the good of others. If suffering is partly defined as a threat to the intactness of the self, there may be occasions when present suffering can be borne for the self's ultimate, whole, long-lasting well-being. Through love and empathy our well-being is intimately connected with the well-being of those we love; so we may choose avoidable threats and pain to our own self's integrity if it benefits the integrity of others. Redemptive morally necessary suffering can be discerned as that suffering which will be looked back upon as worthwhile and not regretted, because it increases one's history of loving and creating—even at times to one's store of ultimate joy. Integrity and wholeness of the person will be served by the enduring of the present pain, the present threat, even the present psychological anxiety and agony. When the child is born, any suffering in the birth process will be forgotten in the joy of producing a new life.

This guideline for morally necessary suffering implies that some dimension of the larger personal self can transcend intense suffering while at the same time experiencing the deepest distress. In a self-conscious being some witnessing "I" can stand apart and observe one's own suffering, even annihilation, and take up an ongoing stance to it—courageous acceptance, or enduring for the good of others, or in the cause of one's moral integrity. So in the history of humankind we have seen persons who have been willing to suffer, and grievously suffer, to avoid doing harm, to demonstrate their love of others, or to serve the common good. The joy in effecting their larger purpose and goal can co-exist with dreadful agony and distress. Joy and suffering may have different well-springs that may co-exist. We remember that the agonizing cry, "My God, My God why have you forsaken me," still calling upon God present in absence and followed by a more triumphant, "It is finished." A Trinitarian view of the mystery of God would also affirm that while "the cross is at the heart of things,"[21] and God suffers with us and for us, there co-exists some greater encompassing Divine reality existing as triumphant Love and Joy.

CAN A CHRISTIAN PERSPECTIVE ON SUFFERING AND REDEMPTIVE SUFFERING BE RATIONALLY ACCEPTED BY NON BELIEVERS?
I think that the essentials of the Christian faith perspective on suffering presented above can be rationally accepted as resonating with what can be recognized as morally and authentically human. Persons would first have to accept the new understandings of human reason that affirm that

reason includes more than just abstract logical thought processes. Emotional, imaginative, and social intelligence must be included as part of the moral resources of reasoning human beings as well as the ability to make deductive and inductive inferences about reality.

Surely then all moral persons can accept that human life cannot be lived without suffering in all of its many different dimensions. Unavoidable suffering is a characteristic of the human condition. It is clear too that much of the world's human suffering is blameworthy and also that much suffering is undeserved and an occasion for lament and sorrow. It is an unjust world and bad things happen to good people. I also think it makes moral sense to rational persons of good will that human beings are morally obligated to relieve human suffering. Following the golden rule or the categorical imperative or the moral principle of beneficence, persons of good will can come to accept that humans have a moral obligation to relieve each other's suffering, to heal, to reduce pain, and to make efforts to end injustice and oppression for all.

Rational persons of good will can also agree that we all belong to the human family and because of our common human membership, we owe each other care and concern for the common good and the moral well-being of the common social world we share. Communal consciousness and the sense of the human community as one family has been furthered by the environmental movement and increasing globalization. Moral concerns and ethical mandates have become evermore recognized as central to our common human flourishing in interconnected systems of influence.

I think it also rationally clear that in order to do no harm and to further good, it is necessary for those committed to the good to endure some suffering and even to behave in ways that will incur suffering that might otherwise be avoidable. For individuals to develop morally and for human communities to flourish in justice, moral persons have to be willing to suffer to maintain their moral integrity and the good of their families and communities. And the behavior of each individual will have an effect on many others.

In sum, in an imperfect world, full of evil human acts, oppressive social structures, and destructive natural forces, human suffering is inevitable. Suffering has many dimensions but we are morally obligated to relieve suffering and to try to counter and prevent blameworthy suffering that occurs from evil actions. We must also attempt to mitigate suffering that arises from unjust social structures, illnesses, and natural disasters. At the same time in order to do no harm, to refrain from killing, and to pursue the common good and the greater integrity of the moral self, human beings must sometimes courageously endure morally necessary suffering.

The success of the prolife movement will be dependent upon how well we can apply these truths about suffering and the interdependent human condition to questions of killing in abortion, assisted suicide, and euthanasia. If we in the prolife movement make every effort to prevent and relieve unnecessary suffering of women, children, the ill, and the dying, our insights about the need for morally necessary suffering can be persuasive—eventually. As a believer I trust humankind's moral resources of reason and conscience to effect moral progress. If it is morally true that human beings should not relieve suffering by killing the unborn or those suffering at the end of life, then it will be eventually be recognized to be true by all those of good will. After moral reflection, reasoned dialogue, and argument within our society, believers and unbelievers can hope to reach a moral consensus on the ethics of life and death.

NOTES

1. For a statement of this position see H. Tristram Engelhardt, Jr., "Suffering, Meaning, and Bioethics" in *Suffering: Christian Bioethics: Non-Ecumenical Studies in Medical Morality* 2 (1996) pp. 129-53; see also Stanley Hauerwas, *God, Medicine, and Suffering* (Grand Rapids: Eerdmans, 1990), esp. ch.2, "Theology, Theodicy, and Medicine,"pp. 39-95.

2. Engelhardt, section 4: "The Non-Ecumenical Alternative: Religion Has to Do with the Truth about Suffering," pp. 137-43.

3. Engelhardt, p. 143.

4. Joseph Fuchs, S.J., "Is There a Specifically Christian Morality?" in *Readings in Moral Theology No.2: The Distinctiveness of Christian Ethics*, ed. Charles E. Curran and Richard A. McCormick, S.J., pp. 3-19. A nuanced discussion of the history and state of the question which essentially agrees with Fuchs but also

elaborates upon his position can also be seen in the same volume in Charles Curran, "Is There a Catholic/Christian Ethic?" pp. 60-76.

5. Fuchs quotes Thomas Aquinas in support of his point, p. 11.

6. See David Burrell, C.S.C., and Elena Malits, C.S.C., *Original Peace: Restoring God's Creation* (Mahwah: Paulist Press, 1997).

7. *Ibid.* See also Elizabeth A. Johnson, C.S.J., "Does God Play Dice? Divine Providence and Chance," *Theological Studies* 57/1 (1996) pp. 3-18; and Catherine Mowry LaCugna, *God For Us: The Trinity and Christian Life* (San Francisco: Harper, 1991).

8. John Mahoney, S.J., *The Making of Moral Theology: A Study of the Roman Catholic Tradition* (Oxford: Clarendon Press, 1987) p. 325.

9. James M. Gustafson, "Can Ethics Be Christian? Some Conclusions" in Curran and McCormick, pp. 146-55. In the same volume see Richard A. McCormick, S.J., "Does Religious Faith Add to Ethical Perception?" pp. 156-73.

10. Hans Urs von Balthasar, "Nine Theses in Christian Ethics" in Curran and McCormick, p. 193.

11. See Daniel Callahan, *The Troubled Dream of Life: Living with Mortality* (New York: Simon and Schuster, 1993).

12. Paul Ricoeur, "Evil, a Challenge to Philosophy and Theology" in *Figuring the Sacred: Religion, Narrative, and Imagination* (Minneapolis: Augsburg Fortress, 1995).

13. Again, see the discussion in Johnson (n.7 above). The same point against a punitive view of suffering can be found in John Paul II's work on suffering. See John F. Crosby, "The Teaching of John Paul II on the Christian Meaning of Suffering" in *Christian Bioethics*, pp. 154-71.

14. See Ricoeur (n.12 above).

15. Roger Haight, "The Social Dimension of Sin" in "Sin and Grace" in *Systematic Theology: Roman Catholic Perspectives*, vol. 2, ed. Frances Schussler Fiorenza and John P. Galvin (Minneapolis: Augsburg Fortress, 1991) pp. 101-06. See also Walter Wink, *Engaging the Powers: Discernment and Resistance in a World of Domination* (Minneapolis: Augsburg Fortress, 1992).

16. Eric J. Cassell, *The Nature of Suffering and the Goals of Medicine* (New York: Oxford Univ. Press, 1991) p. 33. See also the emphasis upon suffering as "the experience of finitude" in Daniel P. Sulmasy, O.F.M., M.D., *The Healer's*

Calling, esp. ch. 6, "Suffering, Spirituality, and Health Care," pp. 93-108.

17. Elaine Scarry, *The Body in Pain* (New York: Oxford Univ. Press).

18. Edward Schillebeeckx, *Church: The Human Story of God* (New York: Crossroad, 1990).

19. M. Shawn Copeland, "Wading through Many Sorrows" in *Feminist Ethics and the Catholic Moral Tradition*, ed. Charles E. Curran, Margaret A. Farley, and Richard A. McCormick, S.J. (Mahwah: Paulist Press) p. 156.

20. Walter Wink, "Jesus's Third Way: Nonviolent Engagement" in *Engaging the Powers: Discernment and Resistance in a World of Domination* (Minneapolis: Augsburg Fortress, 1992) pp. 175-93. See also James W. Douglass, *The Nonviolent Coming of God* (Maryknoll: Orbis, 1991).

21. Bruce G. Epperly and Robert L. Kinast, *Can Suffering Be Redemptive?* (Claremont: Process and Faith, 1995) p. 17.

COMPULSORY STERILIZATION, EUTHANASIA, AND PROPAGANDA: THE NAZI EXPERIENCE

Jay LaMonica

I. COMPULSORY STERILIZATION, 1933-1939

When Adolf Hitler took power in Germany, one of his top priorities was to purify the race and to build the genetically pure Aryan man. It was an objective he had discussed in his early manifesto, *Mein Kampf.* One of the first major laws passed by the Nazi regime in 1934 was the forced sterilization program of those with hereditary illnesses. This program was intended to develop eventually into a full-scale program of euthanasia for those judged "unworthy of life," especially the mentally and physically disabled. To prepare public opinion in greater Germany, a systematic and widespread propaganda campaign was put into effect to provide the scientific and political rationale for these proposals and to build support among the public at large.

The Nazi propaganda program took advantage of a well-developed German film industry that was already being retooled as an instrument of the state in order to maintain and expand backing for the regime. The general pattern of slick, well-produced films utilized repetition of misleading and erroneous scientific information and statistics, coupled with powerful emotional images that confirmed pre-existing prejudices and stereotypes. These techniques were particularly effective when applied to the forced sterilization program and to the euthanasia program that would follow when public opinion was sufficiently prepared. These techniques were also used to inform and indoctrinate those personally involved in carrying out the initiatives and to help maintain their level of commitment.

The scientific and medical communities that would implement these programs were already well-disposed to accept their theoretical underpinnings. Eugenics was firmly established in both the United States and in Europe as a science that claimed to find mental and physical illness to be hereditary and considered certain undesirable anti-social behavior patterns as capable of being passed from one generation to the next. As early as 1920 Karl Binding, a legal specialist, and Alfred Hoche, a psychiatry professor, had published an influential book entitled *Permission for the Destruction of Unworthy Life*. Hoche in particular advocated the idea of an organic state that must amputate any useless or diseased limb in order to assure the survival of the body politic. A series of training films were produced to indoctrinate medical personnel. They were widely shown at medical conferences, and we have evidence of one that was viewed at a 1935 national meeting of the Nazi party.[1]

One early 16mm film *Erbkrank* ("The Hereditarily Ill" or "The Genetically Diseased"), variously dated as 1934 (U.S. National Archives) or 1936 (Bundesarchiv, Koblenz) was presented as an educational documentary by the NSDAP, the agency for racial affairs of the National Socialist Party. It begins by citing the influence of the "Jewish Liberal thinking" that led to a situation in which mentally ill and handicapped patients were being cared for in "palatial" sanatoriums by "the cream" of the medical profession, the best-educated, best-trained, and healthiest nurses and doctors. These idyllic scenes are intercut with contrasting scenes of average, hard-working German families living in abject poverty within over-crowded hovels, and the implication is that their situation is the result of the same misguided policies: "Healthy families are housed in sheds that are falling apart and in dark alleys, but for the insane... palaces have been built." This was a particularly telling argument for the average German worker, impoverished during the terrible economic times of the Weimar Republic.

The film argues that the hereditarily ill become guilty only when they transfer their illness to their offspring. These genetic diseases come from the parents, who may not show any visible signs of it. Jews and Blacks, in particular, are considered to be common carriers of these defective genes and to make up an especially large proportion of the mentally ill population. The only solution is to stop transmission, and it is the duty of the state to do this. Anything else is dereliction of duty on the part of the government. The problem is presented in Darwinian terms: only the healthy will succeed in the new state and become "good Nazis" capable of building the Thousand Year Reich.

Statistics are presented which show the number of mentally ill as having increased by 450% in the previous 70 years while the total population has grown 50%. This information is used to support a projection that within fifty years there will be one mentally ill person for every four healthy people.

Part two of the film *Erbkrank* begins with the portrayal of an idiot "Nigger Bastard" from the Rhine Valley. Mental as well as physical traits, it claims, are inherited and will continue to be inherited. Although silent, the film carefully reinforces the economic burden of the mentally ill and the compounding of this problem over generations by the repeated use of slates in between film clips detailing the health-care costs in ridiculously precise numbers. These slates show how much each person or family is costing the state up to that point and then projects how much caring for them will cost over the course of their lives. For example, "This mother and son, together in institutions, so far has cost 29,016 reichsmarks."

One statistic shows the cost of the upkeep of these mental institutions at 1.2 billion reichsmarks, while the administration of all local and national government costs only 713 million marks. The amount spent to keep one "life-unworthy retard," born out of wedlock in an asylum, for 22 years "could have helped 40 poor families with many children to start a settlement." The idea that these people were an economic drain on the state is not just an exaggeration; it is probably not true at all, for patient-labor is believed to have made most asylums self-sufficient.

The film also charges that "due to the ignoring of natural law and a false view of Christianity, even the worst criminals were not punished but rather kept in an institution if there was any sign of mental deficiency." The film purports to demonstrate how criminal tendencies are hereditary, one of the more extreme claims of eugenics. It also shows a close correlation between illness and criminal behavior.

Erbkrank concludes with the question: "May we burden our future generations with such an inheritance?" The answer is obvious, a new moral imperative: "The prevention of hereditary illness is a moral law. It means practical love of your neighbor and utmost respect for God-given natural laws."

This was all by way of criminalizing and dehumanizing handicapped people with the ultimate object of ridding society of them. The first step was to sterilize, with or without consent, those identified as carriers of bad genes. In 1936 a "talkie" (or sound-film) entitled *Opfer der Vergangenheit* ("Victims of the Past") was made at Hitler's command for mass consumption, co-produced by the NSDAP and the Reich Propaganda Ministry. It enjoyed a mandatory showing in all German theaters after March 1937. It is the first film (part documentary, part drama) for general audiences that addressed the prevention of a new generation of the hereditarily ill through the sterilization of the mentally ill.

Opfer der Vergangenheit again plays on the costs associated with keeping mentally ill or horribly cripped "useless eaters" in "palaces with beautiful gardens" where their criminal tendencies and misery can be passed on to future generations. The Darwinian imperative and the moral obligation to redress past failings are spelled out in the commentary: "Life is a fight for existence. Only the strong will in the long run succeed. All the weak will perish. In the last few decades mankind has sinned. We have not simply preserved unworthy life. We have allowed it to breed. The reproduction of unworthy life is to be prevented by law."

According to the film, the law of natural selection has been misunderstood (and thus violated) to the detriment of society. Such high-quality and expensive care is given to the sick in mental institutions that they reach old age—"this life-span costs the nation thousands." Images of deformed and crippled patients are accompanied by a narrator's voice saying: "All of this suffering could have been avoided if one had simply hindered the further spread of these hereditary sicknesses. The protection against the spread of hereditary illness is a customary command. It basically equals the highest respect for God-given rules of nature."

The film takes the line that it was "ethically required" to feed and care for these people and to keep them from injuring themselves. "But," it says, "we also gave them the capacity to pass on their suffering to their children.... If we restore the important law of selection, we then restore the success of those very laws given us by our Creator." And who is to be the instrument of God's will? Who will restore the natural order and preserve the sacred gene-pool of the Aryan race? The hero of this drama, filmed for viewing by average German citizens, is a highly educated and respected leader of the community: "the physician, who thereby becomes the protector of the people and of hereditary health."

The movie shows its star, the doctor, meeting with a woman who is to be married in order to determine her fiancé's genetic suitability. He tells her that he has come in a new role, not as healer but as consultant, as a trusted guide to the new science, as one who can be told all the family secrets. "The man from yesterday" is portrayed as one ignorant of the scientific advances now available to enrich and protect the race by assuring healthy and productive children. Without specifying the exact deficiency, the doctor explains that the fiancé's case "is always becoming more and more complicated." He warns that "we will hinder your reproduction—such sad cases should no longer live among our healthy children. Sterilization is a heroic approach." He then repeats the statistics on how the number of mentally ill has grown and will eventually destroy the race. "The new law," the doctor concludes, "is not man meddling in God's work, but rather the restoration of laws of nature that humanity has succeeded in breaking."

Other 16mm films like *Das Erbe* ("The Inheritance") hammer home the theme that the weak perish and the strong survive according to the natural law and God's order. Through footage of stag beetles battling and plants fighting for survival, the point is made that "we all live in a battle in which the weak are eliminated." Once again this wisdom is imparted by a doctor, a scientist who studies the natural world where war and survival are the rule. Techniques of horse and dog breeding are explained, with the implication that they can be applied to racial breeding.

The example of an American family called the Kallikaks, a staple of the Nazi propaganda films supporting sterilization, is trotted out to demonstrate how bad genes and illnesses can be widely distributed through otherwise healthy families, bringing misery in their wake. Another often repeated image appearing in the background is a dictum attributed to Adolf Hitler: "He who is not healthy and able, both physically and mentally, may not immortalize his body in that of his child."

Another influential film from the late 1930's, *Was Du Ererbt* ("What you have inherited") set out to demolish the liberal idea that environment could influence physical and mental capabilities. It stressed the correctness of eugenics: "Despite favorable environmental conditions, inferior inherited traits or dispositions cannot be gotten rid of." The film begins thus: "The power and purity of the race are granted only once. Once they decay they can never be regenerated." In this way the importance of protecting against inferior blood is stressed and the history of great cultures that perished because of such mixing is reviewed. Scapegoats are designated: "In order to assure the decay of our race, the Jew preached the glorification of prostitution. Dilapidation, downfall, and agony were the results." In a chilling harbinger of policies to come, reference is made to the "130,000 people vegetating in asylums, ruined in mind and body."

Ultimately, thousands were sterilized and many died during the procedure. By the late 1930's Hitler turned his attention to putting into effect a policy of euthanasia, the mercy-killing of "life unworthy of life." He hoped that several years of sustained propaganda had prepared both the public and the scientific and medical communities to see euthanasia as a logical and reasonable follow-up to the forced sterilization project.

II. EUTHANASIA, THE T-4 PROGRAM, 1939-1945

Hitler understood from the start that the concept of systematically murdering thousands of handicapped German citizens would be controversial and contentious within German society. The Gestapo's vast system of informants provided him with a highly accurate version of public opinion polling, broken down by age, occupation, and religion. The sterilization program had been generally supported by the populace, who came to accept the racial, scientific, and economic arguments that were used to justify it. But the euthanasia program called for a more cautious treatment. Early indoctrination films on supporting sterilization had effectively stigmatized and criminalized the mentally ill and disabled. But these films had also promised that the living ill would be taken care of—only their procreation would be stopped: "The hereditarily sick are innocent of what they inherited from their parents. They will receive the best care until the end" (from *Victims of the Past*).

There is evidence that in 1933 Hitler spoke to Hans Lammers, the chief of the Reich Chancellory about killing the mentally ill. He seems to have been well aware of the political difficulties such a program would face. Professor Karl Brandt, an eminent doctor who would become a key figure in the euthanasia project, quotes a senior doctor as saying that Hitler told him in 1935 that "If war should break out, he would take up the euthanasia question and implement it.... The public resistance which one could expect from the churches would not play such a prominent role amidst the events of wartime as it otherwise would."[2]

In 1939, shortly after the invasion of Poland, Hitler was true to his pledge. He quietly authorized Brandt, his personal physician, and others to begin the murder of the disabled and mentally ill, both adults and children. The project was run from a villa at #4 Tiergartenstrasse in Berlin, hence the name T-4. The primary justifications and themes of the T-4 program were:

1) Racial purity based on scientific eugenics in order to purify the gene-pool and to build a stronger master race by killing off defective genes.

2) Economic efficiency: to save money by cutting excess welfare costs (a big political issue even under the liberal Weimar Republic).

3) Compassion: both the disabled and society would be better off; also, bed space would be freed up for the anticipated casualties of the war.

The project succeeded in at least the last of these objectives. Some 70,000 asylum inmates were killed in a relatively short time, from late 1939 to August 1941. As many as 200,000 may have been killed overall.[3]

The need to develop an efficient, cost-effective means of mass-murder presented something of a challenge. Train crashes were staged, explosives were set off in bunkers filled with Russian psychiatric patients, and so on, but all these initiatives were found wanting in one way or another. The Nazis finally hit on carbon monoxide gas-poisoning, using rooms outfitted with fake shower heads. An efficient transport system was organized, with regional holding asylums channeling patients to six large, relatively remote castles that were converted to the first killing centers.

Hartheim Castle, the center for Austria, was a site where more than 18,000 mentally ill and handicapped people were killed. It proved so effective that several thousand prisoners from a nearby concentration camp were also gassed there. Now it is a residential complex, except for the fake shower room which was recently made into a memorial. Ironically, a brand new state asylum is just across the street, replacing the one whose wards were emptied under the T-4 program.

It was a very well-organized system. In Hartheim they kept elaborate graphs and flow-charts, now known as the Hartheim statistics, in order to show how much money, coffee, bread, and so on would be saved through the projected end of the war in 1951.

Later there was a direct technology-transfer to the mass death camps in Eastern Poland, where Jews were found to have the ultimate disability. Ninety-two key doctors were transferred to make use of the expertise gained in the T-4 program, where all killing was done by doctors. Simon Wiesenthal, the famed Nazi hunter, suggested in an interview with this author that the T-4 program was deliberately overstaffed in order to provide training for the hard-core personnel, mostly doctors, who would help with the scaled-up, much larger gas chambers used in the Jewish holocaust.

The T-4 program needed to identify potential victims, particularly children with mental or physical defects. The Nazis introduced payments to doctors and midwives who notified the authorities about such patients. For deciding which people to kill, there was an intricate centralized system of review by doctors and psychiatrists in order to maintain a veneer of scientific and medical legitimacy. These reviewers never saw the patient but were paid on a piecework basis for each case considered. Thus there was an incentive to go through as many as possible, and one doctor processed some 15,000 in one month.

It is important to remember that no doctor was coerced into participation. They were given time to think it over, and there is no evidence of any sanctions being applied to the few doctors who refused to get involved. The theories that justified the program were generally accepted by the medical community. This was, after all, a society very concerned with race and purity of ancestry, so there was great psychological shame associated with having defective children. Every time someone came up for a job or promotion, a racial taint would come up. There was a 1925 study by an asylum director, showing that many families wanted their insane relatives killed. They just did not want to know about it—they did not want to be part of the decision. They thought it should be done covertly, so that they could simply be told that their child had died—precisely what happened fifteen years later.

Hitler had originally intended for this to be a public program with wide public support, building on his successful propaganda campaign for sterilization. He drafted a law that would legalize the euthanasia program. But the outcry from those whose Christian beliefs and values were offended, mainly Catholic and Protestant Churches, caused him to table the draft legislation. An influential bishop, Clemens von Galen, delivered an impassioned sermon in August 1941, condemning the program from the pulpit of the Lambertkirche. The sermon made the rounds of the diocesan churches as a pastoral message.

Shortly afterwards Hitler ordered the program discontinued. The killing continued, however, on a less formal, decentralized basis and in a more covert fashion, primarily directed against children, since most adult asylum inmates were already dead. The quiet killing of children was particularly sensitive, and so it was carried out by the use of slow overdoses or starvation rather than by mass gassing.

Throughout this period the Nazi propaganda machine was called upon to bolster public support for the euthanasia project and to deflect opposition from organized religion. A popular feature film called *I Accuse* was released in 1940 to support the idea of euthanasia. A woman with multiple sclerosis asks her husband, a doctor, to kill her, and he does so to the accompaniment of another doctor mournfully playing a piano in the next room. It was a huge release—nearly 20 million saw it in wide distribution across greater Germany.

Other films were not intended for public distribution. They took as their audience the staffs of the euthanasia centers. There was a continuing need to indoctrinate the perpetrators of the slaughter in its proper conduct and execution. Most of these films were destroyed by the Nazis before the end of the War. Some of the original raw footage was mislabeled and sat undiscovered in the basement of the East German Archives in Potsdam until 1990 when British scholar Michael Burleigh stumbled across it. The scripts were also found, and they indicate that footage had been shot through a porthole of the early gas chambers while people were actually being gassed and that this footage was intended to be included in the finished films. Although this particular footage has never been recovered, there is some evidence that these films were shown to various audiences, such as the families of T-4 personnel, in order to test their reaction. But the films were never widely released.

An examination of the eight surviving rolls of raw footage for one such film, *Dasein Ohne Leben* ("Existence without Life"), reveals many of the themes established in the earlier propaganda campaign. Images of horribly crippled and deformed patients, babies without arms or legs, an insane inmate banging his head against the wall, animal-like screaming, and so on predominate, along with pictures of healthy, well-trained caregivers feeding and tending their helpless charges.

CONCLUSION

The Nazi propaganda effort in support of forced sterilization and euthanasia was in many ways a classic campaign to win public acceptance and understanding of a controversial policy. It was built on accepted scientific theories current at the time and took them to their logical conclusion. The triumph of eugenics and social Darwinism provided the scientific footing to justify many actions that would otherwise have been reprehensible. The propaganda also provided a moral sanction for these activities by claiming to restore God's order to Christian Germany, an order that was upset by the advent of liberal Jewish doctrine. This was a theme that the Nazis used to great effect.

The message also appealed to base self-interest, stressing the benefits to each individual as well as the greater good of society. Reducing the economic burden of the handicapped while compassionately putting them out of their misery and purifying the race for the coming age of German domination was appealing in many ways. It provided a quiet way for relatives of the handicapped to be relieved of their shameful burden without suffering public reprobation; in fact, they were given to believe that the general interest was served by the disappearance of such people.

It is interesting to note that Hitler was ultimately swayed from carrying out his full euthanasia program because of public opposition, particularly from the religious community. He had to be satisfied with a secret, illegal program rather than the formally approved institutionalized project which he had hoped for. In the final analysis, the propaganda campaign was unable to overcome the moral revulsion of the German people to the killing of the disabled and the mentally ill.

NOTES

1. See Hugh Gregory Gallagher, "'Slapping Up Spastics': The Persistence of Social Attitudes toward People with Disabilities" in *Issues in Law and Medicine* 10/4 (1995) at p. 407.

2. Michael Burleigh, *Death and Deliverance: Euthanasia in Germany, 1900-1945* (Cambridge Univ. Press, 1994) p. 97. I am deeply indebted to Burleigh's book throughout this paper. See also Robert Jay Lifton, *The Nazi Doctors: Medical Killing and the Pathology of Genocide* (New York: Basic Books, 1986).

3. Burleigh, p. 4.

ABORTION AND THE NUREMBERG PROSECUTORS: A DEEPER ANALYSIS

John Hunt

FROM LATE 1945 TO LATE 1946, twenty-one leading Nazis were tried at Nuremberg by an international tribunal made up of American, British, French, and Soviet judges. From late 1946 to the spring of 1949, 185 lesser-known Nazis were tried before American military tribunals. The American military, in the American zone of occupation, held twelve trials before six different military tribunals, with three American judges on each tribunal. The RuSHA[1] or Greifelt Case was No. 8 (of 12), Military Tribunal No.1 (of 6). There were fourteen defendants in the RuSHA or Greifelt Case: Heinrich Himmler's deputy Ulrich Greifelt, after whom the case was alternately named, also Otto Hofmann, the second head of RuSHA, Richard Hildebrandt, the third head of RuSHA, and eleven others. There were some two dozen charges made in this trial, and abortion was one of them. On four different occasions I have given a paper on this trial before scholarly bodies, focusing on the subject of abortion.[2]

What exactly was the nature of the Nuremberg Military Tribunal's condemnation of abortion at this trial? The Tribunal had stated: "The acts and conduct, as set forth in this Judgment, and as substantially charged in the indictment ["encouraging and compelling abortions"] constitute crimes against humanity... and... war crimes."[3]

In my paper I maintained that, according to this judgment, *all* abortions were condemned by the Tribunal as war crimes and crimes against humanity.[4] It was my interpretation of the word "encouraging" in the indictment, but I felt uneasy at my interpretation. I decided then to contact the people who were actually involved in the Nuremberg prosecutions.

The prosecutor who drew up the indictment at the RuSHA Case, James McHaney, died in April 1995 after a long, incapacitating illness, and I never had a chance to speak to him. But I was able to get some input from other former Nuremberg prosecutors for their comments on my interpretation. I sent copies of my paper to sixteen surviving Nuremberg prosecutors. With each manuscript I also sent a questionnaire which had the following three questions:

1) Would you give a biography of yourself?
2) Would you briefly state your role at the Nuremberg Trials?
3) Realizing that you were probably not part of the RuSHA (Greifelt) Case, after having read the enclosed manuscript, do you agree with the prosecutor's arguments and the Tribunal's Judgments in that case concerning abortion?

Of the sixteen individuals to whom I sent manuscripts and forms, ten replied, but two of them stated that they were unfamiliar with RuSHA and thus had no opinion. This left eight who did have opinions, and their replies forced me to give the abortion-Nazism-Nuremberg story a deeper analysis.

WHAT THE FORMER PROSECUTORS SAID ABOUT CONDEMNATION OF ABORTION AT NUREMBERG

Five of the former prosecutors first expressed interest in this paper with comments such as:

- "It presented a great deal of information of which I was previously ignorant."[5]
- "...the RuSHA manuscript is scholarly and objective and contributes a great deal toward understanding the problem of abortion under the Nazis."[6]
- "I found your research article most interesting."[7]
- "Congratulations on your project!"[8]
- "Interesting."[9]

It is nice to know that the paper was respectable in their eyes because all eight of the former prosecutors disagreed with my conclusion that all abortions were condemned at Nuremberg. They stated that abortions were condemned by the tribunals because they were done for genocidal reasons, because they were forced, or both.

Two of the respondents stated that Nazi abortion was wrong only because it was used for racial reasons in Hitler's genocidal plan:

- "...as part of a war effort or as a policy imposed on a conquered territory, I think abortion is a crime against humanity."[10]

- "...the purpose and reason for the abortion was ethnic and racial, and no one could justify that kind of motivation."[11]

Three others stated that the Nazi abortions were wrong only because they were forced or pressured:

- "I believe that the prosecutor stressed... forced abortions.... I believe a pregnant woman should have more to say about [a] possible abortion than any state, church, or male-dominated society."[12]
- "I always assumed that the findings of the Tribunal on abortion referred to involuntary abortion or pressure."[13]
- "I do not believe that the Nuremberg Tribunal ever considered abortion to be a crime against humanity unless the female was forced to submit to the operation, or was coerced to do so."[14]

Two of the eight prosecutors questioned stated that Nazi abortions were wrong for both reasons, racial-genocidal and forced-pressured, but no other:

- "I cannot accept the prosecutor's [James McHaney, the RuSHA Prosecutor] contention that even truly voluntary abortions were a war crime and crime against humanity.... Only when such abortions advanced the Nazi Genocidal plan.... I might be willing to hold those Nazis guilty because, for them, the woman's true consent was an incidental rather than a significant element in the execution of the genocidal plan."[15]
- "I am in complete agreement that if abortion of pregnant women in the occupied territories... was coerced by the Nazi Government *as part of its overall policy of genocide*... such acts constituted both war crimes and crimes against humanity.... The 'encouragement' of abortion was in fact another form of coercion by the Nazi Government and was not a truly voluntary decision [*sic*] by the affected woman, such 'encouragement' can be equated with forced abortions."[16]

Finally, one of the former prosecutors was ambiguous on the question:

- "...the manuscript cannot avoid the ambiguities in the prosecutor's case and in the Judgment on the question.... I have always had some difficulty in following all the arguments of the prosecution and the finding of the Court. [Your] manuscript raises the same questions."[17]

We all have biases and desires about what we would like to see. I should also note, however, the admitted biases in four of the prosecutors:

- "You may not see any difference but my position is that I have no right to dictate moral behavior to anyone. I am personally against abortion, as are our four daughters. They, like myself, arrived at that position by their own free will."[18]

- "I do not regard a fetus as a human being before birth but only as a potential human being.... I do not like abortion as a birth control method; at the same time, medically supervised abortions are preferable to back-alley butcheries.... I also recognize that others may strongly disagree with my views."[19]

- "The Nuremberg Trials should have concentrated more on the problems of women and specific wrongs done to women."[20]

- "I personally disagree with those who believe abortion is a crime *per se*. In my view, whether to abort a pregnancy is a personal and not a political or governmental matter. To equate abortion with murder and illegitimize the procedure would, in my view, penalize the poor and encourage the return to back-alley medical butcheries. I am currently an open-minded, skeptical, secular humanist member in good standing of our local Unitarian Church."[21]

To recapitulate, the eight respondents, some with their own biases (as we all have), thus state that the RuSHA Trial condemned the Nazi use of abortion for one of two reasons or both:

1) Only because the abortions were done for racial-genocidal reasons.
2) Only because the abortions were forced or pressured.

A DEEPER ANALYSIS OF THE RuSHA CASE

In answering these two points made by the respondents, I will look at some old evidence in a new way and present some new evidence. I will then draw a conclusion.

Point One: Nazi abortions were wrong only because they were done for racial-genocidal reasons. Four of the eight respondents stated this.[22]

When I first approached this subject not too long ago, this was also my own initial conclusion about what the Military Tribunals condemned in the RuSHA Case. On reflection, however, I began to look at the trial in a new way by focusing hard on the indictment, something I had not done before. Under "Crimes Against Humanity" is the statement which, upon quick reading, seems to uphold the conclusion that the Tribunal condemned abortion because of racial-genocidal reasons:

The object of the program [RuSHA] was to strengthen the German nation and the so-called "Aryan" race at the expense of such other nations and groups... by the extermination of "undesirable" social elements. This program was carried out in part by... (b) encouraging and compelling abortions on Eastern workers for the purposes of preserving their working capacity as slave labor and of weakening Eastern nations.[23]

Mentioned also, however, were:

(a) Kidnapping the children of foreign nationals in order to select for Germanization those who were considered of "racial value."
(c) Taking away, for the purposes of extermination or Germanization, infants from Eastern workers in Germany.[24]

Kidnapping children and forcefully taking infants from their parents are always wrong! They do not become wrong only when done for racial-genocidal reasons. The indictment of encouraging and compelling abortions, therefore, must be understood in this light. It is quite possible that the prosecutor thought abortion *per se* was wrong, just like kidnapping and the ferreting away of newborns are wrong.

Point Two: Nazi abortions were wrong only because they were pressured and forced. Five of the eight respondents stated this.[25] The Tribunals found "encouraging and compelling" abortions, as charged in the indictment, to be crimes against humanity as well as war crimes.[26] Almost everyone today is against compelling (forcing) abortion. The problem in the indictment and subsequent judgment by the Tribunal, however, concerns the word "encouraging" (*Förderung* in German). Did it mean pressure? If it did, this is close to force. Did it have a broader meaning? Did it mean, in other words, promoting abortions as something positive or progressive? If so, then abortion *per se* was condemned.

The dictionary defines "encouraging" as "to stimulate, ...in a bad sense, to abet, hound on."[27] Thus the dictionary, on the one hand, seems to indicate that "encouraging" can mean *pressure*, so that the Tribunal's judgment on the indictment of "encouraging and compelling" can read as "pressuring and forcing," which is the conclusion of five of the Nuremberg prosecutors. The dictionary also defines "encouraging" as "to allow or promote the continuance or development of."[28] Thus the dictionary, on the other hand, seems to indicate that "encouraging" can mean *condoning*, so that the Tribunal's judgment on the indictment of "encouraging and compelling" could read as "condoning and forcing." The German word used in the indictment was *Förderung*,[29] which can mean the furthering or hastening (pressuring) or promoting or supporting (condoning).[30] Hence, semantics gives us a mixed message.

At this point we should look at the old evidence again, but now with a more penetrating eye. James McHaney, the RuSHA prosecutor at Nuremberg, the one who drew up the indictment "encouraging and compelling," possibly revealed the intention of the indictment in his closing statement when he said:

> Assuming that the abortions performed upon approval of [RuSHA] were made upon request, it is obvious that under the Nazi system of terror the pregnant women had no other choice but to request abortion.
>
> Even under the assumption that her request was *genuinely voluntary*, it constitutes a crime under Section 218, German Penal Code. *At the same time it constitutes a war crime and a crime against humanity* [emphasis mine].[31]

I believe that a fair appraisal of what McHaney said here in the first paragraph is that the Nazis were guilty of pressuring and forcing abortions and of doing so for racial-genocidal reasons, the two points made by the former Nuremberg prosecutors. In the second paragraph, however, he is saying that the practice itself is also wrong, whether it is voluntary or forced, and for whatever the reason. Hence, I think that the word "encouraging" in the indictment, drawn up by Prosecutor McHaney, and the subsequent Judgment of the Tribunal, has a *double meaning*. It means force and pressure, and it also means condoning and promoting.

There is also some new evidence which I have not previously presented, namely, a letter sent to me by Telford Taylor, who was in charge of all twelve American Military Tribunals from 1946 to 1949 and who is the author of the 1992 best-seller, *The Anatomy of the Nuremberg Trials*.[32] He said: "Dear Professor Hunt: I read your paper with pleasure, and general agreement.... I would be interested to see the ultimate result."[33] While not a ringing endorsement, it is still some indication that he thought my conclusions to be correct.

Our story is not over, however. One prosecutor told me: "I know Jim McHaney quite well. I doubt that he would oppose voluntary abortion and deem it a crime were he still alive."[34] McHaney's son expressed similar sentiments to me, describing his father as a moderate, with no particular church affiliation.[35] McHaney's obituary and accounts of his life describe a man who was an ecologist (chief counsel to the Arkansas Department of Pollution Control and Ecology for over twenty years)[36] and who drafted legislation allowing mixed alcoholic drinks to be served in Arkansas, hardly the activities of a staunch conservative.[37]

Despite all of this, however, McHaney said what he said, and it is part of the Nuremberg record. In addition, if one takes a hard look at the trial testimony again, there are indications that more than women's liberties and privacy were being violated:

SS General Richard Hildebrandt: "Up to now nobody had the idea to see the interruption of [any] pregnancy as *crime against humanity*" [emphasis mine].[38]

We also have indications that Prosecutor McHaney, in the trial testimony, considered the unborn as human beings subject to the protection of the law:

McHaney: "But protection of the law was denied to *unborn children* [emphasis mine] of the Russian and Polish women in Nazi Germany. Abortions were encouraged and even forced on these women."[39]

Finally, again referring to the summation, McHaney made clear allusions to lives being taken when there is an abortion: "The performance of abortions on Eastern [female] workers is also a crime against humanity.... It constitutes an 'act of extermination' ...and an 'inhumane act'."[40] James

McHaney, the prosecutor who drew up the indictment and who conducted the trial, was condemning a form of killing as well as condemning the coercion of women.

CONCLUSION

The Nazis performed abortions through RuSHA for two reasons:

1) *To keep women available as slave labor.* These abortions were forced and pressured and, most certainly, they compromised women's liberty and deeply violated their privacy.

2) *To slow down Eastern (Slavic) reproduction.* Here we see that the Nazis saw abortion as an act of killing. They would, so to speak, nip a life in the bud.

Nuremberg, I believe, condemned both the violations of liberty and the violations of life as far as abortion was concerned. Like the kidnapping of children and the seizing of newborns, also prosecuted at this trial, abortions were seen as wrong at any time, not just when done for racial-genocidal reasons.

In 1948, the very year the Nazis were convicted in the RuSHA Case and abortionists were being convicted in the United States,[41] the World Medical Association formulated the Declaration of Geneva, or Geneva Code. This was in deliberate reaction to the Nazi experience and was intended to modernize the Hippocratic Oath. It stated: "I [the physician] solemnly pledge to consecrate my life to the service of humanity.... I will maintain the utmost respect for life from the time of *its conception*" [emphasis mine].[42] Ironically, a quote from the letter of one of the former Nuremberg prosecutors to me can best summarize this paper: "I believe you are correct in pointing out the immense change in American public opinion regarding voluntary abortion during the last half century."[43]

Appendix: the Nuremberg Prosecutors

Those who held abortions wrong because done for racial-genocidal reasons:

Fenstermacher, Theodore. Chief prosecutor in the "Hostage" or "Southeast" Case against two Field Marshals and ten high-ranking generals.

Johnson, Esther Jane. Assistant in the prosecution of the SS Trial and assistant to James McHaney, who later prosecuted the RuSHA Case.

Those who held abortions wrong because pressured and forced:

Harris, Whitney. Presented the case against Ernst Kaltenbrunner, Gestapo Head, at the first (international) trial.

Rockler, Walter J. Prosecuted German bankers in the last (12th) trial, "The Economic Ministries."

Sprecher, Drexel A. Director of the I.G.Farben Trial Team and editor-in-chief of *Trials of War Criminals before the Nuremberg Military Tribunals* (15 volumes of the 12 trials held by the Americans in their zone of occupation).

Those who held abortions wrong for both reasons:

Caming, H. W. William. Prosecutor of members of the German Foreign Office and other governmental ministers of the Nazi Regime.

Meltzer, Bernard D.   The Edward H. Levi Distinguished Professor Emeritus of Law, University of Chicago. Presented the case against Walter Funk, Reich Economics Minister, at the first (international) trial.

Ambivalent position:

King, Robert D. Prosecuted the "Justice Case" against sixteen judges and lawyers of the Nazi Regime.

NOTES

1. RuSHA is a German acronym for *Rasse und Siedlungshauptamt* (Race and Resettlement Office).

2. "Victims Without Names: Abortion and the Nuremberg Trials," Fifth Annual Conference on the Holocaust, Hebrew University, Jerusalem, Israel (Dec. 29-31, 1996); "Nuremberg Revisited: Abortion as a Human Rights Issue," The Fourteenth Annual Conference on the Holocaust (Auschwitz and Modernity), Millersville University, Millersville, Pa. (April 9-10, 1995); The New England Historical Association, Brown University, Providence, R.I. (Oct. 23, 1993); University Faculty for Life, Yale University, New Haven, Ct. (June 6, 1993). The first listed above was a longer version with different title than the other three.

3. *Trials of War Criminals before the Nuremberg Military Tribunals, October 1946-April 1949*, Vols. IV-V, "The RuSHA Case" (Washington, D.C.: U.S. Gov't. Printing Office, 1949), V, 153, 160-61, 166. See also IV, 610, 613. Cited hereafter as TWC.

4. "Nuremberg Revisited: Abortion as a Human Rights Issue," *Life and Learning III: Proceedings of the Third University Faculty for Life Conference*, ed. Joseph W. Koterski, S.J. (Washington, D.C.: University Faculty for Life, 1993) pp. 258-59.

5. Letter from Theodore Fenstermacher to the author, August 2, 1996. Festermacher was chief prosecutor in the "Hostage" or "Southeast" Case against two Field Marshals and ten high-ranking generals.

6. Returned form from Robert D. King to the author, October 16, 1996. King prosecuted the "Justice Case" against sixteen judges and lawyers in the Nazi regime.

7. Returned form from Esther Jane Johnson to the author, August 26, 1996. Johnson assisted in the prosecution of the SS Trial. She assisted James McHaney, who later prosecuted the RuSHA Case.

8. Returned letter from Professor Whitney Harris to the author, July 1996. Harris presented the case against Kaltenbrunner, Gestapo head, in the first (international) trial.

9. Letter to the author from Bernard D. Meltzer, Edward H. Levi Distinguished Service Professor Emeritus of the University of Chicago, July 25, 1996. Meltzer presented the case against Walter Funk, Reich Economics Minister, at the first (international) trial.

10. Returned form from Esther Jane Johnson to the author, August 26, 1996.

11. Letter from Theodore Fenstermacher to the author, August 2, 1996.

12. Returned form from Walter J. Rockler to the author, August 1996. Rockler prosecuted German bankers in the last (12th) trial, "The Economic Ministries."

13. Letter from Drexel A. Sprecher to the author, August 25, 1996. Sprecher's record is outstanding, having directed the I. G. Farben Trial Team and having been the editor-in-chief of *Trials of War Criminals before the Nuremberg Military Tribunals* (15 volumes of the 12 trials held by the Americans in their zone of occupation), and many other posts.

14. Returned letter from Whitney Harris to the author, July 1996.

15. Letter from Bernard D. Meltzer, July 25, 1996.

16. Letter from H. W. William Caming to the author, October 15, 1996. Caming prosecuted members of the German Foreign Office and other governmental ministers of the Nazi Regime.

17. Returned form from Robert D. King to the author, October 16, 1996.

18. Letter from Robert D. King to the author, October 23, 1995. King returned a letter in October 1995 and a form in October 1996.

19. Returned form from Walter J. Rockler to the author, August 1996.

20. Statement of Drexel A. Sprecher to the author, October 16, 1995. I spoke to Mr. Sprecher at a conference called "Fifty Years after Nuremberg: Human Rights and the Law," held at the University of Connecticut, Storrs Campus. I am recalling his remarks from memory.

21. Letter from Theodore Fenstermacher to the author, August 2, 1996.

22. Caming, Fenstermacher, Johnson, and Meltzer.

23. TWC, IV, 609-10.

24. *Ibid.*

25. Caming, Harris, Meltzer, Rockler, and Sprecher.

26. TWC, V, 153, 160-61. See also IV, 610.

27. *Oxford English Dictionary*, 2nd ed. (Oxford: Clarendon, 1989) V, 216.

28. *Ibid.*

29. Records of the United States Nuremberg War Crimes Trials, *United States of America v. Greifelt et al.* (Case VIII), October 10, 1947-March 10, 1948; the National Archives, Washington, D.C., Record Group 238, Microfilm Publication (M) 8945, Roll ® 17, p. 5. Cited hereafter as NWCT. The above is the German version; references on NWCT below will be the English version.

30. *Cassell's German-English English-German Dictionary*, revised (New York: MacMillan, 1978) p. 226.

31. NWCT, M.894, R.31, pp. 13-14. See also pp. 37-42.

32. Telford Taylor, *The Anatomy of the Nuremberg Trials: A Personal Memoir* (New York: Alfred A. Knopf, 1992).

33. Letter from Telford Taylor to the author, June 21, 1993. I wrote to him for a deeper clarification of all this on November 7, 1996, but there was no reply, for he had had a brain tumor by this time.

34. Letter from Theodore Fenstermacher to the author, August 2, 1996.

35. Telephone conversation with son, James McHaney, Jr., June 6, 1996.

36. See *The Arkansas Democrat,* April 15, 1995, p. B6 and March 26, 1983, p. A9.

37. *Ibid.*, December 4, 1968, p. F1.

38. TWC, IV, 1090.

39. *Ibid.*, p. 1077.

40. NWCT, M.894, R.31., pp. 13-14. See also pp. 37-42.

41. *The New York Times*, November 15, 1947, p. 19; July 15, 1948, p. 24; July 16, 1948, p. 40.

42. Quoted in William Brennan, *The Abortion Holocaust: Today's Final Solution* (St. Louis: Landmark Press, 1983), pp. 137-38, 142.

43. Letter from Theodore Fenstermacher to the author, August 2, 1996.

PRINCIPLES OF AMERICAN LIFE:
AN ARCHAEOLOGY OF THE VIRUS OF
NEGATION OF INALIENABLE RIGHTS
AND ITS ANTIDOTE
IN AMERICAN LITERATURE

Jeff Koloze

I. INTRODUCTION

Like a viral infection, a powerful and vicious anti-life "strain" is evident in the national literature of the United States from colonial times to the present, fatal only to those human beings who have been legislatively or judicially removed from the definition of human personhood. Fortunately, however, while the United States has always been infected by an anti-life philosophy, there has also existed a pro-life "antidote" to this anti-life tendency.

Structurally, this paper consists of the two main features of the American dehumanization process: the first, how animal metaphors were used to devalue Native Americans and slaves; the second, the role that race played in the process. I will then illustrate how these two factors joined to permit an action whereby the United States came dangerously close to having Nazi-like death camps. Finally, I will discuss the role that the Declaration of Independence played in civil rights movements of the nineteenth and twentieth centuries.

II. NATIVE AMERICANS DEHUMANIZED AS "BEASTS"

To document the origin of the anti-life philosophy in the literature of the United States, we must begin with the archival evidence of the colonial period. Continuously, the colonists likened Native Americans to animals, not only because of the Native Americans' unique lifestyle, but also because it would be morally easier to possess as much of the new land as possible if the original inhabitants were not equal to the English. As

William Brennan documented in his *Dehumanizing the Vulnerable: When Word Games Take Lives*, "Removal of individuals from membership in the human community and re-classifying them as animals has the effect of consigning them to a lower level of existence where their victimization can be more easily rationalized."[1] The animal metaphor would become a constant factor in the American dehumanization process.

This colonial disregard of the humanity of Native Americans is best illustrated in the account of the killing and butchering of the most famous Native American leader of the time, Metacomet (called "King Philip" by the colonists). Metacomet orchestrated an uprising of the Wampanoag nation against British colonists in 1675. Benjamin Church's 1716 narrative of Metacomet's killing and eventual butchering was meant to delight the colonists, who would, of course, be overjoyed that such an enemy to their way of life had been killed.[2] Church's description of the killing is worth examining in detail:

Capt. *Church* ordered his body to be pull'd out of the mire on to the Upland, so some of Capt. *Churches Indians* took hold of him by his Stockings, and some by his small Breeches (being otherwise naked), and drew him thro' the Mud unto the Upland, and a doleful, great, naked, dirty beast, he look'd like. Capt. *Church* then said, *That for asmuch as he had caused many an English mans body to lye unburied and rot above ground, that not one of his bones should be buried.* And calling his old *Indian* Executioner, bid him behead and quarter him. Accordingly, he came with his Hatchet and stood over him, but before he struck he made a small Speech directing it to *Philip*; and said, *He had been a very great Man, and had made many a man afraid of him, but so big as he was he would now chop his Ass for him*; and so went to work, and did as he was ordered.[3]

Church's narrative continues, relating not only that Metacomet's head but also his "remarkable hand" were shown to those who would pay to see it.

This one passage contains within it several elements of the dehumanizing tendency which would repeat themselves in the following centuries. Metacomet is specifically dehumanized when he is equated with being a "beast." The string of adjectives further compounds the dehumanization. Not only is Metacomet a mere beast; he is a "dirty" beast. Since he had only the most essential clothing on, he is described as "naked" as an animal would be. The fact that he is described as "great" pertains not to his stature within Native American society, but to his dimensions and further adds to the glory of his death, much as a sportswoman might marvel at the size of a wild animal she has trapped. Finally, there would be no concern over the desecration of a corpse since the person whose body has been chopped to pieces has been likened to an animal. Note, too, that Church records a speech in which the body is synecdochically reduced to the name of one of the least esteemed parts.

Mary Rowlandson, a colonist whose captivity occurred during the war instigated by Metacomet, had this to say about her capture by the Native Americans: "I had often before this said, that if the Indians should come, I should choose rather to be killed by them than be taken alive but when it came to the trial my mind changed; their glittering weapons so daunted my spirit, that I chose rather to go along with those (as I may say) ravenous beasts, than that moment to end my days...."[4]

III. SLAVES DEHUMANIZED AS "CRITTERS," "SWARMS OF VAGRANTS," AND "LOCUSTS"

As Native Americans were dehumanized with animal imagery, so also were the nineteenth century's other victims of the anti-life philosophy, slaves. A century and a half after the animal metaphor was used to dehumanize the subjugated Native Americans in New England, a slave trader in Harriet Beecher Stowe's fictionalized account of slavery, *Uncle Tom's Cabin*, suggests to Mr. Shelby, the original owner of Tom, that black slaves can overcome the emotional trauma of losing the sale of their children because "these critters ain't like white folks."[5]

This fictional character may have been repeating a concept first clearly enunciated by one of the Founding Fathers of the nation. In writing his famous *Notes on the State of Virginia* Thomas Jefferson describes slaves not as human beings, but as though they are subjects for his scientific examination:

They secrete less by the kidneys, and more by the glands of the skin, which gives them a very strong and disagreeable odor.... They are more ardent after their female; but love seems with them to be more an eager desire, than a tender delicate mixture of sentiment and sensation.... In general, their existence appears to participate more of sensation than reflection. To this must be ascribed their disposition to sleep when abstracted from their diversions, and unemployed in labor. An animal whose body is at rest, and who does not reflect, must be disposed to sleep of course. Comparing them by their faculties of memory, reason, and imagination, it appears to me that in memory they are equal to the whites; in reason much inferior, as I think one could scarcely be found capable of tracing and comprehending the investigations of Euclid; and that in imagination they are dull, tasteless, and anomalous.... Religion, indeed, has produced a Phyllis Whately; but it could not produce a poet. The compositions published under her name are below the dignity of criticism.[6]

It is difficult to believe that the man who authored the famous clauses of the Declaration of Independence about the "inalienable rights" with which "all men are created equal" would have harbored such opinions about African American slaves. Not even Benjamin Banneker's remonstrance with Jefferson, urging him fully to implement the words of the Declaration, persuaded the future president to alter his views on slavery or the black race.[7]

To compound the animal imagery used to dehumanize slaves further, pro-slavery writer Albert Taylor Bledsoe does double damage to African American slaves, hinting at criminality as well as animality when he compares the slaves in Virginia to "a swarm of vagrants more destructive than the locusts of Egypt."[8]

The resolution of the question regarding the political status of slaves contributed to a civil war. Already we can see that the inalienable clause of the Declaration was used in the war of words which preceded the first gunfire.

IV. THE FACTOR OF "RACE" AS A DEHUMANIZING PRINCIPLE; OR
"WISE CHARITY," AMERICAN STYLE

The late nineteenth century United States saw burgeoning capitalism transform the nation into an economic powerhouse. It is at this time that a change in philosophy can be documented toward the care of the poor. Andrew Carnegie's 1889 essay "Wealth" became a foundational document for the new view of charity toward the poorer citizens. No longer would mere charity be a goal; "wise" was prefixed to the noun, thereby enabling Americans of the last decades of the nineteenth century to distinguish between assistance to the justifiably needy poor and wasted donations to an unmerited underclass. The poor were seen to lack four essential virtues to elevate themselves: courage, frugality, industry, and wise charity. Bizzell and Herzberg summarize the philosophy well in one complex sentence: "If getting rich was the result of virtue, poverty must be the result of vice."[9]

Carnegie's essay makes several references to the term "race" which, viewed neutrally, can mean only a given class of human beings. Viewed negatively, "race" assumes more its modern connotation of the superiority of one ethnic group over another. Carnegie is concerned with "the progress of the race," how "the race is benefitted," what "is best for the race," "essential for the future progress of the race," and he denigrates certain economic theories by stating "the race has tried that."[10]

We who are pro-life now know that the social Darwinism of the late nineteenth century contributed to the views of Margaret Sanger and others who thought that the economic lower classes, especially immigrants, were a different type of human being, almost subhuman. I believe that the demarcation created between the deserving and the undeserving poor assisted in the dehumanization process of the United States, a process which would lead ultimately to an internment of an entire ethnic group.

V. INTERNMENT OF JAPANESE ALIENS AND CITIZENS OF JAPANESE ANCESTRY: THE CONCENTRATION CAMPS OF THE UNITED STATES

Before the era of legalized killing which began in 1973, perhaps no other activity perpetrated by the United States government is more shameful than the incarceration of Japanese aliens and American citizens of Japanese ancestry during World War II.[11] As Nazi Germany had its concentration camps, so too did the United States herd over 110,000 of its own people for the ostensible purpose of neutralizing the "Jap" threat against the western states.[12] The forced removal of the Issei (the term used to designate the original Japanese immigrants) and the Nisei (the term to denote their children) occurred despite the fact that both major groups of human beings of Japanese heritage had proved themselves to be not only respectful citizens, but also persons who had made the areas in which they settled highly productive.

The concentration camps to which the Issei and Nisei were shuffled were comparable to those of Nazi Germany. First, advocates of the internment used words which mirrored Nazi ingenuity in distorting language. Mike Masaoka, leader of the Japanese American Citizens League during the internment, writes:

Sometime during the early part of February 1942, John H. Tolan, an obscure Democratic congressman from Oakland, California, announced formation of what was grandiosely called the Select Committee Investigating National Defense Migration.... As it turned out, its primary function was not to investigate "migration" but to provide a platform for those advocating the removal of Japanese Americans from the West Coast.[13]

Similarly, the United States government used a variety of Nazi-like euphemisms for the internment camps themselves. Michi Nishiura Weglyn, herself an internee whose work on the internment was one of the first written, provides several examples of this euphemistic language:

A theme widely exploited by U.S. propaganda channels, including the Army's own public relations setup, was that relocation centers were wartime "resettle-ment communities" and "havens of refuge," so it is little wonder that the public—and even those who ended up in them—were easily misled. Assembly center internees resentful of searchlights, machine-gun-manned watchtowers, and other repressive paraphernalia were generally reassured that it was all "a temporary measure," that their freedom would be largely restored to them after the move to civilian-controlled "permanent camps" in the hinterland.[14]

The very existence of the camps was based not on objective facts and verifiable military threats, but on logically-distorted suppositions and conjecture steeped in racist ideology. Prominent early twentieth-century racist Montaville Flowers wrote in his 1917 book, *The Japanese Conquest of American Opinion*: "Race mixture has been not only a fundamental cause of war, involving as it does internal convulsions and external complications, but the crossing of races has always resulted in a change of civilisation and lowering of the rank of higher civilisations."[15]

This racism is echoed in the military's justification for internment. One of the documents contained within the U.S. Department of War's *Final*

Report: Japanese Evacuation from the West Coast, 1942 asserts emphatically that: "The Japanese race is an enemy race and while many second and third generation Japanese born on United States soil, possessed of United States citizenship, have become 'Americanized,' the racial strains are undiluted."[16] To respond to any doubt about the need for internment of the Japanese beyond racial concerns, and, after analyzing the population patterns of Japanese immigrants, the Department suggested the following as further justification for the internment:

Such a distribution of the Japanese population appeared to manifest something more than coincidence. In any case, it was certainly evident that the Japanese population of the Pacific Coast was, as a whole, ideally situated with reference to points of strategic importance, to carry into execution a tremendous program of sabotage on a mass scale should any considerable number of them have been inclined to do so. [17]

The use of subjunctive constructions and ambiguous pronouns makes the justification for internment "certainly evident" that it was groundless.

Ultimately, on the command of Lieutenant General John L. DeWitt, the racist commanding officer of the Western Defense Command, with the approval of President Roosevelt, whose Executive Order 9066 authorized the internment, 110,000 human beings were herded into camps hastily built to accommodate the suspect race. Besides receiving approval from the Commander-in-Chief, and encountering little opposition, DeWitt's decision "was also supported by many citizens' groups, including the American Civil Liberties Union."[18]

The speed with which the Japanese were forced out of their homes and businesses is reminiscent of Nazi tactics to remove Jews from occupied countries: "The army moved people out of their homes with no more than a few days' notice, collected them in grimy 'assembly centers' at such places as fairgrounds and racetracks, and then shipped them by train to shabby 'relocation centers'—in reality detention camps—in desolate areas of California, Arizona, Utah, and other states."[19] Like their Jewish victims, once the Japanese internees were at the camps, they were identified not by their names but by an administrative numbering system. One survivor recalls that "Someone tied a numbered tag to my collar and to [my] duffel bag (each family was given a number, and that became our official designation until the camps were closed)."[20]

Of course, such deportation to concentration camps could have only come about after a dehumanization process had been well established. Threats of the "yellow peril" had been promoted by persons like Flowers for several decades before the internment. Perhaps more importantly as a step toward the internment, as one survivor stated, "You cannot deport 110,000 people unless you have stopped seeing individuals."[21]

VI. THE PRO-LIFE ANTIDOTE: THE USE OF THE DECLARATION
A. NINETEENTH-CENTURY DECLARATIONS

Although an anti-life tendency has afflicted American literature since colonial times, over the course of the nation's two centuries those who opposed the anti-life philosophy have advocated the inalienable rights to life, liberty, and the pursuit of happiness of all human beings by using a distinctively American contribution to the world's political literature, the "declaration." The purposes of a declaration are several: first, it is used to recount abuses of an oppressive power; second, it is used to argue for justice—political, economic, or other; finally, it is used as a device to liberate the oppressed group from the tyranny of the oppressor. Of course, Thomas Jefferson's "Declaration of Independence" became the model for future declarations for the oppressed within United States society.[22]

Although Jefferson is credited with writing the Declaration of Independence for the ostensible political purpose of justifying the American colonies' separation from British rule, other powerless individuals and groups used the declaration device as a means of stating their grievances against the government. Specifically, the listing of inalienable rights has been retained by a diverse number of oppressed groups and has been the foundation for their pressure for equal rights.

For example, one of the earliest abolitionist documents to rely on the listing of inalienable rights is William Lloyd Garrison's "Declaration of Sentiments of the American Anti-Slavery Convention" of December 6, 1833. Garrison's version appropriately capitalizes the most significant word for which abolitionists fought:

The corner-stone upon which [the signers of the Declaration] founded the Temple of Freedom was broadly this— "that all men are created equal; that they are endowed by their Creator with certain inalienable rights; that among these are life, LIBERTY, and the pursuit of happiness."[23]

Garrison was able to use accusatory as well as polite language when referring to the chasm between the ideals of the Declaration and the nation's slavery policy. A month before the American Anti-Slavery Society adopted its declaration, in a speech before the Great Anti-Colonization Meeting in London (November 9, 1833), Garrison used a long string of "I accuse" phrases in parallel to indict the United States: "I accuse her [the United States], before all the nations, of giving an open, deliberate and base denial to her boasted Declaration, that 'all men are created equal; and that they are endowed by their Creator with certain inalienable rights; that among these are life, liberty, and the pursuit of happiness'."[24]

Nineteen years later Frederick Douglass used the Declaration as the basis for his argument against slavery. In his 1852 essay "What to the Slave is the Fourth of July?" (one of the most famous in the "Fourth of July sermon" genre), Douglass sternly rebukes his listeners for permitting the intentional legal schizophrenia between a document which espouses that "all men are created equal" and a government which enslaves African Americans:

[The Fourth of July] is the birthday of your National Independence, and of your political freedom. This, to you, is what the Passover was to the emancipated people of God.... What have I, or those I represent, to do with your national independence? Are the great principles of political freedom and of natural justice, embodied in that Declaration of Independence, extended to us? ... What, to the American slave, is your 4th of July? I answer: a day that reveals to him, more than all other days in the year, the gross injustice and cruelty to which he is the constant victim. To him, your celebration is a sham; your boasted liberty, an unholy license; your national greatness, swelling vanity; your sounds of rejoicing are empty and heartless; your denunciations of tyrants, brass fronted impudence; your shouts of liberty and equality, hollow mockery; your prayers and hymns, your sermons and thanksgivings, with all your religious parade, and solemnity, are, to him, mere bombast, fraud, deception, impiety, and hypocrisy—a thin veil to cover up crimes which would disgrace a nation of savages. There is not a nation on the earth guilty of practices, more shocking and bloody, than are the people of these United States, at this very hour.[25]

I have extensively quoted from this speech to illustrate two elements in it: first, reliance on the Declaration of Independence; and, secondly, the use of second-person pronouns at crucial points for the purpose of making the speech sound as accusatory as possible. Such a fiery speech has validity for today: substitute "unborn child" for "slave" and the enumerated paradoxes and contradictions demonstrate that the ideals of the Declaration are still words in contention.[26]

As abolitionist demands increased, so too did demands for the other American slaves, women. Nineteenth-century feminists used the Declaration as a model for their "Declaration of Sentiments and Resolutions" at the 1848 Seneca Falls Convention. Its language would make the contemporary anti-life feminist uncomfortable, for, while it adds the word "women," it maintains the listing of inalienable rights: "We hold these truths to be self-evident: that all men and women are created equal; that they are endowed by their Creator with certain inalienable rights; that among these are life, liberty, and the pursuit of happiness...."[27]

Elizabeth Cady Stanton was not content to have the women merely proclaim their equality. Much as Douglass chastised his audience, when Stanton spoke before the Judiciary Committee of the New York State legislature in 1860, she combined ancient rhetorical accumulation of questions with the tripartite nature of the inalienable rights clause:

It is declared that every citizen has a right to life, liberty, and the pursuit of happiness. Can woman be said to have a right to life, if all means of self-protection are denied her—if, in case of life and death, she is not only denied the right of trial by a jury of her own peers, but has no voice in the choice of judge or juror, her consent has never been given to the criminal code by which she is judged? Can she be said to have a right to liberty, when another citizen may have the legal custody of her person; the right to shut her up and administer moderate chastisement; to decide when and how she shall live, and what are the necessary means for her support? Can any citizen be said to have a right to the pursuit of happiness, whose inalienable rights are denied; who is disenfranchised from all the privileges of citizenship; whose person is subject to the control and absolute will of another?[28]

In the late nineteenth century, the Declaration was often invoked tangentially to combat the growing divergence between rich and poor. In his 1894 *Wealth Against Commonwealth*, Henry Demarest Lloyd uses a phrase at the end of the Declaration to advance his case: "All follow self-interest to find that though they have created marvelous wealth it is not theirs. We pledge 'our lives, our fortunes, and our sacred honor' to establish the rule of the majority, and end by finding that the minority—a minority in morals, money, and men—are our masters whichever way we turn."[29]   Another writer opposed to the "Gospel of Wealth," Henry George, writing in his 1879 *Progress and Poverty,* used the explicit wording of the inalienable rights clause to argue against private owner-ship of land:

All men to her [Nature] stand upon an equal footing and have equal rights.... The laws of nature are the decrees of the Creator.... The equal right of all men to the use of land is as clear as their equal right to breathe the air—it is a right proclaimed by the fact of their existence. For we cannot suppose that some men have a right to be in this world and others no right. If we are all here by the equal permission of the Creator, we are all here with an equal title to the enjoyment of his bounty—with an equal right to the use of all that nature so impartially offers. This is a right which is natural and inalienable.... [He then proceeds in a footnote to blast Malthus's philosophy.] And so it has come to pass that the great republic of the modern world has adopted at the beginning of its career an institution that ruined the republics of antiquity; that a people who proclaim the inalienable rights of all men to life, liberty, and the pursuit of happiness have accepted without question a principle which, in denying the equal and inalienable right to the soil, finally denies the equal right to life and liberty; that a people who at the cost of a bloody war have abolished chattel slavery, yet permit slavery in a more widespread and dangerous form to take root.[30]

Toward the end of the nineteenth century, when capitalist oppression of workers reached fever pitch, the Workingmen's Party of Illinois responded with their own version of the Declaration, also titled "Declara-tion of Independence" (July 4, 1876). Although this declaration omits references to the divine source of rights, it specifically retains the pro-life language of the inalienable rights clause: "We hold these truths to be self-evident: that all men are created equal, that they are endowed with certain inalienable rights; that among these are life, liberty, and the full benefit of their labor."[31]

To summarize this section, what is most significant about nineteenth-century declarations is that the inalienable rights language is almost universally maintained, even though the various declarations may highlight a specific right. This summary statement can be quite useful for the purposes of determining legislative history.[32]

VI. THE PRO-LIFE ANTIDOTE: THE USE OF THE DECLARATION
B. TWENTIETH-CENTURY DECLARATIONS

The twentieth century saw continued publication of declarations, most with an ostensibly political purpose, some serving a primarily didactic function. Since the specific ones I will consider were generated by United States involvement in the Vietnam War, I will discuss how opposition to the war generated two important versions of the Declaration, one of which expressly retained the inalienable rights clause.[33] The "Declaration of Conscience Against the War in Vietnam" (1965) modifies the rights clause slightly: "We believe that all peoples of the earth, including both Americans and non-Americans, have an inalienable right to life, liberty, and the peaceful pursuit of happiness in their own way...."[34]

Except for the title, the other important version I would like to mention (Dr. Martin Luther King's 1967 "Declaration of Independence from the War in Vietnam") bears little resemblance with Jefferson's document.[35] King urged black Americans to disavow involvement in the Vietnam War. As a further break against the rhetorical tradition of the Declaration, it is within this document that King utters what would in today's post-abortion era vocabulary be an apparent pro-life reference. He compares the amount of money financing the Vietnam war to "some demonic, destructive suction tube"; he continues his jeremiad, saying that he "was increasingly compelled to see the war as an enemy of the poor and to attack it as such."[36] Moreover, we in 1997 must recall that the vocabulary describing the technology of abortion in the late 1960's was not as diverse as today. The "curette" and "suction tube" were often metonymies for the one method which was synonymous with abortion, dilation and curettage.[37]

As with their nineteenth-century counterparts, what is most significant about twentieth-century declarations is that the inalienable rights language is almost universally maintained, even though the various declarations can be concerned with issues not directly connected with the right-to-life issues of abortion, infanticide, and euthanasia.[38]

VII. CONCLUSION

Many strategies and means were used to fight the dehumanization which affected certain groups of people since the founding of the colonies over three centuries ago. Perhaps no better antidote to the anti-life virus could have been found than a declaration affirming one of the contested inalienable rights. And yet, although the historical record demonstrates that various oppressed groups have utilized and altered Jefferson's words to accommodate their concerns, there is no declaration which summarizes the views of the American pro-life movement and which argues forcefully that attention must be given to the first of the inalienable rights, the right to life. Perhaps this can be explained by the fact that pro-lifers have been too busy working for protective laws and supportive candidates. Perhaps this indicates that pro-lifers in the United States have made the fatal assumption that such a declaration is not needed, that it is a mere academic exercise and not important to advance the movement.

Especially after the re-election of someone who made it into the White House on a plurality vote (again), today's pro-lifers may feel as marginalized as three other groups: rap singers, "angry white males," and ordinary voters. Pro-lifers may feel as disgusted with American society as rap singers who sing about oppressive poverty and worthless government school education. Pro-lifers may feel as oppressed as those who have been victimized by affirmative-action policies which have crippled their chances for employment. Finally, pro-lifers may be as turned off by their government as the electorate in general, the size of which continues to diminish. If the 1996 elections saw the lowest rate of voters since 1924, then the government of these United States is at a crisis point: it has lost the confidence of its people.[39]

Perhaps the dissolution of the current anti-life government is not far off; things get worse, supposedly, before they can get better. Douglass's nation of slavery collapsed after nearly a half-century of agitation induced by appealing to the ideals of the Declaration—and a civil war. Stanton's nation of slavery for women fell with the passage of the voting rights amendment. Oppression of Native Americans may decrease as they discover that they can achieve something much more powerful than political power (namely, economic power) by opening gambling casinos on their reservations.

It is easy for pro-lifers to be just as angry at the United States as abolitionists and women's suffrage activists were, and as Native American activists are. It is easy to hope that the country would split apart so that the power of what Martin Luther King called ""the greatest purveyor of violence in the world today" would dissipate.[40] It is, after all, not a necessary tenet of the pro-life movement that we must believe that the fifty states should continue as a unified nation in the next century.

It is necessary, however, that we attack the anti-life, dehumanizing virus which has taken over the country, and we can do that by using the same strategies which were used by oppressed groups in the past. We who are now nurtured in a nation which is the greatest threat to peace in the womb, peace in the nursery, and peace in the nursing home can restore the first inalienable right to life by following the examples of history. And if the government does not change, then, as the Declaration asserts, "it is the right of the people to alter or to abolish it, and to institute new government." Whether this means that the separatists of Texas, who are today's outlaws, will be tomorrow's heros; or whether this means that the United States will go the way of its former challenger to imperial hegemony, the Soviet Union; or whether this means that the nation will stay intact and not split apart like the former Soviet Union, is our challenge for the twenty-first century.

NOTES

1. William Brennan, *Dehumanizing the Vulnerable: When Word Games Take Lives* (Chicago: Loyola Univ. Press, 1995) p. 89.

2. It would be left to William Apes's 1836 *Eulogy on King Philip* over a hundred and fifty years later to write a more balanced biography of Metacomet.

3. Quoted in Richard Slotkin and James K. Folsom, eds. *So Dreadfull a Judgment: Puritan Responses to King Philip's War, 1676-1677* (Middletown: Wesleyan Univ. Press, 1978), pp. 451-52. The famous Puritan divine Increase Mather expressed the killing and butchering in similarly glowing language: "Thereupon he [Metacomet] betook himself to flight, but as he was coming out of the Swamp, an Englishman and an Indian endeavoured to fire at him, the Englishman missed of his aime, but the Indian shot him through the heart, so as that he fell down dead.... This Wo was brought upon him that spoyled when he was not spoyled. And in that very place where he first contrived and began his mischief, was he taken and destroyed, and there was he (Like as Agag was hewed in pieces before the Lord) cut into four quarters, and is now hanged up as a monument of revenging Justice, his head being cut off and carried away to Plymouth, his Hands were brought to Boston. So let all thine Enemies perish, O Lord!" Quoted in Patricia Bizzell and Bruce Herzberg, eds., *Negotiating Difference: Cultural Case Studies for Composition* (Boston: Bedford Books of St. Martin's Press, 1996) p. 61.

4. Slotkin and Folsom, p. 325. A different printing of her autobiography states that Rowlandson used the word "Bears" to describe her captors. Cf. Mary Rowlandson, "A True History of the Captivity and Restoration of Mrs. Mary Rowlandson" in *Classic American Autobiographies*, ed. William L. Andrews (New York: Penguin Books, 1992) pp. 20-69. Whether this version is due to copyists' or printers' errors or not, Rowlandson's devaluation of the Native Americans as human beings is obvious.

5. Harriet Beecher Stowe, *Uncle Tom's Cabin* (orig. 1852; New York: Modern Library, 1985), p. 8.

6. Thomas Jefferson, *Notes on the State of Virginia*, ed. Thomas Perkins Abernethy (New York: Harper & Row, 1964) pp. 133, 135.

7. Recent scholarship claims that Banneker "was a primary symbol of the self-evident truth that all men are created equal." See Sidney Kaplan and Emma Nogrady Kaplan, *The Black Presence in the Era of the American Revolution*, rev. ed. (Amherst: Univ. of Mass. Press, 1989) p. 132. More importantly, even though Banneker defended "black dignity against the aspersions of Thomas Jefferson" and had "achieved transatlantic fame... Jefferson never really forgave the sable scientist for speaking out" against slavery and refuting Jefferson's charges about the inferiority of African Americans (Kaplan and Kaplan, p. 132).

8. E.N. Elliot, *Cotton Is King, and Pro-Slavery Arguments: Comprising the Writings of Hammond, Harper, Christy, Stringfellow, Hodge, Bledsoe, and Cartwright, On This Important Subject* (orig. 1860; New York: Johnson Reprint,

1968) p. 324.

9. Bizzell and Herzberg, p. 419. Another element of dehumanization made possible in the whirling industrial development of the United States is the reduction of a human being to a synecdoche. Elizabeth Stuart Phelps documents a prime example in her novel, *The Silent Partner: A Novel* (orig. 1871; Westbury: Feminist Press, 1983), p. 71: "If you are one of 'the hands' in the Hayle and Kelso Mills—and again, in Hayle and Kelso—you are so dully used to this classification, 'the hands,' that you were never known to cultivate an objection to it, are scarcely found to notice its use or disuse. Being surely neither head nor heart, what else remains?"

10. Bizzell and Herzberg, pp. 451-54.

11. Internment of persons who were viewed less than human seems to have been practiced early on in the founding of the United States. During the time of Metacomet's war against the English colonists in 1675, for example, Daniel Gookin reports in *Historical Collections of the Indians in New England* (orig. 1674, New York: Arno Press, 1976) that "the Indians of Natick and other places, who had subjected themselves to the English government, were hurried down to Long Island in the harbour of Boston, where they remained all winter, and endured inexpressible hardships" (p. 88). One can argue also that the numerous efforts to guarantee that Native Americans could have their own "reservations" were similar efforts to control where the population of an inferior or unwanted race would reside.

12. A cursory glance over wartime documents reveals that only the Japanese were often designated by a pejorative abbreviation ("Jap"). In official government material Germans and Italians were not called any of the variety of derogatory names used to refer to their ethnicity (such as "kraut" or "dago") in the same way that the Japanese were referred to by their pejorative term.

13. Mike Masaoka, with Bill Hosokawa, *They Call Me Moses Masaoka: An American Saga* (New York: William Morrow, 1987) p. 85.

14. Michi Nishiura Weglyn, *Years of Infamy: the Untold Story of America's Concentration Camps*, updated ed. (Seattle: Univ. of Washington Press, 1996) p. 89.

15. Montaville Flowers, *The Japanese Conquest of American Opinion* (New York: George H. Doran, 1917) pp. 209-10. Although a cause and effect relationship cannot be established between the two authors, a case for the similarity of racist ideas between Flowers and Hitler can be made. These words in Hitler's first volume of his *Mein Kampf* (published in 1925) approximate

Flowers's summary condemnation of the Japanese: "The result of all racial crossing is therefore in brief always the following: (a) Lowering of the level of the higher race; (b) Physical and intellectual regression and hence the beginning of a slowly but surely progressing sickness. To bring about such a development is, then, nothing else but to sin against the will of the eternal creator. And as a sin this act is rewarded." Adolph Hitler, *Mein Kampf*, tr. Ralph Manheim (Boston: Houghton Mifflin, 1971) pp. 286-87; typographical conventions merged into one quote.

16. Quoted in Bizzell and Herzberg, p. 640. Cited as an appendix to the report, the title of the document is "Final Recommendation of the Commanding General, Western Defense Command and Fourth Army, Submitted to the Secretary of War."

17. Bizzell and Herzberg, p. 632.

18. Bizzell and Herzberg, p. 613.

19. Bizzell and Herzberg, p. 614.

20. Jeanne Wakatsuki Houston and James D. Houston, *Farewell to Manzanar: A True Story of Japanese American Experience during and after the World War II Internment* (New York: Bantam, 1974) p. 13.

21. Houston, p. 114. Fortunately, the internment did not match the function of the Nazi death camps. One example of how such subjugation of a race can make it easier to begin killing occurred only about twenty years after World War II. One of the most horrifying examples of how the dehumanization process blinds the perpetrator to the humanity of another human being, especially if the victim is of a different race, occurred during the Vietnam war. Documenting U.S. soldiers' abuse of Vietnamese villagers, Harold Bryant, an African American soldier, describes how he and two of his fellow soldiers saw "three black pajama bodies start runnin' away from us"; later, after the Vietnamese civilians were killed, one of the American soldiers, a white man, raped one of the dead women. Wallace Terry, *Bloods: An Oral History of the Vietnam War by Black Veterans* (New York: Random House, 1984) p. 29.

22. As used throughout this paper, "Declaration" will be the abbreviation for Jefferson's document, which argued for political liberation from Great Britain. When lower case, "declaration" refers to any manifesto which embodies the criteria for this American rhetorical trope.

23. Bizzell and Herzberg, p. 271.

24. Truman Nelson, ed., *Documents of Upheaval: Selections from William Lloyd Garrison's The Liberator, 1831-1865* (New York: Hill and Wang, 1966) p. 74.

25. John W. Blassingame, ed. *The Frederick Douglass Papers.* Series One: *Speeches, Debates, and Interviews*, Vol. 2: *1847-54* (New Haven: Yale Univ. Press, 1982) pp. 360, 367, 371.

26. Pro-slavery writers were quick to demonstrate the inconsistencies of the Declaration's universal assertions of rights and the practice of slavery in the new nation. After discussing various arguments about the Declaration's "all men are created equal" clause, pro-slavery writer Elliot argues that "Mr. Jefferson was not only opposed to allowing the negroes the rights of citizenship, but he was opposed to emancipation also, except on the condition that the freedmen should be removed from the country. He could, therefore, have meant nothing more by the phrase, 'all men are created equal,' which he employed in the Declaration of Independence, than the announcement of a general principle, which, in its application to the colonists, was intended most emphatically to assert their equality, before God and the world, with the imperious Englishmen who claimed the divine right of lording it over them. This was undoubtedly the view held by Mr. Jefferson, and the extent to which he expected the language of the Declaration to be applied" (Elliot, p. 44). Elliot thus neutralizes the impact of scholarship which demonstrates that Jefferson adopted this principle from ancient Greek writings and Roman codification of natural law. The ancient Romans, like the United States government, allowed slavery, but recognized that even the slave can claim that he is equal to his master according to natural law. Cf. Edward Dumbauld, *The Declaration of Independence and What It Means Today* (Norman: Univ. of Oklahoma Press, 1950) pp. 56-58.

Similarly, another prominent pro-slavery writer, George Fitzhugh, directly challenged the ideals of the Declaration in his *Sociology for the South, or the Failure of a Free Society* (orig. 1854; New York: Burt Franklin, 1965), saying: "It is, we believe, conceded on all hands, that men are not born physically, morally, or intellectually equal—some are males, some females, some from birth, large, strong, and healthy, others weak, small, and sickly—some are naturally amiable, others prone to all kinds of wickednesses—some brave, others timid. Their natural inequalities beget inequalities of rights. The weak in mind or body require guidance, support, and protection; they must obey and work for those who protect and guide them—they have a natural right to guardians, committees, teachers, or masters. Nature has made them slaves; all that law and government can do, is to regulate, modify, and mitigate their slavery" (pp. 177-78). Immediately before this section justifying slavery, Fitzhugh accounts for the presence of the inalienable rights clause of the Declaration by saying that, since they were written in revolutionary times, "men's minds were heated and blinded when they were written" (p. 175).

27. Diane Ravitch, ed., *The American Reader: Words That Moved a Nation* (New York: Harper Perennial, 1991) p. 83.

28. Bizzell and Herzberg, p. 359.

29. Bizzell and Herzberg, p. 503.

30. Bizzell and Herzberg, pp. 521, 523, 525.

31. Philip S. Foner, ed., *We, the Other People: Alternative Declarations of Independence by Labor Groups, Farmers, Women's Rights Advocates, Socialists, and Blacks, 1829-1975* (Urbana: Univ. of Chicago Press, 1976) p. 100.

32. According to primary documents gathered by Foner, other declarations of the period which retain all three of the inalienable rights include: "The Working Men's Declaration of Independence," dated December 26, 1829 (p. 48); "Declaration of Rights of the Trades' Union of Boston and Vicinity," dated June 12, 1834 (p. 53); "Declaration of Rights by Equal Rights Advocates and Anti-Monopolists of New York," dated September 1836 (p. 57); Lewis Masquerier's "Declaration of Independence of the Producing from the Non-Producing Class," dated September 28, 1844 (p. 66); "Declaration of Rights of the Industrial Congress" dated June 21, 1845 (p. 72); "A New Constitution for the United States of the World, Proposed by Victoria C. Woodhull for the Consideration of the Constructors of Our Future Government," dated February 1872 (p. 181); "Declaration of Principles and Bill of Grievances of the Internationals of the United States of America," dated February 14, 1874 (p. 85); "Declaration of the Rights of Man by the Rocky Mountain Division, International Working Men's Association" dated April 12, 1884 (p. 121); "The American Wage-Worker's Declaration of Independence by the Federated Trades of the Pacific Coast," dated July 3, 1886 (p. 131); and "A Declaration by the Representatives of the Wage-Workers of the United States of America in Congress Assembled," dated July 4, 1886 (p. 137).

33. Although the Communist version of the Declaration does not fit into this study of the foundational principles of American life, it is interesting that the avowed enemy of the United States during the war used Jefferson's document to advance the cause of Vietnamese liberation from France. In fact, Ho Chi Minh's formulation of the "Declaration of Independence of the Democratic Republic of Vietnam" (September 2, 1945) begins by expressly quoting Jefferson's crucial rights language almost verbatim: "'All men are created equal. They are endowed by their Creator with certain inalienable rights; among these are Life, Liberty, and the pursuit of Happiness.' This immortal statement was made in the Declaration

of Independence of the United States of America in 1776. In a broader sense, this means: All the peoples on the earth are equal from birth, all the peoples have a right to live, to be happy and free." Quoted in Marvin E. Gettleman, Jane Franklin, Marilyn B. Young, and H. Bruce Franklin, eds., *Vietnam and America: A Documented History*, 2nd ed. revised and enlarged (New York: Grove, 1995) pp. 26-27.

As with the Rowlandson entry above, where "translation" of a difficult-to-read script is necessary, another edition of Ho's Declaration has slightly different punctuation and terminology: "'We hold truths that all men are created equal, that they are endowed by their Creator with certain unalienable Rights, among these are Life, Liberty, and the pursuit of Happiness.' This immortal statement is extracted from the Declaration of Independence of the United States of America in 1776. Understood in the broader sense, this means: 'All peoples on the earth are born equal; every person has the right to live to be happy and free'." Quoted in Bizzell and Herzberg, p. 804.

34. Gettleman *et al.*, p. 306.

35. The strongest parallel to Jefferson's wording is embedded in King's "deem(ing) it of signal importance to try to state clearly" his reasons against the Vietnam War, an echo of Jefferson's "a decent respect to the opinions of mankind requires that they should declare the causes which impel them to the separation." Martin Luther King, "Declaration of Independence from the War in Vietnam" in *Two, Three... Many Vietnams: A Radical Reader on the Wars in Southeast Asia and the Conflicts at Home*, by the editors of *Ramparts*, with Banning Garrett and Katherine Barkley (San Francisco: Canfield Press, 1971) pp. 206-15 at p. 206.

36. King, p. 207.

37. In Charles J. McFadden's 1967 *Medical Ethics*, 6th ed. (Philadelphia: F. A. Davis, 1967), the primary example given for abortion is the use of the curette: "In cases of *direct* abortion, *the very nature of the surgical or medical procedure is aimed at getting rid of the fetus* (*ex gr.*, curettage of the pregnant uterus)" (p. 122, emphasis in original). The dominance of the curette method of killing the unborn child reigned well into the decade after King's declaration. In his 1977 book *This Curette for Hire* (Chicago: ACTA Foundation, 1977) Eugene F. Diamond documents still only three methods of abortion: "When abortion is done at twelve weeks, it is done by the method of dilitation (*sic*) and curettage.... Between the sixteenth and the twentieth week, the preferred abortion procedure would be hysterotomy.... Between twenty and twenty-four weeks gestation, the preferred method of abortion is by the saline amniocentesis or 'salting out' method" (pp. 77-78). And, as today, so in the 1970's "most abortions [were] performed between the eighth and the twelfth week of pregnancy" (p. 77).

38. Again, Foner's collation shows that the following other declarations of the twentieth century retain all three of the inalienable rights: "A New Declaration of Independence by the Continental Congress of Workers and Farmers," dated May 1933 (p. 156); "Black Declaration of Independence by the National Committee of Black Churchmen," dated July 3, 1970 (p. 164); "A Declaration of Independence: an American Response to New Global Imperatives by Henry Steele Commager for the World Affairs Council of Philadelphia," dated October 1975 (pp. 203-04); and "A Declaration of Economic Independence by the People's Bicentennial Commission," dated 1975 (p. 171). Finally, the text of Russell Means's "declaration of independence" for the Oglala Sioux Nation, while referred to in at least one Native American sourcebook, could not be obtained to determine if the inalienable rights language is maintained. Cf. Vine Deloria, *Behind the Trail of Broken Treaties: An Indian Declaration of Independence* (Austin: Univ. of Texas Press, 1985) pp. 77-78.

39. A *Congressional Quarterly* article analyzing the last presidential election reports that "Fewer than 96 million ballots were cast, according to an estimate by the Committee for the Study of the American Electorate (CSAE), which represented just 48.8 percent of the voting-age population. It was the lowest turnout rate since 1924 and the second lowest since 1824.... The rate of presidential-year turnout has been on a steady decline since the closely fought election of 1960... which drew 63 percent of the voting-age population to the polls. The turnout rate stayed above 60 percent through the 1960's, before falling to 55 percent in 1972.... And it has continued to fall since then, with the exceptions of 1984 and 1992, when there were upticks in voter participation that proved only temporary." Rhodes Cook, "Clinton's Easy Second-Term Win Riddles GOP Electoral Map: but both parties claim victory, as voters make historic choice for further split government" in *Congressional Quarterly* (Nov. 9, 1996) pp. 3189-94 at p. 3194.

40. King, p. 208.

THE ROAD TO ROE: CULTURAL CHANGE AND THE GROWTH OF ACCEPTANCE OF ABORTION PRIOR TO 1973

Keith Cassidy

WHEN ABORTION EMERGED as an issue in the 1960's, those who arose to combat the movement first to "reform" and then to repeal the existing abortion laws were struck by two facts: first, that there was controversy over abortion at all—that the protection of fetal life was not a settled and unquestionable social guarantee—and second that this novel and shocking movement seemed to have strong allies in the mass media and in the professions and that it was the opponents of abortion rather than the proponents of its greater accessibility who bore the burden of proof and the stigma of eccentricity and extremism.

For decades no public controversy of any consequence had ever disturbed the widely held belief that abortion was a terrible crime which took an innocent life and which was sharply different from birth control. Indeed an official of the leading organization advocating birth control had carefully distinguished its cause from that of abortion and had referred to it as the taking of a life.[1] Suddenly there was a demand for expanded "therapeutic" abortions, a demand which quickly became transformed into a call for unrestricted access to abortion, "abortion on demand" as one early proponent called it.[2]

The sympathetic treatment of this demand in the media, both print and electronic, and the support which it secured from prominent public leaders, seemed inexplicable to abortion's opponents. These opponents felt like a city's defenders, who upon being awakened by the sound of attack discovered that the foe already held most of the city's key positions and that important allies were suddenly enemies. Any attempt to write a history of the pro-life movement must come to an understanding of two things: the source of this widespread support for ready access to abortion and the fact that the discovery of the existence of such support was a shock to abortion opponents. A history of the right-to-life movement must be set in a number of contexts, and one of these is the process by which what came to be called "pro-choice" forces emerged as a powerful and well-connected element in American society. The character of the right-to-life movement was shaped in large measure by the social circumstances of its birth, and the nature of its opposition was a particularly significant part of those circumstances. Before we ask then about the pro-life movement we must ask, why a pro-choice movement? When and why did it arise, and how did it come to have such powerful friends?

The argument of the following paper is easily summarized: the roots of the pro-choice movement lie much further back in the American past than the 1960's. While that turbulent decade saw forces which triggered the abortion controversy and which aided its speedy triumph, the crucial—and in many respects deeply contradictory—changes in attitude which were the necessary precondition for change had much deeper roots. Where can we find an adequate account of this transformation?

We could begin by turning to the accounts prepared by pro-choice historians. Several are available, but in essence the story they tell is this: throughout history abortion was a long-standing, widely practised and widely accepted means by which women attempted to control their reproductive lives, which encountered a significant campaign to restrict it only in the 19th century. This campaign had some elements of moral concern for the rights of the fetus but was primarily part of a move by doctors to enhance their professional status. It was also part of a move to increase the birth rate of white middle class women, in part because of racist fears of immigrant birth rates but even more because of a fear of women who were not subject to male power. Moreover, the restriction of abortion was an expression of hostility to women and can only be understood in the context of gender relations and a profoundly anti-feminist backlash.

This tale, with variations, can be found in James C. Mohr's *Abortion in America: The Origins and Evolution of National Policy,*[3] Carroll Smith-Rosenberg's "The Abortion Movement and the AMA, 1850-1880,"[4] and more recently and exhaustively in Janet Farrell Brodie's *Contraception and Abortion in Nineteenth Century America.*[5] Brodie argues that techniques of both abortion and contraception were widely available after the middle of the century and that little distinction was made by the public between the two. She makes a strong case for holding that the availability of contraceptive information and indeed the dramatic plunge in the birth rate of native-born whites over the course of the century serve to indicate that birth limitation was being practised. She repeats the Smith-Rosenberg line that the AMA's anti-abortion crusade was "hostile to women and to the power that control of reproduction promised (or threatened) to give them."[6]

The repressive regime created in the 19th century was unable to cope with changes in medical practice in the 20th century and was incompatible with the movement of women into the workforce after World War II. Kristin Luker, in her widely cited work, *Abortion and the Politics of Motherhood*, argues that as the medical grounds for therapeutic abortions shrank with improvements in medicine, a crisis arose within medical circles over the definition of "therapeutic":

So long as some abortions *could* save the physical lives of women, professional pressures kept "strict constructionists" from watching their colleagues (at least those in good standing) very closely to see that their abortions actually *did* save lives. But as abortions necessary to save lives became a medical rarity, one pillar of the medical profession's support for abortion began to crack. The "strict constructionists" began to look forward to the day when abortions would never need to be performed. But neither they nor their "broad constructionists" colleagues fully appreciated just how deep the divisions between them really were.[7]

She argues as well that the large scale entry of married women into the workforce after the 1940's created an increasing demand for control over reproduction, as an unplanned pregnancy's serious impact on work and career became apparent.[8]

A recent and extremely important pro-choice study of the origins of abortion restrictions and their impact up to *Roe v. Wade* is Leslie J. Reagan's *When Abortion Was a Crime: Women, Medicine, and Law in the United States, 1867-1973*. Reagan, unlike Mohr, grants no morally good intentions to the doctors who led the movement to end abortion in the 19th century: "Periods of anti-abortion activity mark moments of hostility to female independence."[9] Her coverage of abortion practice during the period after the 19th century laws were passed is divided into four eras.

The first, from 1880 to 1930, begins with the criminalization of abortion in all States to the Great Depression, a fifty-year period "heavily marked by continuity," when "abortion was widely accepted and practised in women's homes and in the offices of physicians and midwives." During this period, however, "a crackdown on abortion occurred between 1890 and 1920 as specialists in obstetrics renewed the earlier campaign against abortion."[10] The 1930's are the next period, when abortion became "consolidated in medical hands and more visible."[11]

She argues that the period after 1940 saw an increased repression of abortion, both through a tightening of the rules regarding therapeutic abortion and through a crackdown on illegal abortions. "The suppression of abortion in the decades immediately preceding *Roe v. Wade* was unique in the history of abortion. That repressive system, and its deadly results, played a crucial role in producing a movement to legalize abortion. The abortion-rights movement arose out of the deteriorating conditions of abortion and the frustrations of both women and physicians."[12] But "the oppressiveness of the postwar years alone did not produce a movement to legalize abortion"; rather, it "developed at a time when many in the Civil Rights and anti-war movements mobilized for radical change."[13]

The movement to end abortion controls was thus an expression of a desire to return to "normal" practice: women had always sought abortions and regarded them as legitimate but were now facing unprecedented obstacles. The opponents of this abortion reform could best be understood as the analogues of the anti-feminist and reactionary forces who had created the laws in the first place. This interpretation of abortion-law history focuses on an allegedly disrupted tradition: reform is seen as a return to an interrupted past in which abortion had been widely accepted and widely available. Accordingly, this history of the abortion-rights movement stresses the individuals and groups who arose in the 1960's to "restore" this putative right, and since it is seen as a restoration, not a revolution, little attention is paid to its deeper roots.

The work of this group of historians is not without its merits and does add to our knowledge of why and how a pro-choice movement came to be. Reagan's work in particular has contributed considerably to our understanding of how abortion restrictions actually operated over the last century, and thus provides a valuable background to the emergence of an abortion-rights movement in the 1960's. As mentioned earlier, the work of pro-choice scholars has also suggested the connection between women's workforce participation and the demand for access to abortion. David Garrow, among others, has made clear the connection between the birth-control movement and the legitimation of abortion. Further, these scholars have noted the impact of population-control beliefs on the movement to make abortion more accessible, although they do not dwell on the connection.[14] A pro-choice historian of contraception, James Reed, in *From Private Vice to Public Virtue: The Birth Control Movement and American Society Since 1830*, has suggested a deeper root of the acceptance of abortion, insofar as the history of contraception provides an analogue:

In retrospect, the emergence between 1915 and 1921 of a movement to legitimize and spread contraceptive practice might be viewed as a logical, if not inevitable, response to one source of tension in the sex lives of socially ambitious Americans. The essential cultural prerequisite for the success of the American birth control movement was the secularization of society or the celebration of material well-being and pleasure exemplified by the growth of the advertising industry. The progressive rationalization of human relationships in an industrial society was leading toward the acceptance of human sexuality as a means of individual expression divorced from any large social necessity or religious purpose.[15]

Most of all, however, the work of these pro-choice historians provides us with a good picture of the activities of the abortion-rights activists in the decade of the 1960's. This is particularly true of David Garrow's massive and tendentious tome, *Liberty and Sexuality:The Right to Privacy and the Making of Roe v. Wade*[16] and of Suzanne Staggenborn's *The Pro-Choice Movement: Organization and Activism in the Abortion Conflict.*[17]

This focus on the 1960's (and the relative inattention to the larger transformation of American society in the decades preceding that period) is consistent with the theme of a restored tradition—how, after a century, women fought for a return to a long accepted right to abortion. The theme of continuity is explicit in Mohr's account: he argues that the Supreme Court, in its decision on *Roe* was saying in effect that:

Americans would come to recognize the anti-abortion laws of the late 19th century as the real aberrations in the history of their nation's abortion policies and realize that the *Roe* guidelines represented an attempt by the Court to formulate a modern version of the older, though ultimately more appropriate, abortion policies of the past, in the wake of a concerted, though ultimately inappropriate, attempt to impose criminal prescription as the national norm.[18]

...it seems entirely possible that the foregoing book will come to be seen as an examination not of the origins and evolution of America's "normal" or "usual" abortion policies, but rather of how the single greatest period of interruption, or deviation from the norm, came about.[19]

What this approach does not do is to recognize, let alone to explain, the very real revolution in abortion policy undertaken in the 1960's and the way in which it represented not a return to an older tradition but a radical discontinuity, not just with the immediate past, but with several millennia of tradition. The discontinuity is this: even if one accepts without reservation the claim that prior to the 19th century laws there was an unrestricted "right" to abortion prior to "quickening" (a claim which is dubious at best), it is also the case that abortion after quickening was forbidden, and that this arose from a concern for human life.[20] Indeed the less stringent attitude to abortion prior to quickening was the result of the belief that human life was not clearly present prior to fetal movement. It is inappropriate to use the word "abortion" in its modern sense to describe those pre-quickening pregnancy terminations precisely because while we know that they were (in objective fact) abortions, they were not perceived as such by those performing or undergoing them. The claim that the acceptance of pre-quickening terminations in earlier centuries can thus be used as justification for abortion today is insupportable. More importantly, the modern pro-choice movement does not limit itself to a call for a return to a right to terminate an early term fetus. It calls for a right to abort all fetuses at any point in the pregnancy for any reason the mother finds sufficient. The practices and beliefs of an earlier period can provide no support for an unlimited right to abortion. There is clearly a radical discontinuity here.

The story told by pro-choice historians does not recognize or explain this discontinuity. Their failure to deal with the discontinuity, however, makes it impossible for them to understand how truly radical the pro-choice movement was, and it simultaneously makes it impossible for them to understand the nature and role of the pro-life movement. Since abortion-rights advocates cannot recognize that the pro-life movement is much closer to the long-standing tradition of Western society than they are, they must instead force the movement into what is clearly an utterly inadequate explanatory framework: an anti-feminist backlash by those opposed to gender equality. This interpretation of the movement is wrong, or at best only marginally correct, but the interpretive framework used by pro-choicers leads even otherwise able scholars to accept it.

By contrast, I would suggest the following: the 19th century laws against abortion were passed with so little difficulty or debate precisely because they did, to a substantial degree, reflect the moral understanding of the community, namely, that ante-natal life deserved protection. Mohr suggests, to the contrary, that these laws changed rather than reflected public opinion.[21] But it seems unlikely that a change of such magnitude could have occurred if it were not based on a substantial moral consensus. Of course, abortions continued to be practised after the change in the laws, and many were slow to accept the elimination of the quickening distinction, but overwhelmingly abortion was seen as wrong because it did attack human life. At the base of the 19th century crusade to outlaw all abortions lay two assumptions: one was that human life had an absolute value. Secondly, it was assumed that it was only necessary to demonstrate that human life was a continuous process, from conception onward, in order to validate the claim of the early fetus to full humanity. Once the old "quickening" distinction had been discredited, it seemed obvious to the physicians leading the attack on abortion that the nature of the entity was the same, whether one week after conception or fifty years after: it was a human being, which, while admittedly of different size and capabilities, was still in its very nature human. James Mohr touches on both of these points in his account of the 19th century attack on abortion:

The nation's regular doctors, probably more than any other identifiable group in American society during the 19th century, including the clergy, defended the value of human life as an absolute.[22]

...19th-century physicians knew categorically that quickening has no special significance as a stage in gestation. Hence it is not difficult to grant the genuineness of their uneasiness over the continued use of what they regarded as an unimportant, almost incidental, occurrence during pregnancy to distinguish between legal life and legal non-existence in cases of assault against a fetus.[23]

While these views were held with particular intensity by physicians, they were clearly consistent with the dominant philosophical presuppositions of the society, for otherwise they would not have achieved such relatively easy victories throughout the country. It must be stressed that these are in fact *philosophical* presuppositions: the absolute character of the human right to life (which for almost all in society was anchored in the belief that it was conferred by a transcendent God, not by society; that it is a right "endowed by their Creator," as the Declaration of Independence has it) and the belief that the category of "human" was biological, not separate from "human person" and not a social construction. These presuppositions reflected deeply rooted and rarely articulated metaphysical and epistemological beliefs.

The widespread persistence of these beliefs was manifested in the fact that when a right-to-life movement arose in the 1960's, most of its efforts were directed at making precisely these points to the public: the focus on showing the continuity of fetal development was a continuation of the 19th century physicians attack on the quickening distinction. There was this crucial difference: in the 19th century the right-to-life argument could count on the concurrence of the public, or at least the absence of vocal opposition, because the habits of thought and philosophical assumptions of the physicians were almost universally held in society. By the mid-20th century they were not. That pro-lifers were taken aback by this development is a striking reflection of the degree to which American society had split asunder on its understanding of basic words and concepts. Almost inevitably those on both sides of this cultural divide tended to see their opponents as either obtuse or wicked, or possibly both.

The various explanations of why abortion advocates came to prevail—structural changes in women's lives and employment, the acceptance of birth-control and of the sense that control of fertility was a right, population anxieties, the civil-rights and anti-war movements, the youth culture of the 1960's, able leaders and particular events (such as the Finkbine case) are all inadequate to explain the rapid and complete success of the call for an unlimited right to abortion. (As the controversy over the proposed ban on partial-birth abortions has made clear, the right being asserted was to unlimited abortion.) No one factor, of course, is enough to explain the origins of the pro-choice movement and the reasons for its success, but one crucial factor is rarely elaborated by pro-choice historians. James Mohr's remarks about a growing regard for the "quality" of life as opposed to biological life itself gets close to doing so when he writes about:

...an increasing concern in the 20th century for what was called the quality of life, as distinguished from biological life itself as an absolute. When medical research developed the technological capacity to maintain biological life in an otherwise inanimate human body, for example, more and more Americans had to wrestle with the question of whether all forms of life, technically defined, are worth the social, emotional, and financial costs of maintaining them.[24]

The radical shift at the root of abortion's triumph is not just the relativization of human life implied in the "quality of life" argument, but more deeply the changes in Western thought which saw, in general, the waning of the assumptions behind the 19th century attack on abortion. While there is a great deal more to the story than this, it is the contention of this paper that the rise and triumph of the pro-choice movement cannot be understood outside the larger, revolutionary transformation of fundamental patterns of thought over the last century and a half.

Over the course of decades, from the 19th century to the 1960's, the intellectual framework which permitted and indeed required the beliefs that the human right-to-life was a transcendently anchored absolute and that the category of "human" was independent of social definitions of "person" began to fade, first for the intellectual elite and then for a widening circle of the public. It is not possible here to trace in detail the process by which philosophical beliefs of 19th century Americans lost the allegiance of a large part of the intellectual elite. Clearly, in America as elsewhere in the Western world, the revolution which was both (in part) caused and exemplified by Darwinism played a crucial role. A classic expression of this change was given by John Dewey:

In laying hands upon the sacred ark of absolute permanency, in treating the forms that had been regarded as types of fixity and perfection as originating and passing away, the *Origins of Species* introduced a mode of thinking that in the end was bound to transform the logic of knowledge, and hence the treatment of morals, politics, and religion.[25]

Bruce Kuklick's *The Rise of American Philosophy* has examined the early years of this transformation in detail and he makes clear that for America's intellectual elite Darwinism spelled the death of existing philosophical beliefs—in particular for the (until then) dominant school of Scottish common-sense realism.[26] The story of the intellectual revolution which ensued in field after field has often been told, as in Morton White's *Social Thought in America: The Revolt Against Formalism*, and it is the indispensable context for understanding the transformation in American abortion attitudes.[27]

The new philosophical climate made much less plausible the assertion that even in its early stages a fetus was fully human, whatever its appearance, and was entitled to the same absolute protection as any other human. Indeed such a belief came to seem to many not just incomprehensible, but perverse. Eventually it appeared that it was an irrational assertion best lumped under the heading of "religion."

While this trend undermined the fetus's claim to rights, another trend was underway which paradoxically elevated some other rights claims into absolutes. As Mary Ann Glendon has noted, claims to rights under the Constitution have increasingly been made in absolute terms, including (and most notably) in regard to abortion.[28] The woman's absolute right to privacy in this matter overrode all other concerns and created the situation in which the fetus, deemed not to be a person under the Constitution, had no effective rights in any abortion-decision, whereas the woman had absolute rights. The oddity of this situation, when viewed in comparative perspective in the light of other Western countries' experiences, has received Glendon's searching criticism.[29]

This erosion of an absolute right to life and the consequent belief that no claims could be made on behalf of the fetus which were not limited by the social circumstance, in conjunction with the absolutizing of previously limited rights under the Constitution, is one of the most striking and paradoxical features of the events which led to the current triumph of the pro-choice cause. The pro-choice historical accounts of the triumph of their cause do not address it, however. That the weakening—indeed negation—of the idea of fetal rights has to be explained as an historical process is not recognized. Implicit is the assumption that no one had ever really believed in fetal rights. This is, I would submit, inaccurate, but such a belief of necessity leads to the conclusion that those who speak of fetal rights must be hiding other motives, since they could not really believe in them.

Why is it not clearly acknowledged that both the idea of the "human" and beliefs about the origins and nature of human rights have substantially changed in the last century? A tentative suggestion may be advanced here. Perhaps it is because the American polity is based on documents—such as the Declaration of Independence—and on a rhetoric of innate and absolute human rights, which assume the continued vitality of the older philosophical beliefs. If it is held that all humans are from birth fully equal regardless of age, race, or ability but that before birth—even one second before birth—they are not entitled to the protection of the law, both human rights and the very definition of "human" may be taken as social constructions. This apparent tension between the liberal creed and the defense of abortion has drawn the attention of liberals such as Nat Hentoff.[30]

As noted above, pro-lifers insisted on making arguments based on the older view of inherent, inalienable rights, and of a comprehensive definition of "human," based on a traditional set of philosophical understandings. These views could not be attacked unless one was willing to call into question the basis of American liberalism as it was understood by a majority of the public. Radicals might be willing to do so, but others were not, not even to themselves. The right-to-life movement was in large measure a campaign to preserve a traditional understanding of rights, an understanding still shared by many Americans. It could not, however, be attacked, or even understood, as such, so it had to be interpreted and attacked on other grounds: as itself hostile to the rights tradition—thus the claims that it was a repressive movement opposed to gender equality. To say this is not to suggest a deliberate campaign of misrepresentation, but rather that the abortion debate raised issues of the deepest character, going to the heart of American politics and society and that its full implications were rarely recognized by its participants.

This account of the rise of the pro-choice movement has mentioned the work of pro-choice historians and has argued that they do not give an adequate basis for understanding the phenomenon. When that more comprehensive account is written, some very useful material can be found in two books by the pro-life scholar, Marvin Olasky. First in his *The Press and Abortion, 1838-1988*,[31] and then in his *Abortion Rites: A Social History of Abortion in America*,[32] Olasky makes it clear that the anti-abortion consensus of the 19th century began to become unstuck quite early in the 20th century. He maps this change, which was a slow and subtle one, through an exhaustive and detailed review of press coverage of the topic. It is clear from his account that it was in the elite press, such as *The New York Times*, that the acceptance of abortion first became apparent.[33] This is consistent with the suggestion made here that the mindset receptive to abortion first appeared to the educated elite and only gradually spread to wider sections of society.

A history of the pro-life movement will find that it arose in part from a defense of traditional understandings of the nature of human rights and of the idea of the "human." It was thus not a radical, deviant, or pathological phenomenon, as suggested by its opponents and some of its interpreters, but rather was within the mainstream of American history and American society. While its opponents certainly commanded considerable power and prestige, they did not command the support of the majority of Americans. Instead the public was deeply divided, with a majority clearly neither fully pro-life nor pro-choice. The abortion controversy is thus the clearest example of the profound philosophical differences which lie at the root of the "culture wars" of contemporary American society.[34]

NOTES

1. In 1959 Planned Parenthood Federation of America's Medical Director, Mary Calderone, declared that "abortion is the taking of a life" and "explicitly eschewed any call for legal change." David Garrow, *Liberty and Sexuality: The Right to Privacy and the Making of Roe v Wade* (New York: Macmillan, 1994) p. 280.

2. The phrase was used by Garrett Hardin in 1963. See Garrow, p. 295.

3. James C. Mohr, *Abortion in America: The Origins and Evolution of National Policy* (New York: Oxford Univ. Press, 1978).

4. In Carroll Smith-Rosenberg, *Disorderly Conduct: Visions of Gender in Victorian America* (New York: Alfred A. Knopf, 1985) pp. 217-44.

5. Janet Farrell Brodie, *Contraception and Abortion in Nineteenth Century America* (Ithaca: Cornell Univ. Press, 1994).

6. Brodie, p. 272.

7. Kristin Luker, *Abortion and the Politics of Motherhood* (Berkeley: Univ. of California Press, 1984) p. 55.

8. Luker, p. 117.

9. Leslie J. Reagan, *When Abortion Was a Crime: Women, Law, and Medicine in the United States, 1867-1973* (Berkeley: Univ. of California Press, 1997) p.14.

10. Reagan, pp. 14-15.

11. Reagan, p. 15.

12. Reagan, p. 216.

13. Reagan, p. 217.

14. Reagan, pp. 230-31.

15. James Reed, *From Private Vice to Public Virtue: The Birth Control Movement and American Society Since 1830* (New York: Basic Books, 1978) p. 62.

16. See note 1 above.

17. Suzanne Staggenborn, *The Pro-Choice Movement: Organization and Activism in the Abortion Conflict* (New York: Oxford Univ. Press, 1991).

18. Mohr, p. 258.

19. Mohr, p. 259.

20. There is a very large literature which discusses this issue from a pro-life perspective. See, for example, John Connery, S.J., *Abortion: The Development of the Roman Catholic Perspective* (Chicago: Loyola Univ. Press, 1977); John

Noonan, "An Almost Absolute Value in History" in John Noonan, ed., *The Morality of Abortion: Legal and Historical Perspectives* (Cambridge: Harvard Univ. Press, 1970) pp. 1-59; Michael J. Gorman, *Abortion and the Early Church: Christian, Jewish and Pagan Attitudes in the Greco-Roman World* (Downers Grove: Intervarsity Press, 1982); John Keown, *Abortion, Doctors and the Law: Some Aspects of the Legal Regulation of Abortion in England from 1803 to 1982* (Cambridge: Cambridge Univ. Press, 1988); Clarke D. Forsythe, "The Effective Enforcement of Abortion Laws Before *Roe v. Wade*" in Brad Stetson, ed., *The Silent Subject: Reflections on the Unborn in American Culture* (Westport: Praeger, 1996) pp. 179-227; Clarke D. Forsythe, "Homicide of the Unborn Child: The Born Alive Rule and Other Legal Anachronisms" in *Valparaiso Law Review* 21/3 (1987) 563-629; Robert M. Byrn, "An American Tragedy: The Supreme Court on Abortion" in *Fordham Law Review* (1973); Robert Destro, "Abortion and the Constitution: The Need for a Pro-Life Protective Amendment" in *California Law Review* (1975); James Witherspoon "Re-examining *Roe*: Nineteenth-Century Abortion Statutes and the Fourteenth Amendment" in *St. Mary's Law Journal* 17 (1985); John D. Gorby, "The 'Right' to an Abortion: The Scope of Fourteenth Amendment 'Personhood' and the Supreme Court's Birth Requirement" in *Southern Illinois University Law Journal* (1979) 1-36; Joseph Dellapenna, "The Historical Case Against Abortion" in *Continuity* 13 (1989) 59-83; Joseph Dellapenna's "The History of Abortion: Technology, Morality and Law" in *University of Pittsburgh Law Review* 40/3 (1979) 359-428. I have discussed this issue in "The Historical Roots of the Pro-Life Movement: Assessing the Pro-Choice Account" in J. Koterski, ed., *Life and Learning V* (Washington, D.C.: University Faculty for Life, 1996) pp. 350-83.

21. Mohr, p. 262.

22. Mohr, p. 36.

23. Mohr, p. 165.

24. Mohr, p. 252.

25. John Dewey, *The Influence of Darwin on Philosophy* (Bloomington: Indiana Univ. Press, 1965 [1910]) pp. 1-2.

26. Bruce Kuklick, *The Rise of American Philosophy: Cambridge, Massachusetts, 1860-1930* (New Haven: Yale Univ. Press, 1977).

27. Morton White, *Social Thought in America: The Revolt Against Formalism* (Boston: Beacon Press, 1957 [1949]).

28. Mary Ann Glendon, *Rights Talk: The Impoverishment of Political Discourse* (New York: The Free Press, 1991).

29. Mary Ann Glendon, *Abortion and Divorce in Western Law* (Cambridge: Harvard Univ. Press, 1987).

30. A characteristic statement of this view can be found in "Dred Scott, Abortion, and Jesse Jackson" in *The Village Voice* (Feb. 21, 1989), reprinted in *The Human Life Review* 15/2 (1989) 104-08. He argues for the parallels of the abortion issue with that of slavery, in each case working within a framework of inherent rights.

31. Marvin Olasky, *The Press and Abortion, 1838-1988* (Hillsdale: Lawrence Erlbaum Associates, 1988).

32. Marvin Olasky, *Abortion Rites: A Social History of Abortion in America* (Wheaton: Crossway Books, 1992).

33. *Ibid.*, pp. 270-71.

34. The analysis offered here is similar to that given in the book which made the phrase popular, *viz.*, James Davison Hunter's *Culture Wars: The Struggle to Define America* (New York: Basic Books, 1991). See esp. pp. 43-46.

About Our Contributors

Francis J. Beckwith, Ph.D., teaches at the Graduate Center of Trinity International University in California. Among his books is *Do the Right Thing: A Philosophical Dialogue on the Moral and Social Issues of Our Time* (1996).

Mary Ellen Bork speaks on life issues on many campuses and is active with the Catholic Campaign for America.

Joel Brind, M.D., is Professor of Biology and Endocrinology at Baruch College of the City University of New York and Editor of *Abortion-Breast Cancer Quarterly Update*.

Sidney Callahan, Ph.D., is a member of the Psychology Department at Mercy College. She is the author of *With All Our Heart and Mind* and *In Good Conscience*.

Keith Cassidy, Ph.D., is a member of the History Department at the University of Guelph, Ontario. He is at work on a full-length study of the Right to Life Movement.

Rev. John J. Conley, S.J., Ph.D., is the Chair of the Department of Philosophy at Fordham University, Bronx, New York.

John F. Crosby, Ph.D., has taught at the University of Dallas, the International Academy of Philosophy, and is now professor of philosophy at Franciscan University of Steubenville.

John Hunt, Ph.D., has taught history at St. Joseph College since 1965. His primary field of study has been modern European history, with special interest in human rights, definitions of humanity, and truth in academe and the media.

Hanna Klaus, M.D., is the Executive Director of Teen STAR and of the Natural Family Planning Center of Washington, D.C.

Jeff Koloze is completing his Ph.D. in English at Cleveland State University with a dissertation on several right to life issues in American fiction.

Rev. Joseph W. Koterski, S.J., Ph.D., is a member of the Philosophy Department at Fordham University and serves as the Editor-in-Chief of *International Philosophical Quarterly* and as Director of the M.A. Program in Philosophical Resources.

Rev. William S. Kurz, S.J., Ph.D., has been teaching New Testament at Marquette University since 1975. The author of over 25 articles and 4 books, he specializes in Luke-Acts, narrative criticism, and the use of the Bible in the Church.

Jay LaMonica is a journalist and producer for *ABC News Nightline* and the husband of Teresa LaMonica.

Teresa Hanrahan LaMonica is a pediatric nurse practitioner. She has been a member of the nursing faculty at Georgetown University and has recently begun a Ph.D. program in Nursing.

Kevin E. Miller, M.A., has degrees in molecular biology and political science and is currently pursuing his Ph.D. in religious studies at Marquette University with a dissertation on Pope John Paul II's position on capital punishment.

Joseph T. Maloy, Ph.D., is an Associate Professor of Chemistry at Seton Hall University with a specialty in analytical chemistry and the computer modeling of certain chemical processes. For the last three years he has served as the faculty advisor of Seton Hall United For Life, a campus pro-life organization.

John and Barbara Willke have been national leaders in the pro-life movement for many years. Dr. Willke served as president of the National Right to Life Committee for 10 years and recently founded Life Issues Institute in Cincinnati.

UFL Board of Advisors, 1997-98*

Francis Beckwith, PhD
Trinity University
Graduate School
Los Angeles, CA

Claire Z. Carey, PhD
Assistant Dean of College
Georgetown University
Washington, DC

Richard Doerflinger
NCCB Pro-Life Activities
Washington, DC

John F. Griffith, PhD
Georgetown Medical Center
Washington, DC

C. Ben Mitchell
Biomedical and Life Issues
Southern Baptist Conference
Nashville, TN

Edmund D. Pellegrino, MD
Center for Clinical Bioethics
Georgetown University
Washington, DC

Carol Jean Vale, SSJ, PhD
President
Chestnut Hill College
Philadelphia PA

* Institutional affiliation provided for informational purposes only.

UFL Board of Directors, 1997-98*